The American
Vice Presidency

The American Vice Presidency

From the Shadow to the Spotlight

Jody C Baumgartner with
Thomas F. Crumblin

ROWMAN & LITTLEFIELD
Lanham • Boulder • New York • London

Published by Rowman & Littlefield
A wholly owned subsidiary of The Rowman & Littlefield Publishing Group, Inc.
4501 Forbes Boulevard, Suite 200, Lanham, Maryland 20706
www.rowman.com

Unit A, Whitacre Mews, 26-34 Stannary Street, London SE11 4AB

British Library Cataloguing in Publication Information Available

Library of Congress Cataloging-in-Publication Data
Baumgartner, Jody C, 1958-
 The American vice presidency : from the shadow to the spotlight / Jody C Baumgartner and Thomas F. Crumblin.
    pages cm
 Includes bibliographical references and index.
  ISBN 978-1-4422-2889-4 (cloth : alk. paper) — ISBN 978-1-4422-2890-0 (electronic) 1. Vice-Presidents—United States. 2. Vice-Presidents—United States—Election. I. Title.
 JK609.5.B378 2015
 352.23'90973—dc23

                                                         2014048215

∞™ The paper used in this publication meets the minimum requirements of American National Standard for Information Sciences—Permanence of Paper for Printed Library Materials, ANSI/NISO Z39.48-1992.

Printed in the United States of America

Contents

List of Boxes,
Figures, and Tables

Acknowledgments

This book would not have been possible without the help of several people who we would like to acknowledge. Townley Cheek of East Carolina University was most helpful in tracking down sources and organizing notes for this book. Professor Joseph Pika of the University of Delaware was kind enough to review the manuscript and his comments were most helpful. The editorial team at Rowman & Littlefield is also deserving of thanks, including vice president and senior executive editor Jon Sisk, Laura Reiter, and Natalie Mandziuk. Mia A. Leone was instrumental in preparing the index. Although they deserve to share in the credit, any mistakes contained in this book are, of course, ours and ours alone.

On a personal level, each of us would like to thank our wives and children for the support they have given us through the years. In a real sense, they make all of this worthwhile.

We should also note here that portions of this book were previously published in 2006 under the title *The American Vice Presidency Reconsidered*, to which Baumgartner holds all rights.

1

+

Introduction:
The Vice Presidency

It is quite possible that no elected office has been more maligned than that of the Vice President of the United States. Since the beginning of the republic, the office has been the object of ridicule by scholars, pundits, humorists, citizens, and even vice presidents themselves. For example, John Adams, the country's first vice president, referred to it as "the most insignificant office that ever the invention of man contrived or his imagination conceived." The perception among many is that the vice presidency and vice presidents are, at best, irrelevant. The titles of several books about vice presidents reflect this: *Crapshoot: Rolling the Dice on the Vice Presidency, Madmen and Geniuses,* and *Bland Ambition: From Adams to Quayle—The Cranks, Tax Cheats, and Golfers Who Made It to Vice President.*[1]

A look at some of the vice presidents throughout history seems to confirm the poor impression many have of the vice presidency. There have been more than a few subpar vice presidents. One of the commonly cited examples includes Aaron Burr, who was indicted for the murder of Alexander Hamilton while serving as vice president. George Clinton (who served under both Thomas Jefferson and James Madison) was, by most accounts, senile throughout most of his seven years in office. Daniel Tompkins, who served two terms under James Monroe, was drunk throughout his second term. This made little difference because he stayed in his home state of New York the entire time. Richard Johnson, Martin Van Buren's vice president, spent much of his time as vice president running a tavern and had several slave mistresses. Hannibal Hamlin, Abraham Lincoln's first vice president, spent most of his term sequestered in Maine while the Civil War raged on. Lincoln had no better luck with his

1

second vice president, Andrew Johnson, who was intoxicated at the president's inauguration and later impeached after assuming the presidency. Schuyler Colfax and Henry Wilson (Ulysses Grant's first and second vice presidents, respectively) were both implicated in connection with the Crédit Mobilier scandal of 1872.[2]

To focus too much on these early examples might be unfair, but it remains true that many of our vice presidents were less than exemplary statesmen. In general, a list of vice presidents and vice presidential candidates reads like a virtual *Who's Who* of political mediocrities. Harry Truman may have summed up the classical view of the vice presidency best when he said, "look at all the Vice Presidents in history. Where are they? They were about as useful as a cow's fifth teat." Anecdotes and quotes about the vice presidency abound (see box 1.1), but perhaps the best illustration of the low regard for the office is the fact that before the ratification of the Twenty-Fifth Amendment in 1967, if a vice president resigned or died in office he was not replaced. The vice presidency has been vacant for a total of thirty-seven years throughout American history.

All of this might suggest that the vice presidency is unimportant, but nothing could be further from the truth. First, and most obviously, the vice president is one of only two nationally elected officials in the country. Second, one of the only constitutional functions of the vice presidency is to assume the presidency if and when it becomes vacant. This is significant. From 1841 to 1975 more than one-third of all U.S. presidents either died in office or quit, paving the way for the vice president to occupy the White House. Eight vice presidents became president as a result of the death of a sitting president (John Tyler, Millard Fillmore, Andrew Johnson, Chester Arthur, Theodore Roosevelt, Calvin Coolidge, Harry Truman, and Lyndon Johnson) and one, Gerald Ford, became president as the result of presidential resignation. These men served for a total of forty-two years, twenty-nine of which were in the twentieth century. In fact, vice presidents who became president by way of succession occupied the office half of the time from 1945 to 1977.

Third, since 1945 the vice presidency has been seen as a viable springboard to the presidency. Many prominent and qualified individuals who aspire to the presidency now see the vice presidency as a way to gain valuable national exposure and increase their chance of securing their party's presidential nomination. Most vice presidents since 1945 have subsequently made a run for the presidency.

Finally, and perhaps most importantly, it is widely acknowledged that vice presidents now play an integral, if largely informal role, in their presidents' administrations. Since Walter Mondale held office under President Jimmy Carter, the responsibilities associated with the vice presidency have increased dramatically. The vice president is now an

BOX 1.1

The "Conventional" Wisdom:
Some Quotable Quotes on the Vice Presidency

John Adams once lamented, "my country has in its wisdom contrived for me the most insignificant office that ever the invention of man contrived or his imagination conceived."

Theodore Roosevelt was known to have proclaimed, "I would a great deal rather be anything, say professor of history, than vice president."

Woodrow Wilson once wrote that "the chief embarrassment in discussing [the vice president's] office is that in explaining how little there is to be said about it one has evidently said all there is to say."

When he was informed that his party had nominated him for vice president, *Calvin Coolidge* (Warren Harding's running mate in 1920) replied, "I suppose I'll have to take it." After receiving the nomination, Coolidge received a telegram from former vice president *Thomas Marshall* that read, "please accept my sincere sympathy."

One of the more famous quotes about the vice presidency is from *John Nance Garner* (Franklin Roosevelt's first vice president), who stated that "the vice presidency isn't worth a pitcher of warm piss." More generously, he once claimed that vice presidents are "the spare tire on the automobile of government."

Garner, who gave up a position as Speaker of the House to become vice president, also claimed that this decision was the "worst damn fool mistake I ever made."

Charles Dawes (Calvin Coolidge's vice president) once told future vice president Alben Barkley, "This is a hell of a job. [I] look at newspapers every morning to see how the president's health is."

Presidential scholar *Clinton Rossiter* wrote, "I trust it will be thought proper in a book of 175 pages on the Presidency to devote four or five to the Vice Presidency, although even this ration is no measure of the gap between them in power and prestige."

In 1975 Vice President *Nelson Rockefeller* paid to have the vice presidential seal redesigned and later claimed that it was "the most important thing I've done all year." On another occasion, when asked about his duties as vice president, Rockefeller quipped, "I go to earthquakes."

Late night talk show host Johnny Carson: "Democracy means that anyone can grow up to be president, and anyone who doesn't grow up can be vice president."

important assistant to the president. The president is only one man, and as such, is limited in where he can go, who he can meet with, and so forth. Vice presidents now routinely act as a presidential surrogate, helping the president extend his reach. In addition, recent vice presidents are important policy advisers to their presidents. This often means that the vice president is the last person to talk to the president before a policy decision is made. In short, modern vice presidents, unlike their counterparts in previous times, are important actors in American governance.

This is especially true with the three most recent vice presidents—Al Gore, Dick Cheney, and Joe Biden. Each has been a key player in their respective administrations. Cheney, for example, seems to have successfully exerted his influence in a number of policies adopted by President George W. Bush, especially during his first term in office. Bush's reversal of a promise to lower carbon dioxide emissions, the recommendations of Cheney's energy task force, the 2001 budget tax cuts, warrantless wiretapping efforts, and the push to invade Iraq in 2003 are all examples.[3] Some have claimed that despite his campaign promise to act as an "anti-Cheney," Biden has been easily as active as his predecessor. For example in 2009 he was tasked with overseeing the distribution of $787 billion contained in the economic stimulus bill, moved an arms-reduction treaty with Russia through the Senate, took the lead on issues related to the U.S. military presence in Iraq, and was largely responsible for negotiating a deal to avert an end-of-year budget crisis in 2012. He is universally known as the president's most influential foreign policy advisor and chief troubleshooter.

This book focuses on the institution of the vice presidency and the men who have occupied that office. It is comprehensive in the sense that it begins with an examination of the deliberations that took place at the Constitutional Convention over the creation of the office and then traces the history and evolution of the office and its occupants. The book also explores how and why the office has changed during the past half-century. This includes a discussion of the manner in which vice presidential candidates are selected, which has had an impact on the institution itself. Finally the tenures of modern vice presidents are examined and case studies of the past three vice presidents are presented. The final section of this chapter outlines the remainder of the book in more detail.

PLAN OF THE BOOK

Chapter 2 examines the early vice presidency. We look first at the deliberations of the Constitutional Convention regarding the office, highlighting the idea that the office was in many respects an afterthought, a convenient tool to resolve a problem regarding presidential selection. Next, the constitutional provisions for the vice presidency are discussed. Following this the tenures of the first three occupants of the office— John Adams, Thomas Jefferson, and Aaron Burr—are examined. The chapter then examines the circumstances that led to the passage of the Twelfth Amendment. Finally, the consequences of this change, and in particular how it affected the vice presidency, are discussed.

Chapter 3 takes a closer look at the vice presidency during the nineteenth century. During this time, the office was all but insignificant if we ignore vice presidents assuming the presidency. Many vice presidents during this period could hardly be considered model statespersons. The chapter examines this traditional era of the vice presidency (1805–1900) by looking at what kinds of people were considered for the job, how they were selected, their role in the election campaign, what they did in office, and their life after the vice presidency.

Chapter 4 examines the transitional era of the vice presidency. Vice presidents were nowhere near as active during this period as in the modern era, but they were not as passive as in the traditional era. This period can be thought of as setting the stage for the emergence of the modern era and covers most of the twentieth century through the vice presidency of Gerald Ford. Like chapter 3, the discussion includes the types of people who were considered for the office, the way in which they were selected, their role in the campaign, and their tenure in office.

Drawing in part on the discussion in the previous chapter, chapter 5 discusses the various interrelated factors associated with the emergence of the more active modern vice presidency. Before accepting Ford's invitation to be vice president, Nelson Rockefeller insisted on being an integral part of the Ford administration. The fact that he eventually played a much less significant role is less important than the fact that the two men made an agreement defining the vice president's role and that this was to be an active role. This is the hallmark of the modern vice presidency. This chapter also examines the changing nature of vice presidential selection, in large part because the changes in the manner in which vice presidential candidates are selected and the types of people who are selected are related to changes in the institution.

Chapter 6 examines the selection and tenures of modern vice presidents, with a focus on Rockefeller, Mondale, George H. W. Bush, and Dan Quayle. Like previous chapters, the discussion is structured according to the recruitment and selection of these individuals as candidates, their roles throughout the campaign, what they did in office, and how they fared after the vice presidency.

Building on the themes introduced in the previous two chapters, chapters 7 through 9 provide in-depth case studies of the vice presidencies of Al

Gore, Cheney, and Biden. These men have occupied the office of the vice presidency for the past twenty years. During this time the idea that vice presidents are now an active and integral part of a president's administration has become apparent. Each has left an indelible mark on the institution.

Chapter 7 examines the vice presidency of Gore. The former senator from Tennessee was selected mainly because of his similarities to Bill Clinton, particularly their shared centrist ideologies. From the start, Clinton insisted that Gore would be a partner in his presidency. Gore subsequently headed a well-publicized task force to streamline government, was associated with the administration's environmental and technology initiatives, and in order to facilitate relations with Russia was encouraged to develop a relationship with Prime Minister Viktor Chernomyrdin. Gore was also, famously, deceived by the president about the Monica Lewinsky affair, which somewhat soured relations between the two. This said, Gore was easily the most active and visible vice president since Mondale. And because the past three vice presidents have all been quite active, it could be argued that Clinton and Gore were at least partially responsible for helping cement the new role of the vice president.

Chapter 8 turns to the Cheney vice presidency. George W. Bush's selection of Washington D.C. veteran Cheney was applauded by many as a way to add some needed experience to the presidential ticket. However Cheney's vice presidency was the most controversial in recent memory. He was criticized for the various policies he advocated, his secretive manner, his penchant for bypassing standard bureaucratic procedures, and for presumably exercising undue influence over the president. Ignoring for the moment any normative considerations, this chapter attempts to cut through some of this criticism, suggesting that Cheney was fulfilling a modern vice president's most basic function, that of loyal lieutenant.

Since 2009 the office of the vice presidency has been occupied by Biden, the subject of chapter 9. Likely selected for much the same reason as Cheney was selected, Biden brought a wealth of experience to the Barack Obama ticket in 2008. Interestingly, a common refrain on the campaign trail for Biden was that he would adopt a much lower profile than Cheney if elected. This of course would have reversed the developments of the past several decades in the institution. In fact, Biden has been quite active during the past six years, essentially acting as the president's all-purpose handyman.

The final chapter summarizes the state of the modern vice presidency to this point. The vice president is now one of the president's most valued assistants. What are some of the normative questions that emerge in light of this development? Are increased duties for the vice president, however informal, in keeping with the spirit of the Constitution? If so, how can vice presidents be held accountable? In fact, to whom are they accountable, the president or the people? These questions are addressed in this chapter by way of attempting to make some sense of the transformation of this misunderstood institution.

NOTES

1. Jules Witcover, *Crapshoot: Rolling the Dice on the Vice Presidency* (New York: Crown, 1992); Sol Barzman, *Madmen and Geniuses: The Vice Presidents of the United States* (Chicago: Follett, 1974); Steve Tally, *Bland Ambition: From Adams to Quayle— The Cranks, Tax Cheats, and Golfers Who Made it to Vice President* (San Diego, CA: Harcourt Brace Jovanovich, 1992).

2. Michael Nelson, *A Heartbeat Away* (New York: Twentieth Century Fund, 1988), 30; see also Joel K. Goldstein, "Vice President," in Vol. 4, *Encyclopedia of the American Presidency*, ed. Leonard W. Levy and Louis Fischer.(New York: Simon & Schuster, 1994), 1558.

3. Jody C Baumgartner, "Scoundrel or Über-Lieutenant? The Vice Presidency of Dick Cheney," *American Review of Politics* 29 (2008): 235–52.

2

✢

Origins: The Constitutional Convention and Pre-Twelfth Amendment Vice Presidents

The vice presidency is something of an institutional oddity. In the first place, relatively few presidential democracies have elected vice presidents.[1] Secondly, and in terms of its place in our own political system, the office stands out because it is a constitutional hybrid. In a constitution written to separate the functions and power of government institutions, the vice president is assigned both legislative and executive roles. One of the constitutional duties of the vice president is to assume the presidency in the event of presidential death, disability, resignation, or removal. This is clearly an executive function. However the other constitutional duty of the vice president is to act as President of the Senate, which is a legislative role.

So why did the framers create the institution? In the first part of this chapter we address this question. The chapter deals with what we might think of as the original vice presidency, beginning with the creation of the office at the Constitutional Convention. In addition to trying to discern the rationale for the creation of the office, we discuss the few constitutional provisions dealing with the selection, tenure, and functions of the vice president. Following this we examine the vice presidencies of John Adams, Thomas Jefferson, and Aaron Burr, our first vice presidents. Finally the chapter turns to a discussion of why the Twelfth Amendment, which altered the way that the president and vice president are selected, was passed, and the effect the amendment had on the vice presidency.

IN THE BEGINNING

There is little in the historical record referencing the creation of the vice presidency. According to notes taken by James Madison, an office of the vice presidency was not even mentioned until the closing days of the Constitutional Convention.[2] Therefore we can only speculate why the framers created the office. Three alternatives suggest themselves.

First, and perhaps most obvious, the vice presidency could have been created to provide for presidential succession in the event of presidential death, disability, resignation, or removal. There was some precedent in colonial America and the newly independent states for this idea. Several colonies, and then states (New York, Connecticut, Rhode Island, Massachusetts, and South Carolina), had lieutenant governors whose duty it was to act in place of the governor if needed. In the case of New York, the lieutenant governor even presided over its senate. Some believe that the vice presidency was modeled after these lieutenant governorships.[3] In fact, in discussing the vice presidency in *The Federalist* No. 68, Alexander Hamilton specifically referenced New York's office of the lieutenant governor as established in its 1777 constitution.[4]

But having a vice president is not the only way that presidential succession could have been provided for. Originally it had been thought that a president of the Senate (chosen from that body) would act as provisional successor in the case of a presidential vacancy. Relatively late in the Convention both Madison and Gouverneur Morris objected to this idea on the basis that it would violate the principle of separation of powers.[5] Hugh Williamson had previously suggested that Congress be empowered to name a provisional successor; Madison suggested that a Council of State act during a presidential vacancy; and Morris suggested assigning the role to the Chief Justice of the Supreme Court.[6] The point is that there is nothing in the historical record to definitively suggest that presidential succession was used as a rationale for the creation of the vice presidency.

Less likely, but still possible, is that the institution was created to provide for a president of the Senate and to break tie votes in that body. If a senator was selected to perform this function, his state would effectively lack one-half of its representation in the body. Moreover, this presiding officer would be less likely to be neutral. The main argument advanced for having a vice president serve as president of the Senate was that the vice president had a national constituency and would therefore be more apt to be neutral.[7]

But having a vice president serve as president of the Senate was not the only possible solution to the problem of tie votes. For example, Senate rules could have been written to deal with this eventuality, or another neutral party could have been found to break tie votes. It seems more likely that the decision to have the vice president serve as president of the Senate was based on the fact that, as Roger Sherman noted, unless the vice president served as presiding officer of the Senate he "would be without employment."[8]

There is some consensus among historians and presidential scholars that the vice presidency was primarily a by-product of a compromise crafted to satisfy concerns over the issue of presidential selection. On September 4, 1787, the Constitutional Convention's "Committee of Eleven,"[9] which had been appointed to address various issues that had been tabled throughout the summer, began to debate how to select the president. Three approaches had been proposed, but there were concerns over each. One early suggestion involved having Congress select the president. However if Congress selected the president, Congress might also be able to unduly influence presidential decision making. This was a violation of the precept of separation of powers. A related proposal was to have state legislatures elect the president. The concern here was that the president would then be beholden to states. This had the potential to threaten the authority of the national government and the very foundation of the federal system.

The other proposal was some form of popular election. This alternative was also dismissed. First, many of the framers were at least somewhat skeptical of democracy. Although they believed that the new government should rest on a foundation of popular will, they were reluctant to give the people too much power. The evidence in this regard is clear: only members of the House of Representatives were to be popularly elected, whereas Senators were appointed by state legislatures, presidents were selected by the Electoral College, and Supreme Court Justices appointed by presidents and confirmed by the Senate.

Another reason for rejecting the idea of popular election of presidents was the fact that many citizens would be tempted to vote for a candidate from their own state. This is easier to understand if one remembers the context. At this time in American history the first loyalty of most people was to their state. They did not see themselves primarily as "Americans." Relatedly, transportation and communication technology were such that most people did not travel outside their state and knew less about politics and notable political leaders from other states. Therefore, it would be natural for most citizens to cast their vote for president for a "favorite son" from their home state. In this situation it was quite possible that several candidates, from the more populous states, would garner a large number of votes with none receiving a majority. Moreover these more populous states would be more likely to decide the election and marginalize the smaller states in the process.

The solution was the Electoral College, a scheme under which Electors, chosen by states, would select the president.[10] The idea incorporated components of all of the previously proposed plans. Structurally the Electoral College is similar to Congress in terms of how states and state populations are represented; electors were appointed by state legislatures; and popular will was indirectly represented because state legislatures were elected by the people in each state.

Once it was determined that presidents would be selected by an Electoral College, concern shifted to how well it could be counted on to select a capable chief executive. This was where a vice presidency came into play. The main fear the framers had about the Electoral College was that Electors would cast their votes for a candidate from their home state, regardless of his qualifications. Therefore, the Constitution provided that electors should cast two votes, one of which was to be for a candidate from another state. The thinking was that the country thus had a greater chance of selecting a president who was both capable and who represented the entire nation. To provide an incentive for Electors to cast at least one vote for a capable, national leader, there was to be both a first and second place winner. This left the question of what do with the second-place winner, and the answer was to award this individual with the office of vice president.[11]

In short, it seems as if the framers did not deliberately set out to create a vice presidency as part of the constitutional scheme of governance. Rather it is likely that the office was created to provide, in the words of Hugh Williamson, "a valuable mode of election which required two to be chosen at the same time."[12]

However the decision to create a vice presidency was by no means unanimous. Among others, Elbridge Gerry (who, interestingly, served as Madison's second vice president) claimed that the institution was both unnecessary and a violation of the principle of separation of powers.[13] James Monroe saw no need for the office and said as much to the ratifying convention in his home state of Virginia. "The First Congress even wrangled over the question of whether the Vice President should even be paid a salary. Some thought that he should only receive a *per diem* for those days when he actually presided over the Senate."[14]

Many speculated that with few real assigned functions the office would attract men of lesser caliber. This objection would prove to be prescient, at least for the next century or so. But despite objections against it, the idea of a vice presidency provided what seemed to be a neat solution to one of the main problems the framers encountered in the creation of the presidency: presidential selection. The functions assigned to the vice president seem to have been added after the fact. We examine these functions, as well as Constitutional provisions for vice presidential selection and tenure, in the next section.

THE CONSTITUTIONAL VICE PRESIDENCY

Originally there were no eligibility requirements contained in the Constitution to become vice president. However, to safeguard against any succession problems in the event of a presidential vacancy, the Twelfth Amendment stipulated that "no person constitutionally ineligible to the office of President shall be eligible to that of Vice-President of the United States." According to Article II, Section 1, of the Constitution, this means that individuals aspiring to be vice president must be at least thirty-five years old, a natural born citizen, and have been a resident of the United States for fourteen years.[15]

The president and vice president are selected by the Electoral College. The original text of the Constitution (Article II, Section 1) stipulated that Electors cast two separate ballots, both of which would be for president. In other words, each Elector was to specify a first and second choice for president. As noted previously, one of these choices was to be for a candidate who hailed from a different state than the Elector. Under this arrangement, the president was to be "The Person having the greatest Number of Votes," assuming that one of the candidates had received an absolute majority (greater than 50 percent) of Electoral College votes. The vice president was to be the individual receiving the second most votes. If there was a tie vote for second place, the Senate was to select the vice president. The provisions for the selection of president and vice president changed with the passage and ratification of the Twelfth Amendment (discussed later in this chapter).

With respect to term of office, Article II, Section 1, provides that both the president and vice president are to serve for four years. Section 1 of the Twentieth Amendment (ratified in 1933) further specifies that "The terms of the President and Vice President shall end at noon on the 20th day of January [following the election] . . . and the terms of their successors shall then begin."

Vice presidents, like presidents, can be impeached and removed from office. Article II, Section 4, states that the "Vice President . . . shall be removed from Office on Impeachment for, and Conviction of, Treason, Bribery, or other high Crimes and Misdemeanors." This has never occurred, although Spiro Agnew (Richard Nixon's first vice president, from 1969 to 1974) resigned after being charged with bribery and facing the certainty of impeachment and removal from office. Besides Agnew, seventeen other vice presidents did not finish their terms in office. One resigned before his term was completed, seven died in office, and nine assumed the presidency.

There are only two constitutional tasks assigned to the vice president. Easily the most important of these is to assume the presidency in the event of a presidential vacancy. Article II, Section 1, states that in cases of presidential death, removal, resignation, or disability ("inability to discharge the powers and duties" of the office), the "Powers and Duties" of the presidency "shall devolve on the Vice President . . . until the disability be removed, or a President elected." It further stipulates that Congress may, by law, specify details of presidential and vice presidential succession. Accordingly, the presidential succession acts of 1792, 1886, and 1947, as well as Section 3 of the Twentieth Amendment dealt with lines of presidential succession.

All of these presidential succession provisions have been superseded by the Twenty-Fifth Amendment (ratified in 1967), which addresses several aspects of presidential and vice presidential vacancies. One problem the Twenty-Fifth Amendment addressed was the possibility of a dual vacancy in the executive, that is, both the president and vice president being unable to fulfill their duties. Interestingly, it was not until the passage of the Twenty-Fifth Amendment that the issue of how to fill a vice presidential vacancy was addressed. This was likely because until then vice presidential vacancies were not considered to be a problem. Table 2.1 details the various vice presidential vacancies throughout American history.

By the mid-1960s there was growing public and elite sentiment that vice presidential vacancies were unacceptable. Presidential succession crises involving Franklin Roosevelt's death a few months into his fourth term, Dwight Eisenhower's heart problems, and John Kennedy's assassination fed growing concern about presidential vacancies, much of which was focused on the vice presidency. All were made more acute because the United States was in the midst of the Cold War. In the 1960s, concern was magnified because the two individuals in line for the presidency after the vice president, Carl Hayden (President Pro Tempore of the Senate) and John McCormack (Speaker of the House) were in their seventies.[16] Section 2 of the Twenty-Fifth Amendment states that "Whenever there is a vacancy in the office of the Vice President, the President shall nominate a Vice President who shall take office upon confirmation by a majority vote of both Houses of Congress."

Section 1 of the Twenty-Fifth Amendment formalized the practice of vice presidents becoming president "in case of the removal of the President from office or of his death or resignation." The Constitution was originally ambiguous as to whether a vice president was to *act* as president or was to *assume* the presidency in the event of presidential vacancy, stipulating only that the "Powers and Duties of the said Office . . . shall devolve on the Vice President . . . until the disability be removed, or a President elected." The ambiguity was twofold.

Table 2.1. Vice-Presidential Vacancies: Vice Presidents Who Did Not Finish Their Terms

Vice President (Inaugurated)	Reason for Vacancy	Length of Vacancy
George Clinton (1805)	Died in office (during second term)	11 mos.
Elbridge Gerry (1813)	Died in office	2 yrs., 3 mos.
John Calhoun (1825)	Resigned from office (during second term)	2 mos.
John Tyler (1841)	Became president after death of William Harrison	3 yrs., 11 mos.
Millard Fillmore (1849)	Became president after death of Zachary Taylor	2 yrs., 8 mos.
William King (1853)	Died in office	3 yrs., 11 mos.
Andrew Johnson (1865)	Became president after death of Abraham Lincoln	3 yrs., 11 mos.
Henry Wilson (1873)	Died in office	1 yr., 3 mos.
Chester Arthur (1881)	Became president after death of James Garfield	3 yrs., 6 mos.
Thomas Hendricks (1885)	Died in office	3 yrs., 3 mos.
Garret Hobart (1896)	Died in office	1 yr., 3 mos.
Theodore Roosevelt (1901)	Became president after death of William McKinley	3 yrs., 6 mos.
James Sherman (1909)	Died in office	4 mos.
Calvin Coolidge (1921)	Became president after death of Warren Harding	1 yr., 7 mos.
Harry Truman (1945)	Became president after death of Franklin Roosevelt	3 yrs., 9 mos.
Lyndon Johnson (1963)	Became president after death of John Kennedy	1 yr., 2 mos.
Spiro Agnew (1969)	Resigned from office (during second term)	2 mos.
Gerald Ford (1974)	Became president after resignation of Richard Nixon	4 mos.

"Months" are approximate, based on a 30-day month and rounded to nearest month. The Agnew and Ford vacancies were filled under the provisions of the Twenty-Fifth Amendment.

First, did the framers intend that the "powers and duties"—and not the office itself—devolve to the vice president? If this was the intent, the case could be made that they intended that the vice president be acting president only. If, on the other hand, they meant that the office itself should devolve to the vice president, then the vice president would *be* president.

Second, did the phrase "until . . . a President [is] elected" imply that Congress should hold a special presidential election, or did it mean until the next quadrennial election? Both questions were resolved after President William Henry Harrison died in 1841. His vice president, John Tyler, took the oath of presidential office, thereafter taking the position that he was president, not simply acting president. Although this created some controversy, he served the remainder of Harrison's term, setting a precedent for future presidential vacancies.[17]

It is also worthwhile to note that Section 3 of the Twenty-Fifth Amendment provides that a president may transfer power to the vice president in the case of a temporary inability to exercise presidential power. This clause was exercised, although not formally invoked, when in 1985, Vice President George H. W. Bush served as president for eight hours while President Ronald Reagan underwent surgery. In both 2002 and 2007, Dick Cheney was acting president for a few hours while President George W. Bush underwent a colonoscopy.[18]

Beyond their role as presidential successor vice presidents have little to do. The only other function stipulated by the Constitution (Article I, Section 3) is to act as president of the Senate. In that capacity the vice president presides over the Senate and casts a vote in the event of a tie. In the absence of the vice president, "or when he shall exercise the Office of President of the United States," the Senate selects a president pro tempore to preside over the body in his place.

There is one more function that the vice president fulfills as president of the Senate, and that is of certifying the results of the Electoral College vote. Article II, Section 1, states that after the Electors have met and voted ("in their respective States"), the results shall be signed, certified, and transmitted to the president of the Senate—the vice president. Upon receipt, the vice president "shall, in the Presence of the Senate and House of Representatives, open all the Certificates, and the Votes shall then be counted." The vice president, in other words, announces to Congress who the next president will be. Thus, it was that vice presidents John Adams, Thomas Jefferson, Martin Van Buren, and George H. W. Bush announced that they had been elected president. Vice presidents Richard Nixon (in 1961) and Al Gore (in 2001) announced they had lost. In 1969 Hubert Humphrey would have announced his defeat but was out of the country at the time.

THE ORIGINAL VICE PRESIDENTS

The original system for electing presidents worked reasonably well in terms of selecting well-qualified vice presidents. Electors cast two ballots for president without distinguishing between their first and second choices, and because the second-place finisher became vice president, the first vice presidents were arguably the second-best choice for president. The first two vice presidents were the eminently qualified John Adams (1789–1797) and Thomas Jefferson (1797–1801). Both subsequently had distinguished tenures as president. Of these two, Adams was one of only eight vice presidents (of a total of forty-seven) as of this writing to complete two full four-year terms. Adams is also one of the ten vice presidents to have been elected twice with the same president. The third vice president, Aaron Burr (1801–1805) was seemingly competent, although events subsequent to his election suggest that it was fortunate for the fledgling republic that he was never elevated to the nation's highest office.

In this section we examine each of these three men in terms of their (1) qualifications for vice presidential office, (2) selection as vice president, (3) relations with their president, (4) fulfillment of duties as president of the Senate, and (5) life after their tenure as vice president.

Both Adams and Jefferson were fifty-three years old when they became vice president and had served in a variety of political offices before their tenure as vice president. For Adams this experience was mostly at the national level, whereas Jefferson was active in Virginia politics as well as national politics. For his part, Burr brought roughly ten years of political experience to the office, almost evenly divided between New York state politics and the U.S. Senate. While relatively younger (aged forty-four), Burr was also considered a rising star in the emerging Democratic-Republican Party. See table 2.2.

There was nothing straightforward about the selection of the first three vice presidents, in large part because there were neither established political parties nor a system for nominating presidential candidates. Selections were made by prominent political leaders through conversation and correspondence. There were several individuals being actively considered as George Washington's vice president, including John Jay, John Hancock, and John Rutledge. Adams enjoyed the advantage of being one of the nation's leading political thinkers and played a prominent role in the Revolution. Perhaps as importantly, he was a Federalist (a supporter of the new Constitution) from a New England state, serving to regionally balance the candidacy of the Virginian Washington. However there is some indication that Hancock (also a Federalist from New England) could have been the nation's first

Table 2.2.   Political Experience of the Original Vice Presidents

Name (Age at Time of Election)	Political Experience
John Adams (53)	Member Continental Congress (1774–1777) Commissioner to France (1778–1779) Member, Massachusetts Constitutional Convention (1779) Minister to Netherlands (1782–1788) Minister to England (1785–1788)
Thomas Jefferson (53)	Member, Virginia House of Burgesses (1769–1775) Member, Continental Congress (1775–1776) Governor of Virginia (1779–1781) Member, Virginia House of Delegates (1776–1779, 1782) Member, Confederation Congress (1783–1784) Minister Plenipotentiary to France (1784) Minister to King of France (1785–1788) Secretary of State (1789–1793)
Aaron Burr (44)	Member, New York State Assembly (1784–1785, 1798–1799) New York Attorney General (1789–1791) Commissioner Revolutionary Claims (1791) U.S. Senator from New York (1791–1797)

From Warren, Jack D., "John Adams (1735–1826)," in *Vice Presidents: A Biographical Dictionary*, L. Edward Purcell, ed. (New York: Checkmark Books, 2001), pp. 1–13; Sheridan, Eugene R., "Thomas Jefferson (1743–1826)," in *Vice Presidents: A Biographical Dictionary*, L. Edward Purcell, ed. (New York: Checkmark Books, 2001), pp. 14–22; Kline, Mary-Jo, "Aaron Burr (1756–1836)," in *Vice Presidents: A Biographical Dictionary*, L. Edward Purcell, ed. (New York: Checkmark Books, 2001), 23–31; Young, Donald, *American Roulette: The History and Dilemma of the Vice Presidency* (New York: Holt, Rinehart, and Winston, 1965); Hatfield, *Vice Presidents of the United States*.

vice president had he wanted the job.[19] Because of Adams's support of the administration in the Senate at critical junctures his reelection in 1792 was fairly well assured. He did face some opposition from George Clinton of the emerging Democratic-Republican coalition, but Hamilton and other Federalist leaders worked to ensure his reelection. See table 2.3.

By the time Washington retired, the Democratic-Republican Party, opposed to the centralism of the Federalists, had grown in strength and influence. Two of the party's most prominent leaders, and thus obvious choices to run against Adams for president, were Madison and Thomas Jefferson. Madison was the first choice of many, including his fellow Virginian Jefferson, who had retired from politics three years previously. However Madison made it clear that he did not want the presidency. Jefferson reluctantly agreed to stand against Adams, who was running with Thomas Pinckney. Primarily as the result of the machinations of Adams's archrival Hamilton, who wanted Pinckney elected president, Federalist electors split their votes fairly evenly between Adams, Jefferson, and Pinckney. The unintended result was that the Democratic-Republican Jef-

Table 2.3. Pre-Twelfth Amendment Presidential Elections

Year	Candidate	State	"Party"	Electoral College Votes
1788	George Washington	VA	Federalist	69
	John Adams	MA	Federalist	34
	John Jay	NY	Federalist	9
	Robert Harrison	MD	Federalist	6
	John Rutledge	SC	Federalist	6
	(Seven others)	—	—	14
1792	George Washington	VA	Federalist	132
	John Adams	MA	Federalist	77
	George Clinton	NY	Democratic-Republican	50
	(Two others)	—	—	5
1796	John Adams	MA	Federalist	71
	Thomas Jefferson	VA	Democratic-Republican	68
	Thomas Pinckney	SC	Federalist	59
	Aaron Burr	NY	Democratic-Republican	30
	(Nine others)	—	—	48
1800	Thomas Jefferson	VA	Democratic-Republican	73*
	Aaron Burr	NY	Democratic-Republican	73*
	John Adams	MA	Federalist	65
	Charles Pinckney	SC	Federalist	64
	John Jay	NY	Federalist	1

*On February 17, 1801, the House of Representatives selected Jefferson as president (ten states for Jefferson, four for Burr, with two abstaining). From "Historical Election Results," National Archives and Records Administration, www.archives.gov/federal-register/electoral-college/votes/1789_1821.html#1788, accessed Feb. 13, 2013.

ferson was selected vice president with President Adams, a Federalist.[20] Jefferson thus became one of only two vice presidents in history to serve with a president from the opposing party (Andrew Johnson, Abraham Lincoln's second vice president, was the other).

Leading up to the nation's fourth presidential election Adams's Federalists were divided on how the administration was handling relations with France. Although the party seemed to unite behind Adams early on, Hamilton later defected and savagely attacked him, all but ensuring his defeat. His opponent, Jefferson, was the only incumbent vice president in history to run against a sitting president. Jefferson's running mate, Aaron Burr, was an astute politician and had emerged as the leader of the Democratic-Republicans in the North. The way had been cleared for his unanimous nomination by the party's caucus after party elder Clinton indicated a reluctance to join the ticket.

When the Electoral votes were counted it was found that Jefferson and Burr each had seventy-three votes. A scheme to convince several

Democratic-Republican electors to withhold their vote from Burr—and avoid just this result—had failed. On February 11, 1801, the election went to the House of Representatives, where eight of the sixteen states cast their ballots for Jefferson. This was one short of the necessary majority. After thirty-four more ballots failed to produce a majority for either man, the election was finally decided on February 17, when ten states cast their ballots for Jefferson.[21] Burr became the nation's third vice president.

Like many who held the office after him, Adams was frustrated with the job of vice president. Some of this frustration may have been that when he took office, Congress had not yet voted on a salary for the vice president, and when it did so it was half the amount of the president's salary. His relations with Washington, although cordial, were not close. The two men had met as delegates to the Continental Congress, and although Adams had supported Washington's appointment as commander of the Continental Army, he was at times critical of his command. Although Adams did attend a few cabinet meetings, there is little evidence that Washington consulted his vice president with any frequency on matters of public policy. Nor did the president appear to pay much heed to Adams's recommendations regarding judicial nominations or appointments to the executive.[22] However Washington did seem to believe that Adams should be included with him in the ceremonial tasks associated with the executive branch.

Like Adams, Jefferson was not eager to assume the job of vice president. In his case this was because he had retired from public life and was not anxious to return. In fact he was so ambivalent about the job that he considered not attending his own inauguration. His relationship with Adams was professional and cordial but could not be characterized as close. He respected Adams for his role in the Revolution and as a political thinker but disagreed with his views.

The two met briefly on the eve of the inauguration, discussing how to deal with worsening relations with France. One idea reportedly discussed was sending Jefferson, who had spent four years in France as a diplomat, back to the country in an attempt to improve the situation. This idea was vetoed because neither man thought it an appropriate role for a vice president. Jefferson then suggested sending Madison (like Jefferson, a Democratic-Republican), but in the end Adams decided against this plan. This confirmed, in Jefferson's mind, the idea that Adams was a partisan and would govern as such. Subsequently he turned his energies away from the executive and toward the Senate and party leadership.[23]

Despite the fact that they hailed from the same party, Burr's relationship with Jefferson was, if anything, more strained than was Jefferson's with Adams. Jefferson did not completely trust his vice president, suspecting that Burr had his sights on the presidency and had manipulated voting in the House subsequent to the tie in the Electoral College to that end. In addition, Burr did little to endear himself to Jefferson by presenting a number of his supporters' names to the president to be considered for jobs in the federal government. Burr was a consummate politician, having been instrumental in building the New York state Democratic-Republican party machine. And although Jefferson was no stranger to party politics, he was less comfortable with the patronage-heavy aspects of machine politics. The two, in short, were ill-suited to each other.[24]

All three of the original vice presidents focused most of their attention on their role as president of the Senate. In this they were somewhat circumscribed by Senate rules that loosely defined the job as that of a presiding officer only. The president of the Senate was not, to be more specific, expected to take an active role in debate.

Opinionated and somewhat lacking in tact, this role did not befit Adams. He frequently expressed his opinions to the Senate and went so far as to use his position to lecture the body. One of the more notorious examples of this dealt with the issue of formal titles for members of the executive branch. Before Washington arrived in the capital Adams had proposed to the Senate that the president and other high officials in the executive have formal titles, reminiscent of British royalty, and that access to and relations with these officials be governed by formal and restrictive rules. The ensuing debate, in which Adams took an active part, did not endear him to the Senate, or to Washington, for that matter. The proposals were rejected, and the perception that Adams had aristocratic tendencies was furthered.

This said, by all accounts the nation's first vice president took the job of president of the Senate very seriously. He was rarely absent from the chair and did an admirable job in facilitating and conducting the business of the Senate. He also holds the distinction of having cast twenty-nine tie-breaking votes in the Senate, the most of any vice president in history. Five of these votes were during debates over the location of the national capital. Another dealt with the question of whether the president had the power to remove, without Senate consent, officeholders who had been previously appointed and confirmed by the Senate. Adams strongly believed this was an executive prerogative, arguing vociferously in favor of it and lobbying senators to vote accordingly.

Jefferson was the first vice president to preside over a Senate controlled by the opposition party, and Federalist senators were not above attacking him from the floor. Because of this Jefferson was far more constrained in his conduct than was Adams and made little attempt to shape the agenda of the Senate. As vice president Jefferson presided over the impeachment trial of William Blount, a Democratic-Republican senator from Tennessee who had conspired to aid the British in establishing a foothold in

Louisiana and West Florida. Fearful that impeachment would be used as a partisan tool to punish political enemies, Jefferson privately lobbied several senators to have Blount tried in criminal court instead. In the end the Senate decided that senators could not be impeached. In addition he was apparently instrumental in thwarting an attempt by Federalists to try a Democratic-Republican editor, William Duane, for contempt of the Senate. Duane had refused to appear before the body and answer for his unauthorized publication of a highly partisan Federalist bill.

Jefferson's enduring legacy as vice president was his *Manual of Parliamentary Practice for the Use of the Senate of the United States*. Although the Senate had established rules regarding the conduct of its business, these rules were rather vague with respect to how the President of the Senate might decide on a variety of points of order. Jefferson set about consulting precedent from the British Parliament, adapting procedure on fifty-three different points of order. His work has governed the Senate ever since and was later adopted by the House of Representatives as well.[25]

In contrast to his two predecessors, Burr's tenure as president of the Senate was fairly unremarkable. Personal problems kept him from attending legislative sessions as regularly as either Adams or Jefferson. He missed most of the opening sessions (including the very first at which he was to be initiated), as well as most of the debate over the Louisiana Purchase and the Twelfth Amendment. However when present he was widely regarded as an adept and fair parliamentarian. Like Jefferson, he cast only three tie-breaking votes in the Senate, one of which was a vote opposing his president and the repeal of the Federalist sponsored Judiciary Bill of 1801. The repeal would have removed the "midnight" judges appointed by Adams before he left office and was a central plank in Jefferson's campaign.

Burr did have the distinction of presiding over the first Senate trial to successfully remove a federal judge. Federal District Court Judge John Pickering, who suffered from alcoholism and dementia, was impeached in the House in 1803 and removed from office by the Senate in 1804. Later that year Burr presided over the trial of Supreme Court Justice Samuel Chase, who had been impeached on the grounds of judicial misconduct. Chase was not removed from office. Accounts suggest that for the most part Burr handled himself admirably during the proceedings of both. The only other notable act he made as president of the Senate was his farewell address to the body. Delivered on March 2, 1805, behind closed doors, he praised the body in terms so laudatory that several senators were reportedly moved to tears.[26]

The trajectory of the political lives of each of the three original vice presidents subsequent to their tenures in office was varied. It was fairly well understood, for example, that Adams would likely succeed Washington as the nation's second president. Adams and Jefferson are two of the nine vice presidents that were elected president in their own right, and two of only four to be elected to the presidency immediately after serving as vice president. However on taking office, Adams was forced to confront a growing crisis in Franco-American relations. He managed to avert a war, but the crisis divided the country. Adams was also responsible for signing the controversial Alien and Sedition Acts in 1798. After losing in his reelection bid in 1800 he retired from public life, living long enough to see his son, John Quincy Adams, elected president in 1824.

Jefferson served two terms as president and is recognized as one of the better presidents in American history. He was the only vice president to serve two full terms as president. As president, Jefferson was responsible for a significant shift in the orientation of the presidency, from an aristocratic, philosopher king model, to a president more attuned to the needs of the people. He was commander-in-chief during a four year naval war with Tripoli over pirate attacks on American shipping and was responsible for negotiating the Louisiana Purchase, more than doubling the size of the young nation. Consistent with Democratic-Republican ideas opposing centralist tendencies of the Federalists, Jefferson oversaw a gradual movement of power from the central government to the states. Although his second term was dominated by French and British challenges to American neutrality, he avoided war with both. Despite entreaties from his party to stand for a third term he retired to Monticello in 1809. His legacy includes the founding of the University of Virginia and the sale of his personal library to the Library of Congress. After his presidency he resumed his correspondence and friendship with Adams, and in perhaps a fitting historical twist, the two died within hours of each other on July 4, 1826.

Burr's post–vice presidency was far less illustrious than that of his two predecessors. In early 1804 he learned that Jefferson intended to replace him on the ticket with fellow New Yorker Clinton. The vice president then entered and subsequently lost the race for governor of New York. During the campaign it came to his attention that his archrival, Alexander Hamilton, had made certain comments about him at a social event. The ensuing conflict escalated in a series of letters between the two, and in June of 1804, Burr challenged Hamilton to a duel. The event took place in New Jersey on July 11, 1804, where Burr fatally wounded Hamilton. The vice president was indicted for murder in both New York and New Jersey, although he never stood trial. However the event, as might be expected, cast a cloud over his final months in office. Retiring from politics at the age of forty-nine, Burr was heavily in debt. He traveled west and eventually became embroiled in a conspiracy to lure the western states into a new confederacy with several states and territories in the southeast. For this he was arrested and tried for treason. After his acquittal he traveled to Europe, then returning to New York to resume the private practice of law.

THE TWELFTH AMENDMENT

The framers of the Constitution understood that rules had effects and believed that a good constitutional design could help ensure proper functioning of the political system. But designing institutions is not a perfect science. Rules frequently have unintended consequences, especially when circumstances change. Such was the case with the original provisions for selecting presidents.

In the third presidential election in 1796, Jefferson was elected as Adams's vice president.[27] This may not have been a problem except for the fact that both had run with another running mate and identified with different political factions. This outcome was made possible by the fact that Electors cast two votes, undifferentiated, for president. Jefferson made little effort to conceal his differences with the president, shattering the notion that a president spoke for his entire administration.[28] The two were simply not politically compatible. The fourth presidential election (1800) saw a different mutation of the ill-effects that the original Electoral College system could produce: a tie vote between the presidential and vice presidential candidates (Jefferson and Burr). Although it was clear to most that Jefferson was the presidential choice of the majority of Electors who had voted for him, the House took a full week to decide the outcome.

The point is that the results of the elections of 1796 and 1800 brought the flaws of the presidential selection process into sharp relief. The election of 1796 had shown that the system allowed for the possibility of selecting a president and vice president from different parties. The election of 1800 illustrated that under the original system the potential for a tie was unacceptably high. Thus, Congress set about drafting and passing the Twelfth Amendment, ratified in 1804, which stipulates that Electors "vote by ballot for President and Vice-President." In other words, instead of casting two votes for president, Electors were required to "name in their ballots the person voted for as President, and in distinct ballots the person voted for as Vice-President." The vice president, like the president, is "The person having the greatest number of votes. . . . if such number be a majority of the whole number of electors appointed, and if no person have a majority, then from the two highest numbers on the list, the Senate shall choose the Vice-President."

Although there was consensus that the system for selecting presidents needed adjustment, debate over the Twelfth Amendment saw renewed debate over the institution of the vice presidency. Although the amendment solved the problems of presidential selection and presidential and vice presidential compatibility, it created another problem. Under the original system, any individual that received votes from the Electoral College had the potential to become president. Now, Electors specified who was to be president and vice president, which meant that qualified individuals had little incentive to run for the vice presidency. Being assigned the second spot on the ticket meant that if elected they would be relegated to the political sidelines for four years. Many members of Congress, both Federalists and Democratic-Republicans alike, understood the effects the amendment would have.[29] Senator William Plumer of New Hampshire predicted that

> The office of Vice-president will be a sinecure. It will be brought to market and exposed to sale to ambitious, aspiring candidates for the Presidency. Will [a presidential candidate's] friends and favorites promote the election of a man of talents, probity, and (general) popularity for Vice-president, and who may become his rival? No! They will seek a man of moderate talents, whose ambition is bounded by that office, and whose influence will aid them in electing the President.[30]

The debate over the issue eventually culminated in a vote in both houses of Congress to abolish the vice presidency. The vote failed, nineteen to twelve in the Senate, and eighty-five to twenty-seven in the House.[31] But the greatest fears of the proponents of abolishing the office—that candidate quality would suffer as the result of the Twelfth Amendment—were quickly realized. Electoral considerations became the prime, in fact almost the exclusive, consideration in selecting vice presidential candidates throughout the nineteenth century. This was the era that gave rise to the image of vice presidents as "cranks, criminals, tax cheats, and golfers."[32,33] We turn to this period, known here as the traditional era (from 1804 to 1900), in the next chapter.

NOTES

1. Jody Baumgartner and Rhonda Evans Case, "Constitutional Design of the Executive: Vice Presidencies in Comparative Perspective," *Congress and the Presidency* 36 (2009):148–63.

2. James Madison, *Notes on the Debates in the Federal Convention of 1787, with an Introduction by Adrienne Koch* (Athens, OH: Ohio University, 1984), 596–97. The discussion of the creation of the office is summarized nicely in Joel K. Goldstein, "The New Constitutional Vice Presidency," *Wake Forest Law Review* 30(3) (1995): 510–13.

3. Mark O. Hatfield, *Vice Presidents of the United States, 1789–1993* (Washington, DC: U.S. Government Printing Office, 1997).

4. Alexander Hamilton, James Madison, and John Jay, *The Federalist Papers* (New York: Signet Classics, 2003)

5. Madison, *Notes on the Debates in the Federal Convention of 1787*, 427.

6. Ibid. See also Arthur M. Schlesinger, Jr., "On the Presidential Succession." *Political Science Quarterly* 89(3), (1974): 475–506.

7. Goldstein, "The New Constitutional Vice Presidency," 511.

8. Madison, *Notes on the Debates in the Federal Convention of 1787*, 537.

9. Also known as the "Committee on Postponed Matters" or the "Committee on Unfinished Parts."

10. Madison, *Notes on the Debates in the Federal Convention of 1787*. See also Sidney M. Milkis and Michael Nelson, *The American Presidency: Origins and Development, 1776–1998*, 3rd ed. (Washington, DC: Congressional Quarterly, 1998).

11. Milkis and Nelson, *The American Presidency*, 52–53.

12. Madison, *Notes on the Debates in the Federal Convention of 1787*, 596. See also Goldstein, "The New Constitutional Vice Presidency"; Louis C. Hatch, *A History of the Vice-Presidency of the United States*, ed. Earl Shoup (Westport, CT: Greenwood, 1970).

13. Michael Dorman, *The Second Man: The Changing Role of the Vice Presidency* (New York: Delacorte, 1968).

14. See also Arthur M. Schlesinger, Jr., "On the Presidential Succession," 49.

15. This latter provision was probably specified to ensure that a president had an attachment to, or understanding of, the country.

16. Hatfield, *Vice Presidents of the United States, 1789–1993*, xv.

17. Barzman, *Madmen and Geniuses*, 75–76; Schlesinger, "On the Presidential Succession," 495–96.

18. Deb Riechmann, "Bush to Have Colonoscopy at Camp David," *The Associated Press*, July 20, 2007, www.washingtonpost.com/wp-dyn/content/article/2007/07/20/AR2007072001039.

19. Definitive accounts of Adams's vice presidency can be found in see Page Smith, *John Adams*, Volume Two (Garden City, NJ: Doubleday, 1962); Linda Dudik Guerrero, *John Adam's Vice Presidency, 1789–1797:The Neglected Man In The Forgotten Office* (New York: Arno Press, 1982); see also Jack D. Warren, "John Adams (1735–1826)," in *Vice Presidents: A Biographical Dictionary*, ed. L. Edward Purcell (New York: Checkmark Books, 2001), pp. 1–13.; Hatfield, *Vice Presidents of the United States*, 1–14.

20. Jefferson's vice presidency is examined at length in Dumas Malone, *Jefferson and His Time*, Volume Five (Boston: Little, Brown, 1948); Noble E. Cunningham, *In Pursuit of Reason: The Life of Thomas Jefferson* (Baton Rouge: Louisiana State University, 1987); see also Eugene R. Sheridan, "Thomas Jefferson (1743–1826)," in *Vice Presidents: A Biographical Dictionary*, ed. L. Edward Purcell (New York: Checkmark Books, 2001), pp. 14–22.; Hatfield, *Vice Presidents of the United States*, 15–28.

21. See Milton Lomask, *Aaron Burr: The Years from Princeton to Vice President, 1756–1805* (New York: Farrar, Straus & Giroux, 1979); Mary Jo Kline, "Aaron Burr (1756–1836)," in *Vice Presidents: A Biographical Dictionary*, ed. L. Edward Purcell

(New York: Checkmark Books, 2001), pp. 23–31; Hatfield, *Vice Presidents of the United States*, 29–46.

22. Warren, "John Adams (1735–1826)"; Hatfield, *Vice Presidents of the United States*, 1–14.

23. Sheridan, "Thomas Jefferson (1743–1826)"; Hatfield, *Vice Presidents of the United States*, 15–28.

24. Kline, "Aaron Burr (1756–1836)"; Hatfield, *Vice Presidents of the United States*, 29–46.

25. Sheridan, "Thomas Jefferson (1743–1826)"; Hatfield, *Vice Presidents of the United States*, 15–28.

26. Kline, "Aaron Burr (1756–1836)"; Hatfield, *Vice Presidents of the United States*, 29–46.

27. Dorman, *The Second Man*, 6–17.

28. Ibid., 13–15.

29. Schlesinger, "On the Presidential Succession," 491–92.

30. A quoted in Hatch, *A History of the Vice-Presidency of the United States*, 9.

31. Goldstein, *The Modern American Vice Presidency*, 6. See also Goldstein, "The New Constitutional Vice Presidency," 514–15.

32. Tally, *Bland Ambition*.

33. Milkis and Nelson, *The American Presidency*, 456.

3

+

The Traditional Era: Nineteenth-Century Vice Presidents

In 1804 it was still somewhat unclear what role the vice president might play in the new American republic. This changed fairly quickly as the result of the passage of the Twelfth Amendment. Previously there was some incentive for well-qualified statesmen to agree to run for the office because there was a chance, if only a slight chance, that he might be selected president. The Twelfth Amendment changed this: running for vice president meant serving as vice president if the ticket won. Because there are few formal duties assigned to the vice president in the Constitution, this worked as a powerful disincentive for individuals to run for the office. In other words, men of stature did not aspire to the vice presidency. The result? The vice presidency, previously fairly weak, went into "into prompt decline" and became all but irrelevant.[1] If we discount the fact that vice presidents are first in line to assume the presidency in the event of a presidential vacancy, the office was all but insignificant.

As one vice presidential scholar put it, "nineteenth-century vice presidents make up a rouges' gallery of personal and political failures."[2] It was in this traditional era, from 1805 to 1901, that the image of vice presidents as incompetents, or worse, was formed. Although this image is not completely unwarranted, it is somewhat exaggerated. Although many traditional-era vice presidents were not model statespersons, they were far from being political hacks. Table 3.1 lists the twenty-one men who served as vice president during this time.

Two traditional-era vice presidents (George Clinton and John Calhoun) served under two different presidents. Martin Van Buren was the only vice president from this era who was later elected president.

Table 3.1. Traditional-Era (1805–1901) Vice Presidents

In Office	Vice President	President	(Notes)
1805–1812	George Clinton	Thomas Jefferson (1805–1809); James Madison (1809–1812)	Died in office April 20, 1812; vice presidency vacant until March 4, 1813
1813–1814	Elbridge Gerry	James Madison	Died in office Nov. 23, 1814; vice presidency vacant until March 4, 1817
1817–1825	Daniel Tompkins	James Monroe	
1825–1832	John Calhoun	John Adams (1825–1829); Andrew Jackson (1829–1832)	Resigned Dec. 28, 1832; vice presidency vacant until March 4, 1833
1833–1837	Martin Van Buren	Andrew Jackson	
1837–1841	Richard Johnson	Martin Van Buren	
1841	John Tyler	William Harrison	Assumed presidency April 4, 1841, after death of Harrison; vice presidency vacant until March 4, 1845
1845–1849	George Dallas	James Polk	
1849–1850	Millard Fillmore	Zachary Taylor	Assumed presidency July 9, 1850, after death of Taylor; vice presidency vacant until March 4, 1853
1853	William King	Franklin Pierce	Died in office April 18, 1853; vice presidency vacant until March 4, 1857

1857–1861	John Breckinridge	James Buchanan	
1861–1865	Hannibal Hamlin	Abraham Lincoln	
1865	Andrew Johnson	Abraham Lincoln	Assumed presidency April 15, 1865, after assassination of Lincoln; vice presidency vacant until March 4, 1869
1869–1873	Schuyler Colfax	Ulysses Grant	
1873–1875	Henry Wilson	Ulysses Grant	Died in office Nov. 22, 1875; vice presidency vacant until March 4, 1877
1877–1881	William Wheeler	Rutherford Hayes	
1881	Chester Arthur	James Garfield	Assumed presidency Sept. 19, 1881, after assassination of Garfield; vice presidency vacant until March 4, 1885
1885	Thomas Hendricks	Grover Cleveland	Died in office Nov. 25, 1885; vice presidency vacant until March 4, 1889
1889–1893	Levi Morton	Benjamin Harrison	
1893–1897	Adlai Stevenson I	Grover Cleveland	
1897–1899	Garret Hobart	William McKinley	Died in office Nov. 21, 1899; vice presidency vacant until March 4, 1901

Four vice presidents during this period assumed the presidency after the death of the president: John Tyler, Millard Fillmore, Andrew Johnson, and Chester Arthur. Tyler had served only one month before President William Henry Harrison passed away. None of these men were subsequently elected president in their own right. Six died in office, including both of James Madison's vice presidents (Clinton and Elbridge Gerry). One, William King, served as vice president for only forty-six days. Calhoun resigned the office, making him one of only two who have ever done so. In fact, Daniel Tompkins was the only vice president from this period to complete two full terms in office.

In this chapter we examine this traditional era of the vice presidency. The chapter provides an overview of what kinds of people were considered for the job, how they were selected, their role in the election campaign, what they did in office, and their lives after the vice presidency.

SELECTING VICE PRESIDENTIAL NOMINEES IN THE TRADITIONAL ERA

The original method for selecting presidential and vice presidential candidates is known as the congressional caucus system, or "King Caucus." Starting in 1804, party leaders in Congress met to decide which candidates should represent the party in the general election. This system began to unravel by 1820 and by 1824 several factors converged to replace this method of selecting presidential tickets. These included the death of the one-party system that had dominated American politics for two decades and an anti-elite backlash over the legislative caucus nomination system within the states.[3]

From 1828 on, vice presidential nominees, like presidential nominees, were selected at national party conventions by party leaders and convention delegates. "Four categories of people appear to have played a major role [in the selection process:] (1) the convention managers and other personal representatives of the presidential nominee; (2) the heads of major state delegations that had supported the nominee; (3) other important party leaders, such as the Speaker of the House or chairman of the national committee; and (4) anyone else who could worm his way through the proceedings."[4]

Presidential candidates themselves had little or no say in who their running mate would be during this period. This had an effect on how closely, if at all, presidents and vice presidents worked together. Moreover, very little, if any, consideration was given to issues of competence, compatibility with the presidential nominee, succession, and so on, in the selection process. Other aspects of the selection of vice presidential candidates during this period are worthy of note.

First, unlike presidential nominations, the selection of the vice presidential nominee was rarely seen as a matter of much consequence. "Very little pains [were] bestowed on the election of a vice-president."[5] In most cases the nominee was selected after only a single round of balloting,[6] and was "seldom prolonged over two or three ballots."[7] To be more specific, half of the thirty vice presidential nominations during this period were decided on the first ballot, eight were decided on the second, and two on a third ballot. Three nominations were settled without a formal vote. These included William Graham, the Whig candidate of 1852, who was declared the "unanimous choice" by the convention chair because no one seemed to want the nomination, as well as William English (Democrat, 1880) and Whitelaw Reid (Republican, 1892), who were nominated by acclamation. This is in sharp contrast to balloting for the presidential nominee, which usually lasted multiple ballots. In 1860, the Democrats took fifty-seven ballots to nominate Stephen Douglas; in 1852 the Whigs selected Winfield Scott on the fifty-third ballot, whereas Franklin Pierce was chosen by the Democrats on the forty-ninth ballot.

Second, few individuals campaigned for the vice presidential nomination. In fact, it was difficult to convince great men to accept it. "The prospect of spending four years presiding over the Senate, only to be replaced at the end of the term, dissuaded most talented political leaders from accepting vice presidential nominations in the first place."[8] The job was seen as a political dead end. When Arthur was offered the vice presidential nomination in 1880, Republican Party notable Roscoe Conkling warned him to "drop it as you would a red hot shoe from the forge" and refuse the nomination.[9] Daniel Webster, one of the most prominent senators of the nineteenth century, refused the Whig nomination for the vice presidency by claiming "I do not propose to be buried until I am really dead."

A final aspect of vice presidential candidate selection in this era that stands out is that several sitting vice presidents were dropped from the ticket in their respective president's reelection effort. Calhoun was not renominated by John Quincy Adams in 1828, but instead ran with Andrew Jackson (and was victorious, thereby serving his two terms with two different presidents). Hannibal Hamlin was elected in 1860 with Abraham Lincoln but dropped in the president's reelection bid and replaced by Andrew Johnson in 1864. Schuyler Colfax was elected in 1868 with Ulysses Grant but dropped from the ticket in favor of Henry Wilson in 1872. Levi Morton was elected 1888 with Benjamin Harrison, but Harrison ran with Adlai Stevenson I in 1892.[10] This can be attributed to the fact that electoral considerations were paramount in the selection of a running mate in the traditional era. In other words the selection was made to help win the election, and changes in the political environment often demanded a new candidate be chosen in the reelection effort.[11]

In this regard we can think of the vice presidential nomination during this period as a consolation prize, strategically bestowed. Because American political parties are loose collections of various factions (North–South, hard money–soft money, Stalwart–Progressive), selecting a presidential nominee meant that some faction of the party typically "lost." The vice presidential nomination was made to reward the losers, or "console one of the defeated aspirants for the presidential nomination . . . [it was] handed over to his friends to be given to some politician of their choice."[12]

For example, in 1852, the Democratic nomination was initially a battle between James Buchanan and Lewis Cass. After forty-eight ballots the convention finally selected a "dark horse" candidate, Franklin Pierce. To reward Buchanan supporters the vice presidential nomination went to William King, a close friend of Buchanan.[13] In 1880, the Republicans selected James Garfield as a compromise presidential candidate (on the thirty-sixth ballot). They offered the vice presidential nomination to Levi Morton, a close ally of Conkling, who had been promoting a third term for Ulysses Grant. When Morton refused the nomination, it went to the second-ranking New York Stalwart (the Conkling faction), Arthur.[14]

Attempting to unite the party with the vice presidential nomination often took the form of adding regional balance to the presidential ticket. "One of the chief assets of the American party system in the past has been its ability, with the exception of the Civil War period, to reduce conflict by enforcing compromise within the major factions of the party."[15] Using the vice presidential nomination to add regional balance was one such form of intraparty compromise. Only five (of forty-eight) presidential tickets from the traditional era were *not* regionally balanced.[16] After the two-party system was in place (1832), only one ticket (Republicans Ulysses Grant, Illinois, and Schuyler Colfax, Indiana, in 1868) was not regionally balanced.

Geographically, Northern states dominated vice presidential selection in this era, supplying more than half (twenty-six) of the vice presidential nominees. A full third (sixteen) of the tickets during this period had a presidential and vice presidential candidate from the North and the Midwest. In fact, from 1860 to 1896, sixteen of twenty presidential tickets paired a Northerner and a Midwesterner, and all twelve tickets from 1876 to 1896 did so. An additional twenty-two tickets from this era saw a Northerner matched with a candidate from either a Border or Southern state.

The vice presidential choice also seems to have been made with an eye toward selecting a candidate from a state rich in electoral votes. Of the forty-eight major-party tickets in the traditional era, fourteen had a vice presidential candidate from New York, which commanded anywhere from 8 to 15 percent of the available electoral votes throughout this period (a percentage analogous to California's today). Pennsylvania comes in a distant second with five vice presidential candidates. Of course, coming from a state that is electorally rich means little if the ticket does not carry the state in the election. Conventional wisdom holds that the vice presidential candidate should help carry their home state. But conventional wisdom is hard to reconcile with reality in this case.[17] In the traditional era, only 45 percent (twenty-one) of presidential tickets carried the vice presidential candidate's home state.[18]

Table 3.2 lists the forty-five vice presidential candidates from this era.[19] Five of these men ran for vice president with the same presidential candidate in two consecutive elections (George Clinton, 1804 and 1808; Rufus

Table 3.2.   Traditional-Era Vice Presidential Candidates (1804–1896)

Year	Winning Candidate (Presidential Candidate)	Losing Candidate (Presidential Candidate)
1804	George Clinton (Thomas Jefferson)	Rufus King (Charles Pinckney)
1808	George Clinton (James Madison)	Rufus King (Charles Pinckney)
1812	Elbridge Gerry (James Madison)	Jared Ingersoll (Dewitt Clinton)
1816	Daniel Tompkins (James Monroe)	John Howard (Rufus King)
1820	Daniel Tompkins (James Monroe)	Richard Rush (John Adams)
1824	John Calhoun (John Adams)	Nathan Sanford (Andrew Jackson)
1828	John Calhoun (Andrew Jackson)	Richard Rush (John Adams)
1832	Martin Van Buren (Andrew Jackson)	John Sergeant (Henry Clay)
1836	Richard Johnson (Martin Van Buren)	Francis Granger (William Harrison)
1840	John Tyler (William Harrison)	Richard Johnson (Martin Van Buren)
1844	George Dallas (James Polk)	Theodore Frelinghuysen (Henry Clay)
1848	Millard Fillmore (Zachary Taylor)	William Butler (Lewis Cass)
1852	William King (Franklin Pierce)	William Graham (Winfield Scott)
1856	John Breckinridge (James Buchanan)	William Dayton (John Fremont)
1860	Hannibal Hamlin (Abraham Lincoln)	Joseph Lane (John Breckinridge)
1864	Andrew Johnson (Abraham Lincoln)	George Pendleton (George McClellan)
1868	Schuyler Colfax (Ulysses Grant)	Francis Blair Jr. (Horatio Seymour)
1872	Henry Wilson (Ulysses Grant)	B. Gratz Brown (Horace Greeley)
1876	William Wheeler (Rutherford Hayes)	Thomas Hendricks (Samuel Tilden)
1880	Chester Arthur (James Garfield)	William English (Winfield Hancock)
1884	Thomas Hendricks (Grover Cleveland)	John Logan (James Blaine)
1888	Levi Morton (Benjamin Harrison)	Allen Thurman (Grover Cleveland)
1892	Adlai Stevenson I (Grover Cleveland)	Whitelaw Reid (Benjamin Harrison)
1896	Garret Hobart (William McKinley)	Arthur Sewall (William Bryan)

King, 1804 and 1808; Tompkins, 1816 and 1820; Calhoun, 1824 and 1828; and Richard Johnson, 1836 and 1840). After 1840 no traditional-era vice president was retained on the ticket in his president's reelection bid. Two ran for vice president twice, in nonconsecutive elections (Richard Rush in 1820 and 1828; and Thomas Hendricks in 1876 and 1884).

GENERAL CHARACTERISTICS OF
TRADITIONAL-ERA VICE PRESIDENTIAL NOMINEES

One observer noted that in the nineteenth century, parties selected men "in the second rank" as vice presidential candidates.[20] To be fair it is difficult to say with any certainty what the qualifications for an office like the vice presidency might be. But we can come to some determination regarding an individuals' readiness for the position by examining their prior political experience. The assumption here is that those who have held public office, especially at higher levels of government, are more qualified than those who have not. Of course we must acknowledge that although this is a popular metric in weighing vice presidential qualification, it is not without problems. There are several other factors that may speak to this question. For example, which offices (e.g., the U.S. House of Representatives? The U.S. Senate?) better equip one to serve as vice president? What about quality of service? Even if an individual served in office, how well did they perform their duties? And how many years, served in which offices, are necessary? There are no ready answers to these questions, primarily because in the end they are incapable of being answered in any scientific fashion. In other words they are either difficult to measure empirically (e.g., quality of service), based in opinion (which offices are better?), or both.

This said we can get a rough measure of readiness by looking at years served and in which offices. All told, traditional-era vice presidential candidates averaged 17.1 years of political experience before their nomination. Almost three-quarters of the candidates held office at the national level immediately before their nomination. Only one, Arthur Sewall (who ran with William Jennings Bryan in 1896) had never held public office before receiving the vice presidential nomination. Restricting attention to only nonincumbent vice presidential candidates, table 3.3 details the number and percentage of which types of offices these forty-four candidates held, the average years served in those offices (of those who actually held the office in question), and the maximum number of years served.

As table 3.3 reveals, only three of the forty-four individuals (Levi Morton, 1888; Whitelaw Reid, 1892; and Sewall, 1896) who ran for vice president in the traditional era did not serve in either local or state government

Table 3.3. Political Offices Served by Forty-Four Traditional-Era Vice Presidential Candidates

	Number Candidates Served	Percentage Served	Maximum Years Served	Average Years Served**
State and Local Government*	41	91.1	14	5.4
Governor	12	26.7	21	5.0
U.S. House Representatives	29	64.4	20	6.0
U.S. Senate	21	46.7	29	8.8
Other National Government	21	46.7	17	5.4

* Does not include years served as governor (if any).
** Average represents years only of those who served in the office.

at some previous point in their careers.[21] Most (thirty-five, or 79.5 percent) started their political careers at the local or state level of government. The 91.1 percent of those who had been elected to an office served for an average of 5.4 years apiece. The maximum number of years any one candidate (Andrew Johnson, 1864) served at this level was 14. Only six (Jared Ingersoll, 1812; Tyler, 1840; Theodore Frelinghuysen, 1844; Fillmore, 1848; William English, 1880; and Garret Hobart, 1896) were serving in local or state government at the time of their vice presidential nomination.

A full quarter (26.7%) served as governor of their state, for an average of five years. Clinton (1804) served as governor of New York for twenty-one years (1777–1795, and 1801–1804), whereas Tompkins (1816) was governor of the same state for ten years (1807–1817).

Besides state government, the most common office in the backgrounds of these men was service in the U.S. House. Almost two-thirds served as a House representative for an average of six years. The maximum number of years served in the House by any of these candidates was 20 (Richard Johnson, 1836). Almost half (46.7%) served in the U.S. Senate, for an average of 8.8 years, although William King (1852) was a senator for 29 years before running for the vice presidency. A full 40 percent of the candidates from this period were serving in the U.S. House or Senate at the time of their nomination. Finally, many also served in some other national-level office (national judiciary or executive) as well. Nathan Sanford (1824), for example, was a U.S. Attorney for the District of New York from 1803 to 1815. Before running for the vice presidency in 1828, Richard Rush was Attorney General from 1814 to 1817, Minister to Great Britain from 1817 to 1825, and Secretary of the Treasury from 1825 to 1829.

A popular belief about the vice presidency is that vice presidents and vice presidential candidates are political novices, incompetents, or both. However the political backgrounds of these candidates suggest that this may not necessarily be the case. On average a traditional-era vice presidential candidate held their first political office at the age of twenty-seven, and most had multiple years of experience in higher levels of government.

The youngest vice presidential candidate in the traditional era at the time of nomination was John Breckinridge (1856), aged thirty-five. The oldest was Allen Thurman, who at the age of seventy-five ran with Grover Cleveland in 1888. The average age of a vice presidential candidate in this era was fifty-four years old. All of these candidates were white, male, and Protestant. Almost three-quarters had been lawyers before entering politics, and roughly a third had served in the military at one time or another.

VICE PRESIDENTIAL CANDIDATE CAMPAIGNING IN THE TRADITIONAL ERA

The role of traditional-era vice presidential candidates in the campaign was minimal. This was not a function of the low regard held for the office or the men who aspired to it, but rather that fact that until the late 1800s presidential candidates themselves generally did not campaign on their own behalf. Lincoln, for example, was almost invisible from public view during the campaign of 1860.[22] The "front porch campaigns" of Garfield in 1880, Benjamin Harrison in 1888, and William McKinley in 1896 are good examples of how presidential candidates were expected to campaign. In each case the candidate would make speeches, but only to delegations that came to them. In fact it was considered somewhat unseemly for presidential candidates to campaign too actively for the position, a sign that perhaps he wanted the job too much—and was thus a less than desirable candidate. In addition, the state of transportation and communications technology all but demanded that candidates rely on political party organizations (national, state, and local) to conduct the campaign on their behalf. There were no jet airplanes to help candidates travel around the country and no radio or television (or Internet) to broadcast campaign messages to a national audience.

This said, there were exceptions to this norm. For example John Breckenridge toured the mid-Atlantic and Midwestern states in 1856 on behalf of the campaign of Buchanan. Colfax actively stumped for Grant during the campaign of 1868,[23] as did his opponent Francis Blair Jr. (for Horatio Seymour). Generally speaking vice presidential candidates during the traditional era were only expected to carry their home state and their campaign efforts were largely geographically restricted. Arthur, for example, organized the 1880 Republican campaign in New York but did not campaign outside the state.[24]

In fact, it was not unusual for the party to play down the vice presidential candidate's place on the ticket, out of a desire that the mediocre record of the men nominated not be scrutinized too closely. This was the case, for example, in 1876, when the Republican William Wheeler (who successfully ran with Rutherford Hayes) "played a decidedly less prominent part in the campaign" than did his opponent Hendricks.[25] In 1840, Tyler lent the campaign his name in the form of the campaign slogan, "Tippecanoe and Tyler Too." The "Tippecanoe" referred to presidential candidate William Henry Harrison, hero of the Battle of Tippecanoe in the War of 1812. However beyond this contribution, Tyler was asked by Harrison to remain silent and inactive throughout the campaign.[26]

IN OFFICE: THE FORMAL ROLES OF TRADITIONAL-ERA VICE PRESIDENTS

The formal (constitutional and statutory) duties of the vice presidency are minimal. As President of the Senate, the vice president presides over sessions of the Senate (and, with the Speaker of the House, over joint sessions of Congress). This involves recognizing individual Senators (allowing them to speak), enforcing Senate rules, and resolving disputes over procedure by interpreting the rules. This latter power, however, is minimal because the Senate can reject the rulings of the presiding officer. At minimum, the job of presiding over the Senate requires that the vice president be present at the start of each new Congressional session while committees and leaders are being selected.

The Constitution (Article I, Section 3) also stipulates that each Senate select a President pro tempore, or "President for a time," who presides in the vice president's absence. Historically this position is filled by a senior member of the majority party. Modern vice presidents, as a rule, leave the business of presiding over the Senate to this President pro tempore. This was, generally speaking, not the case in the traditional era. During this time it was common for vice presidents to take the job of presiding officer fairly seriously because the dominant view was that the vice presidency was a legislative office. Of course some were less than dutiful in this regard. Clinton, for example, frequently violated Senate procedures and was often simply absent, "[preferring to warm] himself by the fire to presiding over the Senate."[27] Tompkins was also frequently absent. But most traditional-era vice presidents performed their duty as President of the Senate quite admirably.

Gerry was a faithful officer even through poor health later in his term. In fact Gerry was present throughout most of 1813, to the point where the Senate was unable to elect a President pro tempore because the vice president was always present when the Senate was in session. This was a calculated move on his part. President Madison was in poor health and Gerry himself was somewhat elderly (he was sixty-eight at the time of his election). At the time the President pro tempore was third in line for presidential succession. Gerry, loyal to the president, was unwilling to allow a Senate majority hostile to the president to elect a President pro tempore who would also presumably attempt to undo the president's policies were he to assume the presidency.[28] Accounts suggest that Van Buren, a former senator himself, also served faithfully as presiding officer. This was despite the fact that he faced spirited debate and attacks from the opposition party, then in the majority, which included notables such as Daniel Webster, Calhoun, and Henry Clay.[29] Most traditional-era vice presidents were, like Gerry and Van Buren, studious and judicious legislative officers who maintained proper respect for Senate norms.

But presiding over the Senate was also somewhat frustrating for many vice presidents. This is because the Senate has traditionally viewed vice presidents as outsiders and has therefore resisted vice presidential attempts to exert much substantive power from the chair. Vice presidents who were tempted to try and shape the substance or course of debates, outcomes, and so on, have typically been stymied. It should be remembered that although vice presidents may not have been the first (or in some cases even the second) choice for president, most had been in politics for some time, and as the result had well-thought out policy preferences or ideas. In addition, many attempted to find ways to further—or in some few cases, block—their president's agenda in the Senate. But the President of the Senate is essentially an outsider, looking in: tantalizingly close to, but excluded from debate.

It can be argued that the real power of vice presidents as President of the Senate lies in their ability to cast tie-breaking votes. The first vice president, John Adams, still holds the official record for casting the most tie-breaking votes (twenty-nine). The opportunity to break tie votes depends on the political environment and circumstance (e.g., the partisan makeup of the Senate, the issue at hand), and so the number of opportunities to do so vary considerably. However it should be noted that when the Senate had fewer members (as in the traditional era), the probability for tie votes was higher. One early account suggested that approximately two-thirds of tie votes in the traditional era cast pertained to legislative matters, as opposed to procedure, elections of officers, and questions of operation, treaties, and nominations.[30] Table 3.4 lists the number of times traditional-era vice presidents cast a tie-breaking vote in the Senate.

Calhoun, who resigned during his second term as vice president (under Jackson) cast twenty-eight tie votes in the Senate. Because Calhoun, like

Table 3.4. Number of Times Traditional-Era Vice Presidents Broke Tie Votes in the Senate

Vice President	Number of Tie Votes Broken
George Clinton (two terms)	12
Elbridge Gerry	6
Daniel Tompkins (two terms)	3
John Calhoun (one term, resigned during second term)	28
Martin Van Buren	4
Richard Johnson	17
John Tyler (assumed presidency during term)	0
George Dallas	19
Millard Fillmore (assumed presidency during term)	3
William King (died in office)	0
John Breckinridge	9
Hannibal Hamlin	7
Andrew Johnson (assumed presidency during term)	0
Schuyler Colfax	17
Henry Wilson (died in office)	1
William Wheeler	6
Chester Arthur (assumed presidency during term)	3
Thomas Hendricks (died in office)	0
Levi Morton	4
Adlai Stevenson I	2
Garret Hobart (died in office)	1

Source: Senate Historical Office, "Occasions when Vice Presidents Have Voted to Break Tie Votes in the Senate," March 13, 2008 (http://www.senate.gov/artandhistory/history/resources/pdf/VPTies.pdf).

many traditional-era vice presidents, did not enjoy an especially close relationship with either of the two presidents he served under, he often used his vote to stymie the president's agenda while attempting to further his own. This was especially true in Jackson's case.[31] For example he voted three times to oppose Jackson's appointment of Van Buren as Minister to England (twice on procedural matters and once on the question itself).[32] This move furthered the existing rift between Jackson and Calhoun while cementing the already close relationship between the president and Van Buren.[33] This all but assured that Van Buren would be selected as Jackson's vice presidential nominee in 1832.[34]

George Dallas, vice president under James Polk, cast nineteen tie-breaking votes in the Senate. The best known of these votes was on the issue of the tariff law of 1846, a particularly contentious and divisive issue. In this case he sided with the president, voting in favor of the law's passage, despite the fact that he believed the bill went too far and his home state of Pennsylvania was opposed to it. His support represented a true act of political and personal courage: he was burned in effigy back home subsequent to the vote and even considered moving his family to Washington, fearing for their safety.[35] Richard Johnson (under President Van Buren) and Colfax (under President Grant) cast votes that broke ties in the Senate seventeen times. None of these votes were of any special importance and were often used to promote or further the vice president's agenda or make a political statement (often tie-breaking votes by vice presidents were accompanied by statements explaining the vote).[36] Clinton, who served under both Thomas Jefferson and Madison, cast twelve tie-breaking votes. One of these votes, in 1811, helped to defeat the recharter of the National Bank against the wishes of Madison.[37]

The other constitutional function of the vice presidency is to assume the presidency in the event of presidential vacancy. As noted in the previous chapter, there was originally no consensus regarding what to do in a case like this. In other words, the idea that a vice president would assume the office of the presidency and complete the president's term was not widely accepted. Subsequent to the death of President William Henry Harrison, who had become ill delivering his inaugural address, Tyler took the presidential oath of presidential office (in April 1841) and completed Harrison's term as president. This move was somewhat controversial at the time. Harrison's cabinet, for example, as well as many in Congress, first considered him to be the "Acting President" and addressed him accordingly. Others referred to him as "His Accidency." However his ascension to the presidency, although considered a constitutional coup by some historians, was generally accepted by the major newspapers and the public. Within two months Congress passed a resolution that essentially approved of the move, and a precedent was set for future presidential vacancies.[38] Interestingly it was not until the passage of the Twenty-Fifth Amendment in 1967 that this practice was established as being constitutional (box 3.1).

Besides Tyler, three other vice presidents succeeded to the presidency after the death of a sitting president during the traditional era. Fillmore became president after the death (also from illness) of Zachary Taylor in July 1850. Andrew Johnson took office after Lincoln's assassination in April 1865. Finally, Arthur assumed the presidency after Garfield was shot and killed in September 1881. None of these vice presidents who assumed the presidency are remembered for presidential greatness. None subsequently won the presidency—or even their party's nomination—in their own right. One, Andrew Johnson, was the first president ever to be impeached.

One final note with respect to the formal duties of the vice president: Since 1846 the vice president has been a statutory (ex-officio) member of the Smithsonian Board of Regents. The position is largely ceremonial and the job consumes little or no time.

BOX 3.1

Presidential Succession Acts

The original text of the U.S. Constitution (Article II, Section 1) states that in the event of a presidential vacancy ("Removal of the President from Office, or of his Death, Resignation, or Inability to discharge the Powers and Duties of the said Office") the Vice President shall replace the President. However the same section grants Congress the power to determine lines of succession in the event that both the president and vice president are unable to serve. Throughout American history Congress has passed three such Presidential Succession Acts, in 1792, 1886, and 1947.

The Presidential Succession Act of 1792
The Second Congress (1791–1793) passed the Presidential Succession Act of 1792. The act stipulated lines of succession in the event of a presidential and vice presidential vacancy as follows:

- President Pro Tempore of the Senate
- Speaker of the House of Representatives

In the event that the presidency did devolve to the President Pro Tempore of the Senate or the Speaker of the House of Representatives, the act states that there be a presidential election in December of the year in which either man succeeded to the office, or the following December if this occurred later than October 1 but before December.

Presidential Succession Act of 1886
The second presidential succession act removed the President Pro Tempore of the Senate and the Speaker of the House from the line of succession, replacing them with Cabinet Secretaries, in the order in which the Departments were created. Thus, according to the Presidential Succession Act of 1886, lines of succession were as follows:

- Secretary of State (1789)
- Secretary of Treasury (1789)
- Secretary of War (1789)
- Attorney General (1789)
- Postmaster General (1972)
- Secretary of the Navy (1798)
- Secretary of the Interior (1849)
- (Remainder omitted)

This change, although seemingly dramatic, was accepted because six former Secretaries of State subsequently became president. By contrast, only one congressional leader (Speaker of the House James Polk) had done so. The other difference between the 1792 and 1886 acts is that the latter did not require a special election to be held to replace the president if it was invoked.

(continued)

BOX 3.1 *(Continued)*

Presidential Succession Act of 1947
The most recent Presidential Succession Act, passed in 1947, restored the Speaker of the House and the President Pro Tempore of the Senate, although in opposite order than they were specified in 1792. Like the previous act, this one includes Cabinet Secretaries as well. This means that it must be amended to reflect changes in the structure of the president's cabinet. For example, the Department of Defense, created in 1949, replaced the Department of War, the Department of the Navy (created in 1792), and Department of the Army (created in 1947). In terms of order, the Secretary of Defense replaced the Secretary of War. As another example, the Postmaster General was once a cabinet-level position. As such, it was included in the order of presidential succession. This is no longer the case. The order of succession currently reads:

- Speaker of the House
- President Pro Tempore of the Senate
- Secretary of State
- Secretary of Treasury
- Secretary of Defense
- Attorney General
- Secretary of the Interior
- (Remainder omitted)

Source: Feeric, John D., *The Twenty-Fifth Amendment: Its Complete History and Application*, 2nd ed. (New York: Fordham University Press, 1992).

IN OFFICE: THE INFORMAL ROLES OF TRADITIONAL-ERA VICE PRESIDENTS

There are several informal tasks associated with the vice presidency, of all eras, that have little to do with the actual functioning of government. For example vice presidents travel around the country to make appearances, give speeches, attend ceremonies held to open hospitals, libraries, and the like. This is the ceremonial vice presidency, in which the vice president acts as a symbolic representative of the national government. Ironically, until the early part of the twentieth century, the vice presidency itself did not have much by way of ceremonial trappings, such as its own official flag or seal. Another informal role the vice president plays is that of social host. This is especially true in the case of visiting foreign dignitaries, particularly when the president cannot be present. Many vice presidents in this era (for example, Colfax, Morton, Stevenson I, and Hobart) were quite active in Washington social circles, entertaining lavishly and frequently.[39]

Beyond this, traditional-era vice presidents did very little, in part because there was nothing in a formal and legal sense to *stop* them from doing very little. Henry Wilson (Grant's second vice president) spent most of his time in office "writing a three-volume history of slavery in America."[40] Shortly after the election of 1852, King, Franklin Pierce's vice president, traveled to Cuba for respite from a medical condition and took the oath of office there, the only time something like this has ever occurred. He returned to his home in Alabama to die within the month.[41] This is notable in that it was not considered terribly unusual for a vice president to be absent from Washington. Richard Johnson spent an entire summer in his home state of Kentucky running his tavern and spa.[42] Lincoln's first vice president, Hamlin, spent a considerable amount of time during his term in office in his home state of Maine working on his farm. In fact during the summer of 1864 he served in the Maine Coast Guard as company cook. This story is more interesting when we remember that his term of office coincided with the Civil War.[43]

Traditional-era vice presidents could not even be assured of meeting with the president with any frequency. John Breckenridge, for example, did not have a private audience with President Buchanan until his last year in office.[44] This is less surprising if we consider that presidents and vice presidents could go through the entire election campaign without ever having met each other. Lincoln and Hamlin were not introduced to each other until several days after the election,[45] nor were President Polk and Vice President George Dallas.[46] And, even if the president and his vice president knew each other there was no guarantee that they could or would work together. The early history of the vice presidency holds several examples of presidents and vice presidents openly at odds with each other. The best example of this would undoubtedly be Calhoun, who managed to use his position as President of the Senate to work against both presidents he served under (Adams and Jackson). Clinton actually refused to attend Madison's inauguration and publicly attacked the administration.[47] Hendricks (vice president under Cleveland) and Morton (Benjamin Harrison's vice president) are other examples of traditional-era vice presidents who worked to subvert their president's policies.[48]

Of course the fact that these men were not necessarily loyal to their presidents should not be too surprising. Realistically they had little reason or incentive to be loyal to the president. The vice presidential candidate was the choice of the party, not the president. Moreover, as the century progressed it became standard for sitting presidents running for reelection to "dump" their vice president in favor of a new vice presidential candidate.

Having established that vice presidents in the traditional era were largely insignificant in the scheme of governance in the United States, we should note that several vice presidents had good relationships with their presidents. Van Buren, for example, had an extremely close relationship with President Jackson, and "spent a considerable amount of time "advising members of the cabinet, ghosting significant parts of Jackson's messages, [and] acting as the president's chief adviser on patronage and foreign affairs."[49] Although not a "true confidant," Dallas was sought out for advice by President Polk with some frequency, although Polk sought the advice of others as well and did not necessarily follow Dallas's.[50]

Despite the fact that they had not previously met and the fact that the vice president was often absent from Washington, Hamlin and Lincoln had a good relationship as well. Lincoln frequently consulted with Hamlin on a variety of issues, including the conduct of the war and reportedly went so far as to read a preliminary version of the Emancipation Proclamation to the vice president for his approval.[51] Hobart, William McKinley's first vice president, enjoyed both access to and the trust of the president. Hobart "was known as assistant president for his success in advancing the president's program in the Senate."[52] The tenures of these vice presidents, who were acting in both legislative (as President of the Senate) and executive capacities, foreshadowed the emergence of the modern vice presidency.

However even the few traditional-era vice presidents who enjoyed the confidence of their president were not significant actors in their presidents' administrations. They had a limited role in doling out patronage, did not attend Cabinet meetings, nor were they given any important tasks.[53] Their executive roles were extremely limited.

LIFE AFTER THE VICE PRESIDENCY

Six of the twenty-one traditional-era vice presidents died in office. These include Clinton (who served under both Jefferson and Madison), Gerry (Madison's second vice president—apparently serving as Madison's vice president was occupationally unsafe), King (who served under Franklin Pierce), Henry Wilson (Grant's second vice president), Thomas Hendricks (Cleveland's first vice president), and Hobart (McKinley's vice president). Tompkins died within a year of leaving the vice presidency, having retired from public life. Calhoun, who served both John Quincy Adams and then as Jackson's first vice president, resigned late in his second term as the result of differences with Jackson and then successfully ran for the Senate in South Carolina.

What of the others? Did the vice presidency serve as a springboard to future greatness? The answer to this question varies, but in general, the men who occupied the office in the traditional era led average lives after their tenures in office.

As noted, four traditional era vice presidents (Tyler, Fillmore, Andrew Johnson, and Arthur) succeeded to the presidency after the death of their president. None are considered great presidents (one was impeached) and none won even their own party's nomination for the presidency in the next presidential election. One traditional-era vice president, Van Buren, was elected president (in 1836). This puts him and George H. W. Bush in the rather exclusive club of being the only sitting vice presidents in the post-Twelfth Amendment era to win the presidency immediately following their term as vice president. Van Buren did run as his party's nominee in 1840 but lost to William Harrison and in 1848 as the Free Soil candidate for president. He retired from politics afterward. Breckinridge won his party's nomination for the presidency in 1860 but lost to Lincoln. Adlai Stevenson I ran again as a vice presidential candidate with Williams Jennings Bryan—and lost—in 1900.

Four vice presidents from this era continued their public service as members of the Senate. This includes Calhoun, Breckinridge, Hamlin, and Andrew Johnson. After his term in office Morton became the governor of New York and subsequently returned to business. Dallas rebuilt his law practice immediately after leaving the vice presidency and served as Minister to Great Britain under Franklin Pierce. Richard Johnson served in state politics for a few years before his death. Colfax toured the country as a public lecturer; William Wheeler retired.[54]

In all, the lives of these men after the vice presidency or their vice presidential candidacies confirms what we suggested previously. They were neither extraordinary nor completely unqualified, but for the most part relatively competent men who had chosen a life of politics. The office of the vice presidency fit into this picture quite nicely, inasmuch as there was nothing extraordinary about it either. These men were "broadly characterizable as mediocrities, and those who won found little opportunity in the office to develop contrary reputations—from mediocrity to obscurity was the customary progression."[55] This began to change, albeit slowly, around the turn of the century.

NOTES

1. Schlesinger, "On the Presidential Succession," 492.
2. Nelson, *A Heartbeat Away*, 30.

3. William G. Mayer, "A Brief History of Vice Presidential Selection," in *In Pursuit of the White House: How We Choose Our Presidential Nominees*, ed. William G. Mayer (Chatham, NJ: Chatham House, 1996), 319–21.

4. Ibid., 332.

5. James Bryce, *The American Commonwealth*, Vol. 2 (New York: Macmillan, 1893), 46.

6. Allan P. Sindler, *Unchosen Presidents: The Vice President and Other Frustrations of Presidential Succession* (University of California, 1976), 28.

7. Bryce, *The American Commonwealth*, 865.

8. Michael Nelson, "Choosing the Vice President," *PS: Political Science and Politics* Fall [a], (1988), 859.

9. Miller Center Commission, "James Abram Garfield (1881)," (Miller Center of Public Affairs: University of Virginia, 1992).

10. Richard Johnson was technically not renominated by Martin Van Buren in 1840, but was one of three candidates for vice president running on the Democratic ticket with Littleton Waller Tazewell and James Polk. Johnson, however, was recognized as the official nominee.

11. Nelson, "Choosing the Vice President," 858–68.

12. Bryce, *The American Commonwealth*, 865; see also Nelson W. Polsby and Aaron Wildavsky, *Presidential Elections: Strategies and Structures in American Politics*, 11th ed. (Chatham, NJ: Chatham House, 2004), 132.

13. Mayer, "A Brief History of Vice Presidential Selection," 327.

14. Jody C Baumgartner, *Modern Presidential Electioneering: An Organizational and Comparative Approach* (Westport, CT: Praeger, 2000), 20.

15. Polsby and Wildavsky, *Presidential Elections*, 132. See A. James Reichely, *The Life of the Parties: A History of American Political Parties* (Lanham, MD: Rowman & Littlefield, 2000) for a more detailed examination of the history of American political parties.

16. These included Federalists Dewitt Clinton (NY) and Jared Ingersol (PA), 1812; National Republicans John Adams (MA) and Richard Rush (PA), 1820 and 1828; Democratic Republicans Andrew Jackson (TN) and John Calhoun (SC), 1828; and Republicans Ulysses Grant (IL) and Schuyler Colfax (IN), 1868.

17. Robert L. Dudley and Ronald B. Rappaport, "Vice-Presidential Candidates and the Home-State Advantage: Playing Second Banana at Home and on the Road," *American Journal of Political Science* 33(2) (1989): 537–40.

18. Percentages are based on a total of forty-seven presidential tickets, not forty-eight, because elections were not held in 1864 in Tennessee, vice presidential candidate Andrew Johnson's home state.

19. Vice presidents running for reelection (Clinton in 1808, Tompkins in 1820, and Calhoun in 1828) are only counted once.

20. James Bryce, *The American Commonwealth*, Volume 1 (New York: Macmillan, 1893), p. 46.

21. Data on vice presidential candidates in this book were drawn from a variety of sources, including *The National Cyclopedia of American Biography* (New York: J. T. White & Co., 1926); Allen Johnson, et al., eds., *Dictionary of American Biography* (New York: Scriber, 1958); Lee Sigelman and Paul J. Wahlbeck, "The "Veepstakes": Strategic Choice in Presidential Running Mate Selection" *American Political Science Review* 91(4) (1997): 855–64; Hatfield, *Vice Presidents of the United*

States; Leslie H. Southwick, *Presidential Also-Rans and Running Mates, 1788–1996* (Jefferson, N.C.: McFarland, 1998); John A. Garraty and Mark C. Carnes, eds., *American National Biography* (New York: Oxford, 1999); L. Edward Purcell, ed., *Vice Presidents: A Biographical Dictionary* (New York: Checkmark Books, 2001); Lawrence Kestenbaum, "The Political Graveyard: A Database of Historical Cemeteries," Political Graveyard, http://politicalgraveyard.com; "The Biographical Directory of the United States Congress (1774–Present)" Bioguide, http://bioguide.congress.gov/; David Leip, "David Leip's Atlas of U.S. Presidential Elections," US Election Atlas, http://www.uselectionatlas.org; and Goldstein, *The Modern American Vice Presidency*.

22. Jody C Baumgartner, *Modern Presidential Electioneering: An Organizational and Comparative Approach* (Westport, CT: Praeger, 2000), chapter 2; Stephen J. Wayne, *The Road to the White House: The Politics of Presidential Elections* (New York: St. Martin's, 1996).

23. Vance R. Kincade, Jr., *Heirs Apparent: Solving the Vice Presidential Dilemma* (Westport, CT: Praeger, 2000), 7; Patrick J. Furlong and Ann Lenoard, "Schuyler Colfax (1823–1885)," in Vice *Presidents: A Biographical Dictionary*, ed. L. Edward Purcell (New York: Checkmark Books, 2001).

24. Goldstein, *The Modern American Vice Presidency*, 91.

25. Louis C. Hatch, *A History of the Vice-Presidency of the United States*, 300.

26. Hatfield, *Vice Presidents of the United States*, 140–41.

27. Donald Young, *American Roulette: The History and Dilemma of the Vice Presidency* (New York: Holt, Rinehart, and Winston, 1965), 21.

28. Hatfield, *Vice Presidents of the United States*, 67.

29. Ibid., 111.

30. Henry Barrett Learned, "Casting Votes of the Vice-Presidents, 1789–1915," *The American Historical Review* 20 (1915), 571–76.

31. James E. Hite, *Second Best: The Rise of the American Vice Presidency* (San Diego: Cognella, 2013), 44.

32. Hatch, *A History of the Vice-Presidency of the United States*, 106.

33. Jackson had already begun to look on Calhoun with disfavor and favorably on Van Buren, in part as the result of the Peggy Eaton affair. See Mark G. Malvasi, "John Caldwell Calhoun (1782–1850)," in *Vice Presidents: A Biographical Dictionary*, ed. L. Edward Purcell (New York: Checkmark Books, 2001), 61–71.

34. Hatfield, *Vice Presidents of the United States*, 96–97.

35. John M. Belohlavek, "George Mifflin Dallas (1792–1864)," in *Vice Presidents: A Biographical Dictionary*, ed. Edward L. Purcell (New York: Checkmark Books, 2001), 102–12; Hatch, *A History of the Vice-Presidency of the United States*, 106–08.

36. Hite, *Second Best*, 59.

37. Hatch, *A History of the Vice-Presidency of the United States*, 104.

38. Hatfield, *Vice Presidents of the United States*, 143; Boyd M. Coyner Jr., "John Tyler (1790–1842)," in *Vice Presidents: A Biographical Dictionary*, ed. L. Edward Purcell (New York: Checkmark Books, 2001), 90–101.

39. Purcell, *Vice Presidents*.

40. Goldstein, "Vice President," 1559.

41. Daniel Fate Brooks, "William Rufus DeVane King (1786–1853)," in *Vice Presidents: A Biographical Dictionary*, ed. L. Edward Purcell (New York: Checkmark Books, 2001), 122–28.

42. Lindsey Apple, "Richard Mentor Johnson (1781–1850), in *Vice Presidents: A Biographical Dictionary*, ed. L. Edward Purcell (New York: Checkmark Books, 2001), 82–89.

43. H. Draper Hunt, "Hannibal Hamlin (1809–1891)," in *Vice Presidents: A Biographical Dictionary*, ed. L. Edward Purcell (New York: Checkmark Books, 2001), 138–46.

44. Hite, *Second Best*, 54.

45. Ibid., 56.

46. Ibid., 52.

47. Nelson, *A Heartbeat Away*, 30.

48. Hite, *Second Best*, 62.

49. As quoted in Hatfield, *Vice Presidents of the United States*, 111.

50. Belohlavek, "George Mifflin Dallas (1792–1864)."

51. Hite, *Second Best*, 56–57.

52. William G. Mayer, "A Brief History of Vice Presidential Selection," in William G. Mayer, ed., *In Pursuit of the White House: How We Choose Our Presidential Nominees* (Chatham, NJ: Chatham House, 1996), 340.

53. Nelson, *A Heartbeat Away*, 29.

54. Hatfield, *Vice Presidents of the United States*.

55. Allan P. Sindler, *Unchosen Presidents: The Vice President and Other Frustrations of Presidential Succession* (Berkeley: University of California Press, 1976), 28.

4

+

Setting the Stage: Transitional-Era Vice Presidents

This chapter examines the transitional era of the vice presidency. This period, which begins in 1900 and extends through the vice presidency of Gerald Ford, can be thought of as setting the stage for the emergence of the modern era. During this era we see vice presidents becoming more active in terms of their involvement in governmental affairs. In particular, vice presidents begin a movement away from a strictly constitutionally defined legislative role to a more active executive presence. Some presidents, although certainly not all, begin to vest their vice presidents with actual responsibilities. This executive presence, the vice president as a presidential assistant of sorts, is what defines the modern vice presidency.

The division of vice presidents into traditional and transitional eras may seem somewhat arbitrary. However, most would agree that Theodore Roosevelt, one of the first transitional-era vice presidents, was a breed apart. As one text noted,

> There have been other ambitious vice-presidents: Burr, Calhoun, Nixon. And intelligent vice-presidents: Jefferson, Wallace. And charismatic vice-presidents: Stevenson, Breckenridge. There have been patriotic vice-presidents: John Adams, Andrew Johnson. And verbose vice-presidents: Humphrey, Dawes. There have been others who were lucky, who had large families, and who had wealthy, privileged backgrounds. But there had never been a vice-president who embodied all these qualities until Theodore Roosevelt.[1]

After succeeding to the presidency on the assassination of President William McKinley in September 1901, Roosevelt also became the first vice president since Martin Van Buren to win election to the presidency in his own right. He would not be the last transitional-era vice president to do so.

There are other characteristics that set the transitional era of the vice presidency apart from the traditional era. During this time, presidential candidates began to assert some control over the vice presidential selection process, especially as the period progressed.[2] This resulted in vice presidential candidates who were more competent, loyal to, and compatible with their running mates. Vice presidential candidates in the transitional era also began to play a larger role in the presidential campaign. How and why these changes came about will be discussed in greater detail in the following chapter. This chapter is devoted simply to describing the vice presidency during this period. Table 4.1 lists the sixteen transitional-era vice presidents.

Of the sixteen vice presidents from this era, three served two full terms in office: Thomas Marshall, John Garner, and Richard Nixon. In the traditional era, only one vice president (Daniel Tompkins) could make this claim. Seven of these men did not complete their terms in office. One, James Sherman, died in office, far fewer than the six who did so in the traditional era. Like John Calhoun in the traditional era, Spiro Agnew resigned during his second term, although under completely different circumstances. In all, the transitional-era vice presidency seems to have been a much more stable job. The exception to this is the fact that five vice presidents (31 percent) from this period succeeded to the presidency as the result of a presidential vacancy. During the traditional era this number was four (19 percent). Transitional-era vice presidents who assumed the presidency included Theodore Roosevelt, Calvin Coolidge, Harry Truman, Lyndon Johnson, and Ford. All but Ford were subsequently elected to the presidency in their own right, something that no traditional-era vice president was able to claim.

Like the previous chapter our examination of the transitional era proceeds by presenting an overview of how vice presidential candidates were selected, what kinds of people were selected, the role these candidates played in the campaign, their terms in office, and their lives afterward.

SELECTING VICE PRESIDENTIAL
NOMINEES IN THE TRANSITIONAL ERA

Until 1940 the method for selecting vice presidential candidates was roughly the same as in the traditional era. In other words, party leaders

Table 4.1. Transitional-Era Vice Presidents (1901–1973)

In Office	Vice President	President	(Notes)
1901	Theodore Roosevelt	William McKinley	Assumed presidency Sept. 14, 1901, after assassination of McKinley; vice presidency vacant until March 4, 1905
1905–1909	Charles Fairbanks	Theodore Roosevelt	
1909–1912	James Sherman	William Taft	Died in office Oct. 30, 1912; vice presidency vacant until March 4, 1913
1913–1921	Thomas Marshall	Woodrow Wilson	
1921–1923	Calvin Coolidge	Warren Harding	Assumed presidency August 2, 1923, after death of Harding; vice presidency vacant until March 4, 1925
1925–1929	Charles Dawes	Calvin Coolidge	
1929–1933	Charles Curtis	Herbert Hoover	
1933–1941	John Garner	Franklin Roosevelt	
1941–1945	Henry Wallace	Franklin Roosevelt	
1945	Harry Truman	Franklin Roosevelt	Assumed presidency April 12, 1945, after death of Roosevelt; vice presidency vacant until Jan. 20, 1949
1949–1953	Alben Barkley	Harry Truman	
1953–1961	Richard Nixon	Dwight Eisenhower	
1961–1963	Lyndon Johnson	John Kennedy	Assumed presidency Nov. 22, 1963, after assassination of Kennedy; vice presidency vacant until Jan. 20, 1965
1965–1969	Hubert Humphrey, Jr.	Lyndon Johnson	
1969–1973	Spiro Agnew	Richard Nixon	Resigned Oct. 10, 1973; vice presidency vacant until Dec. 6, 1973
1973–1974	Gerald Ford	Richard Nixon	Assumed vice presidency according to provisions of Twenty-Fifth Amendment on Dec. 6, 1973; assumed presidency Aug. 9, 1974, after resignation of Nixon

selected the vice presidential candidate at the national party convention. The transition away from the convention system of vice presidential selection began in 1920, when James Cox had some input into the decision to tap Franklin Roosevelt for the second slot.[3] In 1940, Roosevelt himself essentially coerced the Democratic Party into allowing him to choose his running mate. He and his first vice president, Garner, had been at odds throughout their second term and Garner had actually declared his candidacy for the presidency in late 1939. At the pinnacle of his power, Roosevelt made it clear that if he did not get his choice of running mate (Henry Wallace) he would not accept the nomination.

However the convention system of selecting vice presidential candidates was not replaced immediately. Indeed, although he again made his choices for running mate known in 1944, Roosevelt allowed the convention to select Truman. However after 1940, presidential nominees began to attend their party's convention and thus were present when the choice of vice presidential nominee was being discussed. Several made their preferences known, and these preferences were often considered or accommodated. For example in 1948 Thomas Dewey played a central role in the selection of Earl Warren (then governor of California) as his running mate. Truman attempted to persuade Supreme Court Justice William Douglas to share the ticket with him in 1948. After that effort failed, Truman deferred to the convention, who selected Senate Minority Leader Alben Barkley.

So, from 1940 until 1956, presidential candidates and their parties generally shared responsibility for the selection of the vice presidential nominee. It should be noted that the party convention is still responsible for formally nominating the presidential and vice presidential candidates. But the last time a presidential nominee (Adlai Stevenson, III) refused any involvement in the selection of his running mate was at the Democratic convention of 1956. Although this may have been a ploy to energize the party, by this time the presidential nominee's inclusion in the process was so accepted that Stevenson's announcement that he would defer to the convention was a bombshell.[4] And "by 1960, neither presidential nominee sought to maintain even a pretense of noninvolvement" in the choice of vice presidential candidate.[5] It is now standard practice to allow the presidential nominee to choose his running mate.

Of course, party leaders are not excluded in the decision-making process.[6] Presidential candidates, especially in the early years of the modern era, typically consulted with a variety of party leaders in the making of their decision. For example the fact that Republican Party leaders were favorably disposed toward former party chairmen William Miller in 1964 probably had some effect on his eventual selection that year.[7] Similarly, Democratic Party leaders were quite supportive of the choice of Hubert

Humphrey in 1964. In the end, however, the choice remained the presidential nominee's.

At the 1960 Democratic convention, presidential candidate John Kennedy met with several groups, each lobbying for their own candidate. Southern leaders were promoting Johnson. Representatives of the labor and liberal wings of the party were opposed, and Kennedy's own campaign staff was somewhat wary of Johnson as well. This was because Johnson was a bit conservative and had been Kennedy's prime contender for the presidential nomination. Despite these objections, Kennedy selected Johnson, although there remains some question as to whether he actually expected Johnson to say yes, and why Johnson actually did.[8] Several weeks before Nixon's nomination he had concluded that Henry Cabot Lodge, Jr., would be his vice presidential choice. However after he officially received the nomination he convened a meeting of thirty-six party leaders in his hotel suite. Having already discussed the matter privately with each he knew that Lodge was agreeable to the majority of them. He allowed those present to indicate their choice, and in the end most approved of the selection of Lodge.[9]

In January 1964, President Johnson began an extensive search for a running mate, considering a wide array of choices.[10] He also consulted with party leaders and went even further by letting the press and public know who was being considered. Despite the pretense of consulting others, his choice of Humphrey was probably made in advance of the announcement at the convention.[11]

In 1968 Humphrey convened a series of meetings with party leaders where he made his high regard for Edmund Muskie clear. He did eliminate one possible choice (Sargent Shriver) after opposition from the Kennedy family and other party leaders, but the final choice was made by he and his top aides. Similarly, Nixon seems to have reached his decision to select Agnew in 1968 more through private discussions with top aide John Mitchell than by any consideration of the preferences of party leaders. In 1972, George McGovern's choice of Shriver to replace his first choice (Senator Thomas Eagleton) may have been influenced by a petition organized by Democratic Representatives Lester Wolff, Sam Gibbons, Wayne Hays, and Shirley Chisholm. But his original choice of Eagleton was made after a meeting with a number of his campaign staffers alone.[12]

In the traditional era, incumbent vice presidents were typically jettisoned in the president's reelection effort. Not so in the transitional era (table 4.2). Only one incumbent vice president, Garner, was dropped from the ticket in the transitional era, and as noted, this was a special case. Garner had already served two full terms, had openly broken with the president, and was challenging Roosevelt for the Democratic Party presidential nomination. On the other hand, five transitional-era vice

Table 4.2.   Transitional-Era Vice Presidential Candidates (1901–1973)

Year	Winning Candidate (Presidential Candidate)	Losing Candidate (Presidential Candidate)
1900	Theodore Roosevelt (William McKinley)	Adlai Stevenson (Williams Bryan)
1904	Charles Fairbanks (Theodore Roosevelt)	Henry Davis (Alton Parker)
1908	James Sherman (William Taft)	John Kern (Williams Bryan)
1912	Thomas Marshall (Woodrow Wilson)	Hiram Johnson (Theodore Roosevelt)*
1916	Thomas Marshall (Woodrow Wilson)	Charles Fairbanks (Charles Hughes)
1920	Calvin Coolidge (Warren Harding)	Franklin Roosevelt (James Cox)
1924	Charles Dawes (Calvin Coolidge)	Charles Bryan (John Davis)
1928	Charles Curtis (Herbert Hoover)	Joseph Robinson (Alfred Smith)
1932	John Garner (Franklin Roosevelt)	Charles Curtis (Herbert Hoover)
1936	John Garner (Franklin Roosevelt)	Frank Knox (Alfred Landon)
1940	Henry Wallace (Franklin Roosevelt)	Charles McNary (Wendell Wilkie)
1944	Harry Truman (Franklin Roosevelt)	John Bricker (Thomas Dewey)
1948	Alben Barkley (Harry Truman)	Earl Warren (Thomas Dewey)
1952	Richard Nixon (Dwight Eisenhower)	John Sparkman (Adlai Stevenson)
1956	Richard Nixon (Dwight Eisenhower)	Estes Kefauver (Adlai Stevenson)
1960	Lyndon Johnson (John Kennedy)	Henry Cabot Lodge (Richard Nixon)
1964	Hubert Humphrey (Lyndon Johnson)	William Miller (Barry Goldwater)
1968	Spiro Agnew (Richard Nixon)	Edmund Muskie (Hubert Humphrey)
1972	Spiro Agnew (Richard Nixon)	R. Sargent Shriver (George McGovern)

*Roosevelt and Johnson ran under the Progressive Party label and received eighty-eight Electoral College votes. William Taft and James Sherman were the Republican presidential and vice presidential candidates and received eight Electoral College votes.

presidents remained on the ticket for their presidents' reelection bid. Two of these ran again and lost. James Sherman, who was William Taft's vice president ran again and lost (if he had won he would not have taken office because he died shortly before the election). Charles Curtis, Herbert Hoover's vice president ran again and lost in 1932. The other three won a second term: Marshall (Woodrow Wilson's vice president), Nixon (Dwight Eisenhower's vice president), and Agnew (Nixon's vice president). Technically, Garner belongs on this list as well because he ran (and won) with Roosevelt in both 1932 and 1936.

A different political strategy is in part responsible for the increased job security of sitting vice presidents. In the traditional era, a new candidate was needed to accommodate shifting political environments. In the transitional era, it became bad politics to drop the sitting vice president. For example, in 1956 there was a movement shortly before the Republican convention to dump Nixon. Eisenhower eventually seems to have concluded that dropping Nixon would have been interpreted as a sign of political weakness.[13] On the other hand, despite the fact that many prominent Republicans were pressuring Nixon to replace Agnew on the ticket in 1972, Nixon appreciated his vice president's ability to galvanize far right support with his fiery rhetoric on the campaign trail.[14] Thus, Agnew was retained.

Another difference between candidate selection in the traditional and transitional eras is that as the transitional era proceeded, the vice presidency became a more attractive office. Marshall did not want the vice presidential nomination, but as the century progressed it became common for prominent individuals to quietly campaign for the second spot. In 1956, for example, three well-known senators, Kennedy, Humphrey, and Estes Kefauver, actively but quietly campaigned to be included on the ticket with Adlai Stevenson III.[15] In large part this was because the office came to be seen as a stepping stone to the presidency.

Why this shift in perception? First, the vice president is the constitutional successor to the president, who by the early twentieth century had become the most visible and central actor in American politics. Aided by a news media that had by this point become nationalized (mass circulation magazines, newspaper wire services, radio, and television), this gave vice presidents increased visibility.[16] "That national figures of the caliber of Jack Kennedy and Estes Kefauver should battle each other for second place on what few observers expected to be a winning ticket was no small tribute to the newfound prestige enjoyed by the vice presidency."[17] Second, the ratification of the Twenty-Second Amendment in 1951 limited presidents to two terms, therefore eliminating speculation as to what a sitting presidents' intentions were after the second term. A vice president could therefore position themselves as heir apparent to outgoing presidents.[18]

In terms of geography, transitional-era vice presidential candidates were somewhat more diverse. In the traditional era, forty-four nonincumbent vice presidential candidates were drawn from only seventeen states. In the transitional era, thirty-three nonincumbent vice presidential candidates represented a total of twenty states. However like the traditional era, a few states seemed to be more likely to supply candidates than others. In particular, Indiana and New York (four candidates) and Illinois (three) were again overrepresented. California had three, Massachusetts and Maryland had two apiece. No other state could claim more than one vice presidential nominee. Midwestern states supplied twelve vice presidential candidates (36 percent) during this period, Northern states seven (21 percent), whereas ten (30 percent) were drawn from the Southern and Border states combined.

Another regional pattern evident in examining presidential tickets from this era is that the Midwestern and Northern state combination of presidential and vice presidential candidates that dominated in the latter half of the traditional era continued to be popular in the transitional era. Twelve of the thirty presidential tickets from this era paired Northern and Midwestern presidential and vice presidential candidates. No other regional patterns are evident, especially because as the century progressed more candidates (presidential and vice presidential alike) came from the Southern and Western regions. This is largely because comparatively speaking, fewer candidates came from the South in the traditional era as the result of the Civil War and Reconstruction and many of the Western territories had yet to become states.

All but four of the thirty-eight presidential tickets from this era were regionally balanced. Three paired two candidates from Midwestern states: William Bryan and Adlai Stevenson I in 1900, William Bryan and John Kern in 1908, and Alfred Landon and Frank Knox in 1936. The fourth was a Border-state ticket (Truman and Barkley in 1948).

In both the traditional and the transitional eras vice presidential candidates were typically selected from different ideological factions within the party (ideological factionalism in the United States is sometimes, though not always, congruent with region).[19] Thus, although Kennedy was a moderate-liberal, his vice presidential selection, Johnson, was a moderate-conservative. Not every ticket from this era was ideologically balanced. Notably, in 1964, Barry Goldwater, running on a platform of principled conservativism, could hardly have afforded to select a more moderate (or liberal) running mate, and thus tapped fellow conservative Miller. But in 1968, the liberal Humphrey selected the relatively moderate Muskie. Similarly, in 1972, the liberal McGovern balanced his ticket with his selection of the more moderate Shriver (and Eagleton before him).

Closely related to ideology, depending on the political environment, is a focus on particular salient issues. A vice presidential candidate who is identified with a certain important issue may be chosen to signal a president's commitment to or stand on that issue or focus attention on it. In 1960 Nixon selected United Nations' Ambassador Lodge to help focus the campaign on foreign affairs. In 1968 he selected Agnew, who took a strong stand on domestic law and order, an issue that complemented Nixon's focus on foreign policy.[20]

Most vice presidential candidates' home states were fairly rich in Electoral College votes. On average they were from states that represented a fair percentage (7.2 percent) of the Electoral College votes needed to win the presidency. Exceptions to this include the candidacy of Muskie from Maine in 1968 (1.5 percent), Charles McNary of Oregon in 1940 (1.9 percent), and Henry Davis from West Virginia in 1904 (2.9 percent). On the other end of the spectrum, candidates from New York during this period brought approximately 16 percent of Electoral College votes needed to win to the ticket; those from California and Illinois represented roughly 10 percent of the required total.[21] As a final note, the notion of a vice presidential "home state advantage" fared slightly better in the transitional era. Vice presidential candidates carried their home states 60 percent of the time, but still lost in thirteen of thirty-three cases.

GENERAL CHARACTERISTICS OF
TRANSITIONAL-ERA VICE PRESIDENTIAL NOMINEES

Vice presidential candidates in the transitional era generally started their political careers a bit later than those in the traditional era. Although many (thirteen) held their first public office before the age of thirty, the average vice presidential candidate in this era was thirty-three years old when he held his first political office, as opposed to twenty-seven in the traditional era. Twenty-two of the thirty-three started their political careers at the local and seven at the state level. The remainder began their careers in national politics. Two of these candidates entered public office at a fairly high level. Marshall, Wilson's vice president, started his political career as governor of Indiana. Charles Fairbanks, Theodore Roosevelt's vice president, began his political career in the U.S. Senate.

The average vice presidential candidate in the transitional era served a total of 17.9 years in public office before being nominated for the vice presidency, almost 1 more year than in the traditional era. One, Barkley (Truman's vice president), served a total of 44 years in other political offices before becoming vice president. Only one, Frank Knox (Alfred Landon's vice presidential candidate in 1936) had no prior political experience. Of the thirty-three candidates, more than two-thirds (twenty-three) had served in local or state government at one point in their career, for an average of 7.6 years (see table 4.3). John Kern (William Bryan's running mate in 1908) served a total of 29 years in various subnational government offices. A total of nine candidates from this era served as governor of their state, for an average of 2.9 years and a maximum of 6 years (John Bricker).

One-third of the candidates from this era served in the U.S. House of Representatives before running for vice president. The average number of years served by these eleven was 12.7. Garner, Franklin Roosevelt's first vice president, was a member of the House (from Texas) for 30 years before his vice presidential tenure. Fifteen of these individuals were members of the U.S. Senate for an average length of service of approximately 12 years. Charles McNary of Oregon, who ran with Wendell Wilkie in 1940, was a member of the Senate for 23 years. Finally, a total of twelve transitional-era vice presidential candidates served in the national executive in one capacity or another. Theodore Roosevelt served on the U.S. Civil Service Commission, his cousin Franklin Roosevelt was Assistant Secretary of the Navy, and Lodge was Ambassador to the United Nations, each for 7 years.

Of these thirty-three men, twenty-four were serving in national political office immediately before their vice presidential bid. Twelve were Senators, whereas two, Adlai Stevenson and Charles Fairbanks, had previously been vice president. Thirteen had prior executive experience, either in the private or the public sector. In sum, it would seem that based on their previous political experience, candidates from this era were slightly better qualified than those from the traditional era.

Looking beyond political experience, the average age of a vice presidential candidate in this era was fifty-six years old. At the age of eighty-one, Henry Davis, who was Alton Parker's running mate in 1904, was the oldest individual to run for the vice presidency in the transitional era. The youngest was Franklin Roosevelt, James Cox's vice presidential nominee in 1920, aged thirty-eight. All but one candidate (Davis) had a college education. Fifteen, or 45.5 percent, had military experience, as opposed to the 32 percent in the traditional era. About 60 percent (twenty) were lawyers before holding public office, slightly more than in the traditional era.

Finally, similar to the traditional era, most candidates (85 percent) from this era were white, male, Protestants, and of Northwest European descent. The exceptions included Charles Curtis (1928), who was at least one-eighth and as much as one-half American Indian[22]; Miller (1964) and Shriver (1972), who were Catholics; Agnew (1968), who was of Greek descent; and Muskie (1968), a Catholic of Polish descent.

Table 4.3. Political Offices Served by Thirty-Three Transitional-Era Vice Presidential Candidates

	Number Candidates Served	Percentage Served	Maximum Years Served	Average Years Served**
State and Local Government*	23	69.7	29	7.6
Governor	9	27.3	2.9	6
U.S. House Representatives	11	33.3	30	12.7
U.S. Senate	15	45.5	23	12.1
Other National Government	12	36.4	4.4	7

* Does not include years served as governor (if any).
** Average represents years only of those who served in the office.

CAMPAIGNING IN THE TRANSITIONAL ERA

In general, the conduct of presidential campaigns during the traditional era was the responsibility of political parties. Neither presidential nor vice presidential candidates were expected to do much campaigning on their own behalf. This began to change around the turn of the century. Theodore Roosevelt, for example, was seemingly indefatigable, delivering 673 speeches in twenty-four states throughout the 1900 campaign.[23] But the change did not take place immediately. In the 1920 campaign, Calvin Coolidge did little campaigning outside his native New England, and Garner made only two speeches in the campaign of 1932.[24] But as the transitional era progressed it became the norm for vice presidential candidates to take to the campaign trail on behalf of the presidential candidate. "Campaigns [became] national efforts in which both members of the ticket [were required to] travel widely and speak frequently to enlist support."[25] Marshall traversed the country during the 1912 campaign—paying his own way as he did so—beginning in late August in the Northeast and moving west. In 1924 Charles Dawes assumed most of the responsibility for the campaign for President "Silent Cal" Coolidge, in part because the president's son had recently passed away. By his own account, Dawes delivered 108 speeches and traveled fifteen thousand miles throughout the campaign. Although many questioned his effectiveness on the campaign trail, Charles Curtis made a whistle-stop campaign tour in 1928 promoting the Republican ticket. During the campaign of 1948 Barkley "captured the attention of the electorate by his novel use of the airplane": in all he "flew 150,000 miles and delivered 250 speeches."[26]

In some respects, 1952 was a watershed for the vice presidency, and this was certainly the case with respect to the vice presidential candidate's role in the campaign. One reason for this was the selection by Eisenhower and the Republican Party of Nixon as vice presidential candidate. Nixon was already known as a consummate politician with an effective and often fiery rhetorical style. Campaigning, in other words, was something Nixon not only enjoyed but did fairly well. He traveled the country in 1952 and 1956 leveling any number of charges against his Democratic opponents. Eisenhower and the party were quite content with this arrangement because the president remained unsullied by any controversy generated by Nixon's speeches. In 1956 Kefauver traveled more than fifty-four thousand miles to thirty-eight states (210 cities and towns in all), making 450 speeches throughout the campaign. His specific task was to counter charges that Nixon was making.[27]

Vice presidential candidates were often assigned the responsibility for campaigning to what was thought to be their natural constituency. And because some attention has historically been paid to uniting the party by selecting a vice presidential candidate from a different faction of the party, region of the country, or both, this was frequently a constituency that may not have been completely comfortable with the presidential candidate. In this way the vice presidential candidate could broaden the appeal of the ticket. Most analyses of the electoral impact of the vice presidential candidate ignore this.[28] The vice presidential candidate may help bring votes to the ticket that may have otherwise been difficult to get.

This also meant that vice presidential candidates focused their attention on the region from which they came. This typically translated into regions where the presidential candidate was not as strong. In 1960 Johnson spent almost 50 percent of his time campaigning in the South, including a five-day "whistle-stop" train trip through eight Southern states. By contrast, Kennedy spent less than one-fifth of his time in the South.[29] Lodge, a Northeasterner, spent about half of his time there, including six of the last seven days of the campaign. In 1964, Humphrey, a Midwesterner, spent almost 40 percent of his time during the campaign in that region, as compared with roughly 20 percent in the Northeast, South, and West.[30] Agnew, from the border state of Maryland, was expected to help Nixon carry the South in 1968, and therefore spent much of the campaign there.[31]

Similarly, certain vice presidential candidates helped mobilize support from various interests and other groups. In 1964, Humphrey used his relationships with a variety of labor, farm, and black leaders to the financial advantage of the campaign. Shriver courted many of these same groups, as well as Jewish and Catholic organizations concerned about some of McGovern's policy stances.[32] In other cases vice presidential candidates meet with party leaders to shore up party support for the ticket. This is especially true after there has been a contentious nominating season. In 1960 Johnson was instrumental in healing a rift in the Democratic Party over the presidential nomination by paying a visit to former President Truman (who thereafter supported Kennedy). Shriver was similarly valuable to McGovern in 1972 when many mainstream party leaders seemed leery of their more extremist candidate. Miller also helped heal intraparty rifts.[33]

Like candidates for any political office most of what vice presidential candidates do during the campaign is speak to crowds, reporters, and so on. A few vice presidential nominees in the transitional era were a disappointment in this regard. For example Lodge was a lackluster campaigner in 1960, perhaps because he was reportedly not terribly fond of Nixon, or perhaps because his mother had died in July. Agnew was energetic but not terribly skilled. Others excelled on the campaign trail and may have been selected in part for that skill. Johnson, Miller, Humphrey, Muskie, and Shriver were notably vigorous campaigners.

One of the main functions of vice presidential candidates on the campaign trail that emerged during this era was that of aggressor, or attacker.

This is because vice presidential candidates can say things about the opposition that might be impolitic for presidential candidates to say. In other words, they can be harsher in their attacks while the presidential candidate appears to stay above the fray. Nixon perfected this element of the modern presidential campaign in 1952 and 1956. Referred to variously in campaign accounts as "hit man," "hatchet man," and "attack dog," vice presidential candidates are now given the primary responsibility of criticizing the opponent.[34]

This role was not immediately and universally embraced. For example, Lodge restricted his criticism of the Kennedy–Johnson ticket to suggestions that Kennedy was inexperienced in foreign affairs.[35] But by this point this was the exception to the rule that the vice presidential candidate would take the lead role in attacking the opposition. That same year Johnson criticized Nixon for being inconsistent on civil rights and inept in the area of foreign policy as well as deriding him for having changed the Republican platform after his preconvention meeting with Nelson Rockefeller.

Johnson's vice presidential candidate Humphrey pulled no punches in his attack on Barry Goldwater. He accused him, variously, of being "fiscally irresponsible," "the Republican pretender to the Presidency," a "radical of the far right," and implied that Goldwater was nuclear-weapon trigger happy. Of course, Goldwater had his own attacker in Miller, chosen for his ability to irritate President Johnson. Miller did not disappoint, accusing Johnson of "playing politics with national security," being gullible with respect to communism, of allowing violence in the street to escalate, and employing heavy-handed techniques to silence him (Miller).[36] Miller's accusations were often so harsh and far-fetched that other Republicans distanced themselves from him.

Agnew was known as an especially vigorous attacker. In 1968 he labeled Humphrey "soft on Communism" and on the Nixon–Agnew ticket's signature issue, law and order. Interestingly, Agnew was the target of one of the most well-known political advertisements in the television age. The ad featured a shot of a television screen that displayed the words, "Agnew for Vice President" and a soundtrack of a man laughing, at first softly, and then, increasingly loudly.[37] In 1972 Agnew's target was McGovern, whom he ridiculed for his ideas about national defense. His opponent in 1972, Shriver, accused Nixon of being power hungry and "the number one war-maker in the world today."[38]

In short, as the transitional era wore on, vice presidential candidates became partners in the campaign effort, expected to share in the work of carrying the message to various regions and groups throughout the country and to factions and leaders within the party. In this they were expected to attack the opposing ticket with vigor.

FORMAL ROLES OF TRANSITIONAL-ERA VICE PRESIDENTS

The formal roles of the vice president increased during the transitional era, although not in a uniform fashion. Consistent with the increased role of vice presidential candidates in the election campaign, vice presidents began to take on more responsibilities. To be sure, vice presidents remained minor players in the overall scheme of governance. However as the transitional era wore on, they were increasingly given formal duties associated with the executive branch, signaling a shift from the vice presidency being primarily a legislative office, as President of the Senate, to one associated with the presidency.

One important change during this period was that the vice presidency was given formal ceremonial trappings that symbolize other official institutions. In particular, in 1936 the vice presidency was given its own flag and in 1948 its own official seal of office. See box 4.1.

Similarly, the institutional resources available have increased incrementally throughout the twentieth century. During the vice presidency of Agnew, the office first received funding for its own staff. Previously, vice presidents relied on staff from the Senate, previous political posts, or others assigned for various executive assignments. And in 1972 the office of the vice presidency was listed for the first time in the *United States Government Organization Manual* as part of the Executive Office of the President.[39]

Office space is part of the formal vice presidency as well. Nixon had three different offices in the Capitol building, but when at the White House worked in conference rooms.[40] Johnson was given a suite of six offices in the Executive Office Building (EOB), next door to the White House. One, now called the Vice President's Ceremonial Office, is quite grand, formerly serving as the office of the Secretary of the Navy.[41] Humphrey had multiple rooms in the EOB as well. Agnew had an office in the White House for a short time until Nixon moved him.

In the transitional era vice presidents continued to preside over the Senate. Some handled this task better than others; some had difficulty. Dawes, for example, was openly contemptuous of Senate rules that allowed for filibuster and used his position as President of the Senate as a bully pulpit of sorts to publicly advocate changing the rules to disallow this parliamentary stalling tactic. Wallace, who was by all accounts not a natural politician, "never quite fit into the Senate's club-like atmosphere," which frequently put him at odds with the body. He found the duties of presiding over the Senate tedious and his performance reflected this. Nixon was also not interested in this constitutional aspect of the vice presidency and spent increasingly less time in his duties as presiding officer of the body as his tenure progressed.[42]

BOX 4.1

Symbols of the Office:
The Vice Presidential Seal and Flag

The early history of the vice presidential seal and flag are not completely clear. This is primarily because (consistent with most things associated with the vice presidency) seal historians have generally ignored the vice presidential seal. Seals were mainly used to seal envelopes used for vice presidential correspondence, and because envelopes were usually thrown away after being opened, not much by way of historical evidence exists. There is, however, evidence that suggests that a vice presidential seal existed well before the middle of the nineteenth century, and a wax impression of an early seal dated to 1850. This is the only known version of the vice presidential seal that exists before 1948.

Since the Civil War, the presence of the vice president on a seagoing craft had been symbolized by flying the national ensign, a version of the national flag used to identify the nationality of seagoing vessels. This changed in 1915, when an unofficial flag consisting of a reversal of the colors of the presidential flag was made and flown for Vice President Thomas Marshall's visit of the USS Colorado in San Francisco Bay.

In 1936, Franklin Roosevelt issued Executive Order 7285, which provided for an official flag for the vice president. In 1948, President Truman issued Executive Order 10016, which defined an official seal for the vice presidency. This had the practical effect of forcing a new flag design as well. The 1948 seal and flag were used until 1975.

The Vice Presidential Seal,   *The Vice Presidential Seal,*
1948–1975   *1975–Present*

See Joe McMillan, "Overview" and "Unofficial Flag of 1915," and Rick Wyatt, "First VP Flag (1936–1948), from Rob Raeside, *Flags Of The World* (available at http://flagspot.net/flags/us-vpres.html, 2005); Richard S. Patterson and Dougall, Richardson, *The Eagle and the Shield* (Washington, D.C.: Department of State, 1978).

What Dawes and Wallace had in common was the fact that neither had served in the Senate. As such, they likely would have found it difficult to fit in even if they were inclined to do so. Their performance reflected this. This was not the case with other vice presidents from this era who had previously been senators. Johnson, who had been Senate Majority Leader, worked closely with the Senate and when in Washington, "made it a practice to open the sessions of the Senate at noon as presiding officer . . . [and] remained in the chair until the conclusion of any significant business during the 'morning hour.'"[43] Humphrey spent a good deal of time in the Senate, especially early in his term. This however was less in the role of presiding officer but rather as President Johnson's legislative lobbyist.[44]

This said, toward the latter part of the transitional era vice presidents seemed to spend less time in the Senate. In part this was because "Senators [began to] view vice-presidents as semi-intruders . . . as a member of the executive branch."[45] Being seen as an outsider is made worse when vice presidents break established Senate customs. Early in his tenure Agnew presided over the Senate more frequently than any other vice president since Barkley. He made a point of mastering Senate rules and meeting with the Senate parliamentarian every morning. However he knew little of Senate norms. During debate over the ratification of the Anti-Ballistic-Missile Treaty, Agnew approached Republican Senator Len Jordan of Idaho about the vote. Jordan was outraged, seeing this as a transgression of separation of powers. Soon afterward he formulated what became known as the "Jordan Rule": "When the Vice-President lobbies on the Senate floor for a bill, vote the other way."[46] Shortly after this, Agnew concluded that his time would be better spent at the White House.

Compared with the traditional period, the number of tie votes the vice president broke declined in the transitional era. This is in part a product of the fact that tie votes are less likely with more (e.g., one hundred) members. Marshall and Nixon, who served two full terms in the office, each broke eight tie votes, as did Barkley. Only three other vice presidents cast as many as half that number. Five of the sixteen did not break any tie votes in the Senate, although to be fair, of these five, four assumed the presidency during their term as vice president. Some tie-breaking votes cast by modern vice presidents were significant. For example, Agnew broke one in 1969 that approved the Safeguard missile defense for ICBM silos and one in 1973 that allowed construction of the Alaskan pipeline to begin (one of his last acts in office).[47] However few tie-breaking votes during this period were of any lasting import. See table 4.4.

Five transitional-era vice presidents succeeded to the presidency during their terms as vice president: Theodore Roosevelt, Coolidge, Truman, Johnson, and Ford. All subsequently ran for the presidency and all except

Table 4.4.   Number of Times Transitional-Era Vice Presidents Broke Tie Votes in the Senate

Vice President	Number of Tie Votes Broken
Theodore Roosevelt (assumed presidency during term)	0
Charles Fairbanks	0
James Sherman	4
Thomas Marshall (two terms)	8
Calvin Coolidge (assumed presidency during term)	0
Charles Dawes	2
Charles Curtis	3
John Garner (two terms)	3
Henry Wallace	4
Harry Truman (assumed presidency during term)	1
Alben Barkley	8
Richard Nixon (two terms)	8
Lyndon Johnson (assumed presidency during term)	0
Hubert Humphrey, Jr.	4
Spiro Agnew (resigned during second term)	2
Gerald Ford (appointed and assumed presidency during term)	0

Source: Senate Historical Office, "Occasions When Vice Presidents Have Voted to Break Tie Votes in the Senate," March 13, 2008 (http://www.senate.gov/artandhistory/history/resources/pdf/VPTies.pdf).

Ford won a single term. Although it is indirect evidence at best, this fact suggests that vice presidents in the transitional era were somewhat better suited for or qualified for high political office. And although disagreement may exist over the question of whether any or all were great presidents, few argue that any were especially bad presidents.

Vice presidents in the transitional era "handled presidential succession more efficiently. . . . Roosevelt and Coolidge essentially retained top administration officials [after assuming the presidency], thereby lending stability to the government."[48] This was in stark contrast to presidential succession in the traditional era, when vice presidents typically came from a different faction of the party and Cabinet members were either quickly replaced or resigned. Major shifts in fundamental policy direction usually followed presidential succession, and worse, the new president typically governed from a position of weakness.[49] This was not the case in the transitional era.

Part of the dilemma of presidential succession is how prepared a vice president is in case of a presidential vacancy. The record in this regard during the transitional era is mixed. On the negative side of the ledger, Wilson, who suffered two strokes in the fall of 1919, served the remainder of his term (until 1921) virtually incapacitated. Although many urged Marshall to be more aggressive in assuming control of government, he was adamantly opposed to doing so without a congressional resolution and Mrs. Wilson's signed consent.[50] Absent presidential leadership, the League of Nations was defeated, many government vacancies went unfilled, and better than two dozen bills became law by default. This was a case in which the vice president was completely unprepared for presidential succession, as was the case of Truman, who assumed the presidency knowing very little about the major decisions Franklin Roosevelt was making concerning the war effort.

On the other hand Eisenhower made it clear that he wanted Vice President Nixon appraised of the workings of the administration in the event he could no longer fulfill his duties. This was fortunate, considering his heart attack in 1955, abdominal operation in 1956, and stroke in 1957. Eisenhower also spelled out the conditions under which Nixon should assume the powers of the presidency and when he himself would resume office in a series of letters with the vice president in February 1958.[51]

The major development with regard to presidential succession was the passage of the Twenty-Fifth Amendment, ratified in 1967. After Johnson became president, pressure mounted to deal with both presidential disability and vice presidential vacancy. Presidents Eisenhower and Kennedy both had written agreements with their vice presidents regarding provisions for their incapacity. Johnson, who suffered a heart attack in 1955 and had been president for fourteen months without a vice president, had a similar agreement with House Speaker John McCormack (next in line to succeed to the presidency) and subsequently with Vice President Humphrey after he was elected to the presidency.[52] The Amendment provides that in the event of a vice presidential vacancy, the president shall appoint a vice president who must then be confirmed by a "majority vote of both Houses of Congress."

The amendment also codified the tradition started by John Tyler in 1841 (and subsequently followed by seven others) that the vice president is the president—not the acting president—in the event of presidential vacancy. The other major provision of the amendment establishes procedures for the vice president and Cabinet to remove the president if and when they deem him to be incapacitated.

A formal duty was added to the vice president's job description in 1949 when Truman successfully lobbied Congress to make the vice president a statutory member of the National Security Council (NSC).[53] Truman was motivated by the fact that he had assumed the presidency with almost no knowledge that the United States had developed and was ready to deploy an atomic bomb. Barkley was the first vice president to regularly attend meetings of the NSC. Nixon attended 217 such meetings, presiding over 26.[54] This greatly enhanced the vice president's preparedness to assume the presidency in the event of a presidential vacancy.[55]

During the transitional era it also became common to assign the vice president to a special domestic policy area or post. These responsibilities are referred to as line assignments and include heading various programs, agencies, or commissions. Wallace was the first in this regard, named Chair of the Board of Economic Warfare. Nixon's domestic duties included chairing the Cabinet Committee on Price Stability for Economic Growth and the President's Committee on Government Contracts.[56] Johnson was named head of the newly constituted Space Council and was influential in shaping the goal of placing a man on the moon. He also headed the Peace Corps Advisory Council and the Presidential Committee on Equal Employment Opportunity, a position he used to advance civil rights.[57] Humphrey headed the National Aeronautics and Space Council, the President's Council on Economic Opportunity, the Office of Economic Opportunity, the Peace Corps, the President's Council on Youth Opportunity, and the President's Council on Recreation and Natural Beauty. In most cases Humphrey was the titular head of these agencies, exercising little actual influence over policy.[58]

Executive assignments of the vice presidency during the 1960s tended to accumulate. "Those that Johnson had taken over from Nixon and those added later were in turn passed on to Humphrey. Eventually the Committee on Equal Employment Opportunity was dismantled . . . But new assignments included chairmanship of the President's Council on Youth Opportunity . . . responsibility for White House liaison with the mayors, and somewhat later the chairmanship of the National Council on Marine Resources and Engineering Development."[59]

But unlike his two predecessors, Spiro Agnew was given few responsibilities. He did head a newly created Office of Intergovernmental Relations. Nixon gave him this job in hopes that an ex-governor would be more attuned to the problems of other state executives. However Agnew was less than diplomatic in his dealings with other governors (Rockefeller, for example, refused to talk to him). This made the agency largely irrelevant. Agnew headed the renamed Space Advisory Committee but angered the administration with his constant advocacy of a manned trip to Mars. He also headed the National Council on Indian Opportunity and was a member of the Council for Urban Affairs, the Council for Rural Affairs, the Cabinet Committee on Economic Policy, and the Domestic Council.[60] Ford managed to jettison the intergovernmental relations and Indian affairs assignments but was a member of the president's Domestic Council, as well as chair of the Committee on the Right to Privacy and the Energy Action Group.[61]

As the transitional era evolved vice presidents began a gradual, if not steady, movement toward becoming more associated with the executive branch. This trend was mirrored in their informal duties as well.

INFORMAL ROLES OF
TRANSITIONAL-ERA VICE PRESIDENTS

Unlike many of their traditional-era predecessors, transitional-era vice presidents stayed in Washington. In addition to their formal duties, most were expected to perform various ceremonial and social, diplomatic, and political tasks for their presidents as the transitional era wore on. Some vice presidents resisted performing these tasks. For example, Garner was protective of what he considered to be his private time.[62] But most understood that as one of only two nationally elected political figures, the vice president had certain ceremonial and social responsibilities. Johnson, for example, was sent to the funerals of Dag Hammarskjold (former Secretary General of the United Nations) and Pope John XXIII.[63] Johnson himself created a bit of a stir when he did *not* send his vice president, Humphrey, to Winston Churchill's funeral in 1965.[64]

Vice presidents also began to travel overseas, meeting with other state leaders, either on state business or otherwise. This can be thought of as a diplomatic function of the vice presidency. Starting with Nixon, vice presidents have been sent abroad, primarily for ceremonial (e.g., funerals, inaugurations) but sometimes for state purposes (e.g., policy-oriented) as well. The precise mix in this regard has been dependent on how much the president trusted the vice president. In either case the vice president was acting as a presidential envoy overseas, increasingly important given expanding U.S. global interests. Presidents and vice presidents also began to view vice presidential travel abroad as a way to burnish the credentials of vice presidents who harbored presidential ambitions.

Garner was the first vice president to travel abroad for his president.[65] Wallace traveled to Central and South America as well as China and the Soviet Union.[66] Nixon made a total of seven trips abroad during his eight years as vice president to a total of fifty-four countries. His function in these trips was mainly symbolic,[67] but he did engage in "extended discussions with nine prime ministers, 35 presidents, five kings, two emperors, and the Shah of Iran."[68] Johnson traveled even more than Nixon, in fewer years.[69] This was the result of a prenomination agreement made between Kennedy and Sam Rayburn on Johnson's behalf. His first trip was in May 1961 to Asia. Later that year he was sent to Berlin to show support after the Berlin Wall went up. In 1962 he traveled to Greece, Turkey, Cyprus, and Iran to notify their governments that U.S. aid would be reduced and minimize fallout from that policy change.[70] Johnson made almost a dozen trips overseas during his abbreviated term and was given "responsibility for specific negotiations and the issuance of policy communiqués on the spot."

Humphrey visited thirty-one countries on a total of twelve trips. On one such trip he met with the leaders of Great Britain, France, and West Germany to discuss nuclear proliferation, the North Atlantic Treaty Organization (NATO), and trade.[71] He also made several "fact-finding" trips to Southeast Asia, which were actually little more than a way for the administration to generate favorable publicity for the U.S. action in Vietnam (for the most part his reports were actually ignored).[72] Agnew made fewer trips (seven) than Humphrey, and several were apparently intended to help him avoid troubles he faced at home. One month-long trip included stops in South Korea, Singapore, Kuwait, Kenya, the Congo, Morocco, and Portugal.[73] These trips were more symbolic than substantive. For example, in South Korea he attended the inauguration of South Korean President Chung Hee Park but still had plenty of time for golf.[74] Arthur Schlesinger probably had Agnew's trip in mind when he claimed that vice presidential travel overseas was a way of "getting Vice Presidents out of sight."[75]

In the transitional era vice presidents extended the practice of acting as a political extension of the president and the party. These political roles included campaigning at midterm elections for congressional candidates of their party, fund-raising, and helping to promote the president's agenda on the road and in the halls of Congress. Marshall stands out in this regard, although Nixon set the standard for midterm campaigning with his efforts in 1954 and 1958.[76] Johnson made some four hundred speeches in thirty-five different states during his vice presidency.[77] In 1966, Humphrey "campaigned in almost every state" in support of "Democrats seeking congressional seats."[78]

Ford was constantly on the road, speaking to more than five hundred groups in forty states during his eight months in office. He also granted eighty-five formal interviews and held fifty-two press conferences during this time.[79] His mandate was both simple and clear: to help Nixon save his presidency. A secondary objective was to support various Republican members of Congress during a time when Nixon's troubles were negatively affecting the entire party.[80]

Vice presidents in the transitional era also began to take to the road in an effort to promote the policies of the administration. In this regard vice presidents can often help shape public debate, doing what the president cannot, either because of the constraints of time or for political reasons. For example, presidents may not have time to campaign for congressional candidates, or it may not be a good use of their political capital. Vice presidents can also lead hard-hitting attacks that the president cannot by virtue of his position as national leader. For example, Marshall campaigned throughout the country during World War I to promote the Liberty Loan effort.[81] Johnson made some four hundred speeches in thirty-five different states during his vice presidency.[82] Humphrey worked with mayors around the country to deal with various inner city and civil rights issues. In addition, Johnson expected him to help promote his Vietnam policy to the American public. Despite his own reservations about the war, Humphrey did this with his usual vigor.[83]

Agnew's political contribution to the Nixon administration was his hard-hitting attacks on the news media. After media criticism over Nixon's Vietnam policies in the fall of 1969, speech writer Pat Buchanan proposed sending Agnew out on the road to counterattack. For the next two years Agnew became the equivalent of a political "assault weapon."[84] To audiences around the country he lashed out at the media and intellectuals opposed to Nixon's policies. His speeches, largely written by Buchanan, were filled with memorable phrases, many of which became known as "Agnew-isms." Liberal university professors who were "misleading" the nation's youth and criticizing American policy were labeled the "effete corps of impudent snobs," and the media were referred to as "nattering nabobs of negativity," and "Radiclibs." In one speech Agnew claimed that, "Ultra-liberalism today translates into a whimpering isolationism in foreign policy, a mulish obstructionism in domestic policy, and a pusillanimous pussyfooting on the critical issue of law and order."

His campaign "struck a chord in middle America" and was so successful that he became one of the most popular men in the United States. In fact, unwilling to share the spotlight, Nixon soon reined him in.[85] Beyond this Agnew's political contributions to the Nixon administration were limited. For example because of his brash style he was ineffective on the congressional campaign trail, so much so that many congressional candidates asked him to stay clear of their campaigns.

Transitional-era vice presidents were also active legislative lobbyists. Garner understood when he accepted the vice presidential nomination that he would be an executive-legislative liaison for Franklin Roosevelt. Wallace was also active in pushing Roosevelt's legislative agenda.[86] Nixon claimed to have attended a total of 173 meetings between Eisenhower and legislative leaders. Johnson used his influence as former Senate Majority Leader to broker many deals between the Kennedy administration and Congress, one of which was a high profile wheat sale to the Soviet Union.[87] Johnson was also vocal in promoting the administration's civil rights agenda.

Humphrey played chief legislative liaison for President Johnson, enjoying even more success in this respect than Johnson had. This was in part because before becoming vice president he had been actively involved with Johnson's legislative agenda. He was instrumental in helping push through various Great Society and civil rights acts associated with the

Johnson administration (Head Start, Medicare, Food Stamps, Model Cities program, the Voting Rights Act of 1965).[88]

Starting with Vice President Marshall, most vice presidents in the transitional era also began to attend Cabinet meetings. Marshall actually presided over Cabinet meetings while Wilson was in Paris for peace talks.[89] Coolidge was the first vice president to attend Cabinet meetings on a regular basis, and although his own vice president Dawes refused to do so (believing it was not appropriate),[90] most have done so ever since.[91] Nixon attended 163 Cabinet meetings, presiding over 19.[92]

Despite the expansion of their duties, transitional-era vice presidents fared little better than their traditional-era counterparts in terms of their relationships with their presidents. For example, although he advocated a more active vice presidency, Theodore Roosevelt did not enjoy an especially close relationship with President McKinley, nor with his own vice president, Charles Fairbanks.[93] Coolidge was not especially close to President Harding.[94] Garner openly split with Franklin Roosevelt during their second term. Although President Eisenhower acknowledged Nixon's value to the Republican ticket he was at times dismissive of him. In late August 1960, in the midst of Nixon's presidential campaign, Eisenhower responded to a question about Nixon's major policy contributions to the administration by saying, "if you give me a week, I might think of one."[95] This said, Eisenhower was committed to ensuring that Nixon was informed about all relevant policy in the event that he had to assume the presidency.

Johnson did not have an especially good relationship with Kennedy and was never fully accepted in his administration. He was not trusted by the presidential staff and Kennedy was also a bit wary of him (though generally supportive). In this regard it probably mattered that the two came from completely different backgrounds. However he did have access to the president, attending meetings with the Cabinet, the NSC, with legislative leaders, and others regarding policy. He did not have much input at these meetings but could exchange views with the president in their frequent meetings alone.[96] But as an advisor he was only marginally influential and his tenure as vice president was, in short, miserable.[97] He once claimed to have "detested every minute" as vice president.[98]

Johnson treated his vice president in a similar way. Although Humphrey was probably the hardest working vice president in history, in his first two years in office Johnson never really trusted him. The president was unquestionably the boss and treated Humphrey accordingly. Humphrey frequently sought more substantive assignments, only to be refused. By 1966 he was being excluded from policy discussions, mainly because of his opposition to Johnson's Vietnam policy. Johnson also thought his vice president talked too much in public. Like Johnson, Humphrey left office embittered about the experience.[99] One positive thing that came out of it was that he advised subsequent vice presidents on how to minimize their own frustration with the job.

Nixon barely knew Agnew before he selected him as vice presidential candidate. Once in office, Nixon (and his staff) found him shallow and politically inept and quickly proceeded to lock him out of the inner circle. He gave Agnew few assignments of any importance. Agnew found it difficult to see the president and was once told by staffers that the president did not want him to disagree with him in meetings.[100] Agnew probably stands out as the least influential of all recent vice presidents.[101] Nixon also kept his second vice president, Ford, locked out of White House affairs. This is no surprise because by that time Nixon was completely preoccupied with his own political survival.

As the transitional era progressed, vice presidents became increasingly active, expected to carry out any number of ceremonial, social, diplomatic, and political tasks on behalf of their presidents. These increased responsibilities, with the added formal executive responsibilities of vice presidents in the transitional era, all but ensured that the vice president would come to be seen as an executive rather than a legislative post.

LIFE AFTER NEAR-GREATNESS IN THE TRANSITIONAL ERA

Perhaps the most obvious change in the vice presidency that occurred in the transitional era was that the vice presidency was "no longer a dead end for the ambitious."[102] Four of the five transitional-era vice presidents (all but Ford) who succeeded to the presidency subsequently won election on their own. Theodore Roosevelt, Coolidge, and Truman are considered by most to have been good, if not great, presidents. The most recent, Johnson, is known for implementation of the Great Society programs designed to assist in health care, education, environmental protection, and the protection and promotion of minority rights. It was the single greatest package of domestic legislation since Roosevelt's New Deal. Despite Johnson's success there were riots and racial unrest in several cities under his watch and under him the war in Vietnam continued to escalate. Consequently Johnson shocked the country in March 1968 by announcing he would not run for reelection.[103]

Ford assumed the office of the presidency after the resignation of Nixon, succeeded in securing his party's nomination in 1976, but lost in the general election. Only one incumbent vice president, Garner, was dropped in the president's reelection bid in 1940. Were it not for President Theodore Roosevelt's opposition, Charles Fairbanks may have secured the presidential nomination in 1908. Fairbanks ran for the vice presidency again in 1916 (with Charles Hughes) and lost.

Many began to see the vice presidency as a "stepping stone" to the presidency. Marshall and Dawes enjoyed some support for their party's presidential nomination but fell short, and Garner unsuccessfully challenged Roosevelt in 1940. Nixon secured his party's nomination for the presidency (in 1960), lost the general election, but eventually won the presidency in 1968 and again in 1972. Humphrey opposed Nixon in 1968 as his party's candidate. He returned to Minnesota and briefly taught at Macalaster College and University of Minnesota. In 1970 he was reelected to the U.S. Senate, winning the seat vacated by Eugene McCarthy. He made a credible but unsuccessful run for the Democratic presidential nomination in 1972 but declined to run in 1976. Later that year he was diagnosed with bladder cancer but was still reelected to the Senate. He passed away in January 1978, ending a distinguished career of public service. He was only the twenty-second person to lie in state in the Capitol Rotunda.[104]

Marshall retired after his brush with near-greatness. Several other vice presidents (Dawes, Charles Curtis, Wallace) remained active, either in public or private life. Wallace ran for president in 1948 under the Progressive party label, after which he retired to a farm in upstate New York. Vice President Barkley, who had been a visible and popular vice president, had a short-lived television show, *Meet the Veep*. It was Barkley's ten-year old grandson who coined the term *veep*, complaining that *vice president* or *VP* was too difficult to say. Barkley ran for and won a seat in the U.S. Senate in 1954 but died two years later.

Agnew, Nixon's first vice president, was charged with accepting bribes and falsifying federal tax returns and eventually pleaded *nolo contendere* to the latter charge in federal court. He resigned in October 1973 and subsequently withdrew from public life. Although he had difficulty finding immediate employment, he eventually became a fairly successful international trade executive. Although he attended Nixon's funeral in 1994 he refused to accept any calls from the former president. In 1995, a bust of Agnew was placed in the Capitol with those of the other vice presidents. He attended the ceremony, while acknowledging that many did not believe the bust should be there. Agnew died on September 17, 1996, in Ocean City, Maryland.[105]

CONCLUSION

The traditional-era vice presidency was marginal to the business of government. Most of the bad press, so to speak, the vice presidency has gotten throughout the years has come as the result of traditional-era vice presidents. The increased centrality of the presidency as a political institution, the growing visibility of presidents in the national media, the decline of political parties, and various succession crises in the first half of the twentieth century all combined to make the vice presidency more important. Political leaders and the public began to pay more attention to vice presidents, and the institution began to grow, if only incrementally and in many ways informally, in its functions. In part this was possible because presidential nominees began to exert more say in who their running mate would be, helping to ensure their compatibility with the second selection.

Several, although not all, vice presidents during this period were responsible for various vice presidential "firsts." All of these changes, cumulatively, meant that by the time Nixon left office, the institution had been transformed from a hybrid legislative-executive office to an executive institution. Nixon estimated that 90 percent of his time was spent on executive as opposed to legislative duties.[106]

In the next chapter we begin our exploration of the modern vice presidency in earnest, exploring the factors that converged to give rise to the modern vice presidency.

NOTES

1. Diana Dixon Healy, *America's Vice-presidents: Our First Forty-three Vice-presidents and How They Got to Be Number Two* (New York: Atheneum, 1984), 132.

2. Goldstein, "Vice Presidents," 1560.

3. Mayer, "A Brief History of Vice Presidential Selection," 329–31.

4. Ibid., 333–36.

5. Ibid., 336.

6. Marie D. Natoli, *American Prince, American Pauper: The Contemporary Vice Presidency in Perspective* (Westport, CT: Greenwood, 1985), 23.

7. Goldstein, *The Modern American Vice Presidency*, 81.

8. Ibid., 56; Natoli, *American Prince, American Pauper*, 31.

9. Theodore H. White, *The Making of the President, 1960* (New York: Atheneum, 1961), 225–26.

10. Since the Twenty-fifth Amendment had yet to be passed, Johnson had no incumbent vice president.

11. Goldstein, *The Modern American Vice Presidency*, 56, 60; Mayer, "A Brief History of Vice Presidential Selection," 347.

12. Goldstein, *The Modern American Vice Presidency*, 53, 55–58.

13. Paul T. David, "The Vice Presidency: Its Institutional Evolution and Contemporary Status," *The Journal of Politics* 29 (4) (1967):721–48, 728; Joan Hoff, "Richard Milhous Nixon (1913–1994)," in *Vice Presidents: A Biographical Dictionary*, ed. L. Edward Purcell (New York: Checkmark Books, 2001), 326. See also Goldstein, *The Modern American Vice Presidency*, 51, and George S. Sirgiovanni, "Dumping

the Vice President: An Historical Overview," *Presidential Studies Quarterly* 24 (4) (1994):765–82.

14. John Robert Greene, "Spiro Theodore Agnew (1918-1996)," in *Vice Presidents: A Biographical Dictionary*, ed. L. Edward Purcell (New York: Checkmark Books, 2001), 350–55.

15. Goldstein, *The Modern American Vice Presidency*, 49–51.

16. Nelson, "Choosing the Vice President," 860.

17. Richard Norton Smith, "'You Can Be President Someday': Richard M. Nixon as Vice President," in *At the President's Side: The Vice Presidency in the Twentieth Century*, ed. Timothy Walch (Columbia: University of Missouri, 1997), 85.

18. Mayer, "A Brief History of Vice Presidential Selection," 344.

19. Of course, classifying a candidate's ideological position is not an exact science. In this regard I rely on the analyses of various scholars and political observers.

20. Natoli, *American Prince, American Pauper*, 28, 59; Goldstein, *The Modern American Vice Presidency*, 81.

21. Figures here are approximations because the number (and percentage needed to win) of Electoral College votes that states represented changed several times during this period because the Electoral College grew in size, and as the result of changing population patterns in the United States, which resulted in reapportionment among the states over time.

22. William E. Unrau, "Charles Curtis (1860–1936)," in *Vice Presidents: A Biographical Dictionary*, ed. L. Edward Purcell (New York: Checkmark Books, 2001), 283–88.

23. Nelson, "Choosing the Vice President," 860.

24. Paul L. Silver, "Calvin Coolidge (1872–1933)," in *Vice Presidents: A Biographical Dictionary*, ed. L. Edward Purcell (New York: Checkmark Books, 2001), 266; Hatfield, *Vice Presidents of the United States*, 388.

25. Goldstein, *The Modern American Vice Presidency*, 91.

26. Peter R. Harstad, "Thomas Riley Marshall (1854–1925)"; Robert A Waller, "Charles Gates Dawes (1865–1951)"; Unrau, "Charles Curtis (1860–1936)"; and James K. Libbey, "Alben W. Barkley (1877–1956)," in *Vice Presidents: A Biographical Dictionary*, ed. L. Edward Purcell (New York: Checkmark Books, 2001).

27. Charles L. Fontenay, *Estes Kefauver: A Biography* (Knoxville: University of Tennessee, 1991).

28. Most recently, see Stacy G. Ulbig, *Vice Presidents, Presidential Elections, and the Media: Second Fiddles in the Spotlight* (Boulder: Lynne Reinner, 2013).

29. David, "The Vice Presidency," 736.

30. Goldstein, *The Modern American Vice Presidency*, 98.

31. Hatfield, *Vice Presidents of the United States, 1789–1993*.

32. Goldstein, *The Modern American Vice Presidency*, 95–96.

33. Ibid.

34. Goldstein, *The Modern American Vice Presidency*, 105.

35. Ibid.,108–9.

36. Ibid., 109.

37. Nelson, "Choosing the Vice President," 864.

38. Ibid., 110.

39. Paul C. Light, *Vice-Presidential Power: Advice and Influence in the White House* (Baltimore: Johns Hopkins University, 1984).

40. David, "The Vice Presidency," 773.

41. Ibid., 739, 744.

42. Hatfield, *Vice Presidents of the United States, 1789–1993*, 365, 402–3, 442.

43. David, "The Vice Presidency," 736–37.

44. Hatfield, *Vice Presidents of the United States, 1789–1993*, 469–70.

45. Cronin, "Rethinking the Vice-Presidency," 328.

46. Cronin, "Rethinking the Vice-Presidency," 329; Hatfield, *Vice Presidents of the United States, 1789–1993*.

47. Steven A. Hildreth, "Ballistic Missile Defense: Historical Overview," CRS Report for Congress, April 22, 2005, www.fas.org/sgp/crs/weapons/RS22120.pdf; Robert B. Bluey, "Bush Administration to Renew Fight for ANWR Drilling," January 09, 2003, *CNSNews.com*, www.cnsnews.com/ViewPolitics.asp? Page= 5CPolitics 5Carchive 5C200301 5CPOL20030109a.html.

48. Goldstein, "Vice President," 1560.

49. Goldstein, "Vice President," 1559.

50. Birch Bayh, *One Heartbeat Away: Presidential Disability and Succession* (Indianapolis: Bobb-Merrill, 1968), 21.

51. David, "The Vice Presidency," 727–29.

52. David, "The Vice Presidency," 729.

53. Mayer, "A Brief History of Vice Presidential Selection," 340, Table 9.1.

54. David, "The Vice Presidency," 727.

55. Hite, *Second Best*, 98.

56. David, "The Vice Presidency," 725, 731–32.

57. G. L. Seligman, "Lyndon Baines Johnson (1908–1973)," in *Vice Presidents: A Biographical Dictionary*, ed. L. Edward Purcell (New York: Checkmark Books, 2001), 336–38; David, "The Vice Presidency," 739–40.

58. Hatfield, *Vice Presidents of the United States, 1789–1993*; Karen M. Hult, "Hubert H. Humphrey, Jr. (1911–1978)," in *Vice Presidents: A Biographical Dictionary*, ed. L. Edward Purcell (New York: Checkmark Books, 2001).

59. David, "The Vice Presidency," 744.

60. John Robert Greene, "'I'll Continue to Speak Out': Sprio T. Agnew as Vice President," in *At the President's Side: The Vice Presidency in the Twentieth Century*, ed. Timothy Walch (Columbia: University of Missouri, 1997).

61. John Robert Greene, "Gerald Rudolph Ford (b. 1913)," in *Vice Presidents: A Biographical Dictionary*, ed. L. Edward Purcell (New York: Checkmark Books, 2001).

62. Hatfield, *Vice Presidents of the United States*, 391.

63. Goldstein, *The Modern American Vice Presidency*, 165.

64. Joel K. Goldstein, "More Agony than Ecstasy: Hubert H. Humphrey as Vice President," in *At the President's Side: The Vice Presidency in the Twentieth Century*, ed. Timothy Walch (Columbia: University of Missouri, 1997), 107–8.

65. David, "The Vice Presidency," 725.

66. Hatfield, *Vice Presidents of the United States*, 403.

67. Pika, "The Vice Presidency," in *The Presidency and the Political System*, ed. Michael Nelson, 4th ed. (Washington, D.C.: Congressional Quarterly, 1995), 504; Hoff, "Richard Milhous Nixon (1913–1994), 325–26.

68. Pika, "The Vice Presidency."

69. The tales of Johnson's lavish trips abroad (e.g., traveling with his own king-size bed and cases of whiskey) and his often less than strict following of diplomatic protocol are legend. See, for example, Robert Dalleck, "Frustration and Pain: Lyndon B. Johnson as Vice President," in *At the President's Side: The Vice Presidency in the Twentieth Century*, ed. Timothy Walch (Columbia: University of Missouri, 1997).

70. David, "The Vice Presidency," 737–38.

71. The leaders were Prime Minister Harold Wilson, President Charles de Gaulle, and Chancellor Kurt George Keisinger, respectively; Light, *Vice-Presidential Power*, 161.

72. Goldstein, *The Modern American Vice Presidency*, 165.

73. Light, *Vice-Presidential Power*, 160.

74. Goldstein, *The Modern American Vice Presidency*, 166.

75. Schlesinger, "On the Presidential Succession," 481.

76. Peter T. Harstad, "Thomas Riley Marshall (1854–1925)," in *Vice Presidents: A Biographical Dictionary*, ed. L. Edward Purcell (New York: Checkmark Books, 2001), 251–261; Joan Hoff, "Richard Milhous Nixon (1913–1994)," in *Vice Presidents: A Biographical Dictionary*, ed. L. Edward Purcell (New York: Checkmark Books, 2001), 322–331.

77. Goldstein, *The Modern American Vice Presidency*, 186; David, "The Vice Presidency," 740.

78. Hatfield, *Vice Presidents of the United States*, 470.

79. Hatfield, *Vice Presidents of the United States, 1789–1993*, 498.

80. Goldstein, *The Modern American Vice Presidency*, 189.

81. Harstad, "Thomas Riley Marshall (1854–1925)," 258.

82. Goldstein, *The Modern American Vice Presidency*, 186; David, "The Vice Presidency," 740.

83. Hatfield, *Vice Presidents of the United States, 1789–1993*, 469.

84. Greene, "I'll Continue to Speak Out," 127.

85. Ibid., 128–29; Hatfield, *Vice Presidents of the United States, 1789–1993*, 484.

86. Hatfield, *Vice Presidents of the United States*.

87. Goldstein, *The Modern American Vice Presidency*, 179.

88. Hatfield, *Vice Presidents of the United States*, 469.

89. Harstad, "Thomas Riley Marshall (1854–1925)," 258.

90. Hatfield, *Vice Presidents of the United States*, 364.

91. Mayer, "A Brief History of Vice Presidential Selection," 340, Table 9.1.

92. David, "The Vice Presidency," 732.

93. Goldstein, "Vice President," 1559; Ray E. Boomhower, "Charles Warren Fairbanks (1852–1918)," in *Vice Presidents: A Biographical Dictionary*, ed. L. Edward Purcell (New York: Checkmark Books, 2001), 240.

94. Silver, "Calvin Coolidge (1872–1933)," 267.

95. Nixon implies in his memoirs that Eisenhower may have been misunderstood. See Richard Nixon, *RN: The Memoirs of Richard Nixon* (New York: Simon & Schuster, 1990), 276.

96. David, "The Vice Presidency," 739.

97. Cronin, "Rethinking the Vice-Presidency," 334.

98. Dalleck, "Frustration and Pain," 99.

99. Thomas E. Cronin, "Rethinking the Vice Presidency," in *Rethinking the Presidency*, ed. Thomas E. Cronin. (Canada: Little, Brown and Company, 1980), 335; Hatfield, *Vice Presidents of the United States, 1789–1993*.

100. Spiro T. Agnew, *Go Quietly . . . or Else* (New York, William Morrow, 1980).

101. Cronin, "Rethinking the Vice-Presidency," 334; Hatfield, *Vice Presidents of the United States, 1789–1993*.

102. Goldstein, "Vice President," 1560.

103. Seligman, "Lyndon Baines Johnson (1908–1973)"; Hatfield, *Vice Presidents of the United States, 1789–1993*.

104. Hult, "Hubert H. Humphrey, Jr. (1911–1978)," 348.

105. Hatfield, *Vice Presidents of the United States, 1789–1993*.

106. David, "The Vice Presidency," 731.

5

The Rise of the
Modern Vice Presidency

In the previous chapter we saw that during the transitional era the vice presidency gradually became more integral and important in terms of its place in the American system of governance. Although this development occurred in fits and starts there is no question that the vice president's job description is different than it was fifty years ago. Modern presidents, vice presidents, and the public now understand that the vice president must be prepared to assume the presidency at a moment's notice. Modern vice presidents are better prepared for office, have better relationships with their presidents, and have more resources with which to do their jobs. Collectively, these developments define the modern vice presidency. What accounts for this change?

The rise of the modern vice presidency can be attributed to three factors. The first is increased concern over presidential succession, which in turn related to the growth of national government and the concurrent rise of the presidency as its focal point. In other words the presidency became, or was perceived to have become, more important to the business of government. As the century progressed there were several presidential successions resulting from presidential death or vacancy. Vice presidents who became president by way of succession occupied the office half of the time from 1945 to 1977. Another vice president (Richard Nixon) served under a president (Dwight Eisenhower) who had serious heart problems. These developments, combined with the resignation of Vice President Spiro Agnew and the withdrawal of vice presidential candidate Thomas Eagleton from the Democratic ticket in

1972, highlighted the issue of presidential succession and vice presidential readiness and competence.

The manner in which vice presidential candidates are selected has also contributed to the emergence of the new model of the vice presidency. It is no longer the case that vice presidential candidates are selected at the last moment with little thought given to their qualifications or compatibility with the presidential candidate. Because the presidential primary system typically produces a presumptive presidential nominee by late spring or early summer (at the very latest) these candidates have ample time to search for, research, and select a running mate. Jimmy Carter set the precedent for the modern selection process in 1976, winnowing down a long list of possible running mates to a final few, who he then personally met with to determine who would be the best fit in terms of personality, policy orientation, and so forth. Most presidential candidates since Carter have employed this "Carter model" of vice presidential selection. Moreover, most vice presidential candidates now reach some sort of explicit agreement with the presidential candidate with respect to what role the vice president will play in the administration if elected. At minimum this helps ensure that vice presidents will not be irrelevant.

The final factors associated with the emergence of the modern vice presidency center around the institution itself. These include, for example, office space in the West Wing of the White House, which helps ensure access to the president. Vice presidential staffing levels, salary, and other perquisites have also grown in the past forty years. These institutional factors include the role of precedent and institutional memory. New vice presidents generally take office with the formal and informal resources that their predecessors had, which over time have increased. In addition, many now consult with previous vice presidents about what the job entails.

In this chapter we will review each of these developments in more detail, showing how each has contributed to a more active, visible, and arguably consequential vice presidency.

PRESIDENTIAL SUCCESSION CONCERNS

The twentieth century saw dramatic changes in the political environment in the United States. Many of these changes affected the presidency, and either directly or indirectly, the vice presidency as well. Two of these changes are of particular interest here: the growth of the national government and presidential power. Together these two developments combined to increase the centrality and visibility of the presidency in the American system of government, and by virtue of the succession function of the institution, the vice presidency.

The Civil War was the most significant event in the growth of the national government in the nineteenth century. This is because the conflict settled, once and for all, the question of the supremacy of the national government over the states. Government, in other words, increasingly began to mean the *national* government as opposed to state governments. The second reason the Civil War was important in this regard was the decision of the national government to pay the pensions of Civil War (specifically Union) veterans. This laid the groundwork for large government programs and monetary transfers. Conventional wisdom holds that the growth of government began in earnest with Franklin Roosevelt's New Deal, but reforms during the Progressive Era immediately before and shortly after the turn of the century continued the pattern of growth begun by the program to assist Civil War veterans. These included the passage of the Sherman Antitrust Act (1890), the establishment of the Interstate Commerce Commission (1887), the Food and Drug Administration (1906), the Federal Reserve (1913), and the Federal Trade Commission.[1]

However the growth of the national government was severely constrained by the fact that it had limited resources at its disposal. This changed with the ratification of the Sixteenth Amendment to the Constitution in 1913, which instituted a national income tax. With more money at its disposal the government could now do more. During the 1920s spending by the national government increased at a rate of approximately 10 percent per year (sometimes more) in areas like commerce, agriculture, education, labor interests, and public improvements.[2] Spending accelerated again with the New Deal and World War II. Whether measured by government spending as percentage of gross domestic product, number of government agencies, programs, and such, the national government was increasingly larger and responsible to its citizens for more.[3]

Concurrent with this change was the increased prominence of the president's role in the federal government. Most presidential scholars agree that this resulted from the convergence of a few developments. First, expectations of the president began to grow in the era after Franklin Roosevelt. Perhaps this was natural. After all, Roosevelt was perceived as having navigated the country successfully through two of its biggest crises to date, namely the Great Depression and World War II. As a result, people began to look to the president to solve any number of national problems. The presidency became, or was perceived to have become, more important to the business of government.[4] Relatedly, presidential candidates began to stoke these expectations during longer and more public campaigns by promising more. By the end of the twentieth century it was expected that someone running for president would have a proposed solution or issue position on virtually all matters of public policy. Second, changes in communications technologies, in particular radio and television, made it possible for presidents to become a more personal figure in the lives of citizens.[5] As the century wore on presidents began to be the focal point of national news coverage.

Together these changes combined to make the presidency a more prominent and visible institution. By the 1960s presidents had become a "central . . . symbol for public emotions and aspirations,"[6] "by far the most visible [actor] in the political system, overshadowing even the most influential legislators."[7] In other words, presidents had become the most important figure in a larger central government.

What made these two developments more important with regard to the vice presidency were various presidential successions or succession issues as the century wore on. The twentieth century began with Vice President Theodore Roosevelt assuming the presidency after the assassination of President McKinley in September 1901. Woodrow Wilson suffered a stroke in 1919 that left him all but incapacitated for the remainder of his second term. In August 1923 Calvin Coolidge succeeded to the presidency after the death of President Harding. Presidential succession was clearly an issue.

But this was even more evident, at least to the political elite, with the death of Franklin Roosevelt in 1945. Vice President Harry Truman, on assuming the office of the presidency, had little knowledge about the development of an atomic bomb or "the agreements Roosevelt had reached with the Russians and British at Yalta."[8] Because vice presidents were not considered central actors in the administration, he was at first seriously underprepared to make foreign policy decisions. Succession concerns continued with the presidency of Eisenhower. During his first term Eisenhower was hospitalized for six weeks after suffering a serious heart attack. In 1956 he underwent surgery for a bowel obstruction and was still recovering at the time of the Suez Canal crisis. Finally, in 1957 he suffered a mild stroke during a Cabinet meeting.[9] Following this was the assassination of John Kennedy in 1963. Although the Twenty-Fifth Amendment dealing with presidential succession and disability was ratified in 1967, concerns over presidential succession, and particularly vice presidential readiness, remained in the public eye

In part this was the result of what has become known as "the Eagleton affair." The shift away from the convention system to the primary system of selecting presidential candidates began in earnest in 1972. Among other things this meant that because of his primary victories Democrat George McGovern appeared to have the Democrat presidential nomination secured well in advance of the party national convention, which was scheduled for July. However there was some controversy within the party surrounding the seating of some convention delegates and this controversy consumed all of McGovern's attention.[10] He officially received the nomination around midnight on July 12. Shortly afterward he called Senator Edward Kennedy, asking him to be his running mate (why he did so is unclear because Kennedy had repeatedly refused McGovern's previous invitations to join the ticket).

Party rules dictated that the vice presidential nominee's name be announced to the party national committee by 4:00 PM, July 13. Clearly it was impossible to comprehensively review all possible choices in that short a period of time. A list of about three dozen prospects was quickly reduced to seven: Walter Mondale, Abraham Ribicoff, Thomas Eagleton, Patrick Lucey, Kevin White, Larry O'Brien, and Sargent Shriver. McGovern received this list about noon, and for the next ninety minutes or so consulted with various interest group leaders who had been instrumental in his campaign. Several of the individuals on the list declined his invitation to join the ticket, and several others were ruled out. McGovern then asked—and was turned down by—Senator Gaylord Nelson, a friend who was not on the list. Nelson in turn suggested that McGovern ask Missouri Senator Eagleton, the only name left on the list.

McGovern barely knew Eagleton and had spoken with him but a few times. Although McGovern's aides had heard rumors that Eagleton might have had a history of mental illness and alcoholism, they conducted a quick background check (recall that this was all occurring in a single afternoon) and found nothing to substantiate those rumors. McGovern called Eagleton and offered him the nomination, and Eagleton accepted. One of McGovern's top aides, Frank Mankiewicz, then got on the phone and asked Eagleton if there were any skeletons in his closet. The Senator claimed that there were none. The entire phone conversation lasted a few minutes.[11]

Subsequent to his nomination the media began investigating rumors about Eagleton's mental health. Shortly afterward Eagleton admitted that he had been hospitalized for nervous exhaustion in the past, and during the course of his treatment had received electric shock therapy. Although McGovern originally stood by Eagleton, the pressure to replace him built and within two weeks he requested that Eagleton withdraw his candidacy.

The Eagleton affair came right before the resignations of Vice President Agnew in 1973 and President Nixon in 1974, followed by an assassination attempt on Ronald Reagan in 1981 and his temporary disability as a result of an operation in 1985. All of these occurrences, although spread out over several decades, served to highlight the importance of the vice presidency in terms of the constitutional role of presidential succession. The media and the public now subject vice presidential candidates to a level of scrutiny previously "enjoyed" only by presidential candidates. Ideas about what type of person is capable and competent to serve as vice president, and potentially as president, have changed. There is now a greater focus on the vice presidency and the issue of vice presidential readiness.

A final effect related to the increased visibility of the vice presidency and a greater focus on vice presidential competence is that by 1960, the office has come to be viewed as a stepping stone to the presidency. More will be said about this in subsequent chapters, but for now it is sufficient to note that because of this the office has become more attractive, thereby attracting men and women of greater caliber.

VICE PRESIDENTIAL SELECTION

Presidential candidates can no longer ignore background, qualifications, and experience in their selection of a running mate. This is related to a larger, second development responsible for the emergence of the modern vice presidency. The shift to the primary system of selecting presidential candidates has resulted not only in vice presidential candidates who are generally better qualified, but who also have quietly campaigned to be selected and will be loyal to their president if elected.

Before 1972 presidential nominations were decided at the party convention. In 1972 the rules changed. The number of delegates to the party national conventions (originally in the Democratic Party) selected by way of party primaries and who were pledged to support a particular candidate increased dramatically. This meant that henceforth the presidential nominee would be known in advance of the convention. It also meant that presidential nominees were no longer dependent on the party for their nomination and thus had little need to consult the party about their vice presidential choice.[12] In addition, with the presidential nomination decided in advance of the convention, presidential candidates now had more time to formally examine their choices. This led, in 1976, to the emergence of the Carter model of vice presidential selection.

Carter captured the 1976 Democrat nomination five weeks before the Democratic convention, giving him ample time to research possible running mates. A list of four hundred possible candidates, compiled in April, was narrowed to about a dozen. The relative strengths of these names were then tested by Carter pollster Pat Caddell. From this list, seven finalists emerged. Carter aide Charles Kirbo then interviewed several of them, asking them to fill out questionnaires about their financial, health, personal, and political backgrounds. He also asked Democratic senators for their evaluations of each. Starting in July, Carter himself began interviewing the finalists, several in New York City, the rest (including the eventual nominee, Walter Mondale) in Plains, Georgia. The interviews allowed Carter and the vice presidential aspirants to exchange views on various policy matters, and just as importantly, gave Carter some sense of what each man would be like to work with.

The Carter model of research and interviews did not catch on immediately. In 1976 the incumbent Vice President Nelson Rockefeller was asked by President Gerald Ford to withdraw his name from consideration in his reelection bid. Ford's decision was the result of pressure from party conservatives to jettison one the nation's leading liberal Republicans. Ford had faced a strong challenge to his own renomination bid from the conservative Reagan. Previously, Ford had consulted key Republican leaders and had polled convention delegates about their choice for a vice presidential running mate. Because no consensus candidate emerged from this he went to the convention without having settled on a final choice. As the result of Reagan's challenge, Ford did not secure the presidential nomination until the convention itself. After meetings which lasted until 5:00 AM, he chose Robert Dole. It was, in other words, a last-minute selection.

Ford deviated from another aspect of the Carter model not yet discussed. Throughout his campaign Carter had kept the media fairly well appraised about who was being considered for the vice presidential nomination. This allowed them to do their own research on potential candidates. After the Eagleton affair, inclusion of the media seems to have become a new norm in vice presidential selection. Obviously Ford was hardly in a position to do this because his own nomination was secured at the last minute.

Another exception was Reagan's selection of George H. W. Bush in 1980. This case also underscores the new role of the media in vice presidential selection. At the Republican convention speculation was rampant that former President Ford would be selected as Reagan's running mate. As unlikely as this seemed, Ford had expressed interest during a televised interview with Walter Cronkite during the convention. The Reagan organization had approached Ford and negotiations were underway as to how such an arrangement might work. Ford, however, made it clear that he wanted a central role—agreed upon in advance— in the administration. He stated, "If I go to Washington . . . I have to go there with the belief that I would play a meaningful role, across the board, in the basic, crucial, tough decisions that have to be made in the four-year period."[13] This was asking more of Reagan than he was willing to accept. However the media hype about this so-called "dream team" had reached a fevered pitch, so Reagan had to appear before the convention to drum up support for what turned out to be a last-minute choice, Bush.

If Mondale had turned out to be a poor vice president, the Carter model of vice presidential selection may have met a quick demise. However Mondale is widely acknowledged as being one of the best vice presidents of the modern era. So it was that most presidential candidates since Carter have followed a similar process of selecting vice presidential candidates, whereby one or a few trusted aides compile and extensively research a list of candidates, keeping members of the press reasonably well informed throughout the process. In fact prospective nominees are now asked to submit to extensive and intrusive background checks and answer lengthy questionnaires before being considered.

This shift in how vice presidential candidates are selected has had two effects related to the emergence of the modern vice presidency. First, it has resulted in higher standards, and thus, more qualified vice presidential candidates. The public has come to expect this. "The presidential candidate who pays insufficient attention to competence . . . pays a price in the election."[14] Second, because vice presidential candidates are now beholden to presidential candidates for the nomination, the "process greatly increased the vice president's incentive to remain loyal to the president."[15] Presidential candidates look for compatible running mates and can expect them to be loyal on the campaign trail and in office if elected.

A final aspect of vice presidential selection that has had an effect on the emergence of the modern vice presidency is the fact that most presidential and vice presidential candidates reach some sort of preelection agreement regarding the role the vice president will play in office if elected. Although Mondale is often credited with this development, Rockefeller was actually the first.

One of the primary reasons Rockefeller was selected for the office by Ford was that he was the well-known four-term governor of New York. Ford selected him to restore some of the luster to the offices of President and Vice President in the wake of the Watergate scandal and Agnew resignation. This gave Rockefeller, who was not eager to be vice president, some bargaining power when approached about taking the job. He used this leverage, seeking and receiving from Ford the post of chair of the Domestic Policy Council, created by Nixon to be the domestic equivalent of the NSC. Rockefeller hoped to direct domestic policy much in the same way Henry Kissinger directed foreign policy. Rockefeller also set an institutional precedent by having regular weekly meetings with the president, during which he was able to share his ideas with him.

Mondale built on these precedents. When he accepted the vice presidential nomination, he and Carter agreed to discuss Mondale's role after the election. After taking office Mondale first avoided taking on any line assignments, or the various executive statutory and appointive positions that his immediate predecessors had taken (e.g., Lyndon Johnson's heading up of the newly created NASA). Based on conversations with Hubert Humphrey and Rockefeller, he had determined that these were a waste of the vice president's time.[16] He too had regular weekly meetings with the president.

Others have followed suit. For example, before he won the vice presidency, Al Gore's father (a former senator who had himself aspired to the vice presidency) suggested that he and President Bill Clinton have a clear understanding of his place in the administration. Gore had also commissioned a study of the vice presidency (by Peter Knight and Reed Hundt), which unsurprisingly concluded that vice presidents were generally unsuccessful and frustrated in their jobs. Clinton and Gore met after the election and forged a two-page document outlining the vice president's role. Gore generally followed the Mondale model of avoiding line assignments. For example, he declined an early opportunity to head the president's task force on health care reform.[17]

INSTITUTIONAL FACTORS AND THE ROLE OF PRECEDENT

Another factor related to the expansion of the vice presidency is that as each new vice president takes office, the resources available to and roles played by previous vice presidents are assumed. Moreover these resources have tended to increase, albeit incrementally, over time. For example before Agnew, vice presidents had relatively small staffs, which were drawn from other offices. Nixon had a total staff of about sixteen people.[18] During Agnew's vice presidency the office first received funding for its own staff. By the time Mondale took office he had a staff of between sixty and seventy. It has remained at about this level since. In 1972, the office of vice president was listed for the first time in the *United States Government Organization Manual* as part of the Executive Office of the President.[19] The vice presidential budget increased substantially during Vice President Ford's tenure,[20] and by the time Gore took office, the budget was more than three million dollars.[21]

As of 2013 vice presidents earn $231,000 per year, roughly the same as the Chief Justice of the Supreme Court and about half what the president earns.[22] By contrast, the first vice president (John Adams) earned $5,000 per annum compared with Washington's $25,000; in 1964 Vice President Humphrey earned $43,000, President Johnson, $100,000. Vice presidents also receive a $20,000 taxable expense account (the president's expense account is nontaxable),[23] free transportation (limousines, air travel aboard Air Force Two), Secret Service protection, and housing (the vice presidential mansion).[24]

Office space is also an important resource. Previous vice presidents shared office space in the Senate wing of the old Capitol building. When the building was expanded in the 1850s the vice president was given his own office (in his function as President of the Senate).[25] This began to change late in the transitional era. Nixon had three different offices in the Capitol but was able to work in various conference rooms at the White House as well.[26] Johnson was given a suite of six offices in the Executive Office Building (EOB) next door to the White House, and Humphrey had multiple rooms in the EOB as well. Mondale had an office in the White House in close proximity to the president, as have all vice presidents since.[27] Vice presidents continue to use EOB offices, mainly for ceremonial events (in fact, Second Ladies now have offices in the EOB as well).[28]

Finally, the vice presidency came of age in July 1974 when Congress designated the Naval Observatory as the official vice presidential residence (see box 5.1). By the time renovations were complete, Rockefeller was vice president. Mondale was the first vice president to live in the vice presidential mansion (the Rockefellers mainly used it for art displays and receptions).[29]

The institutionalization of a resource base for the vice presidency meant that vice presidents had more potential power. A vice presidential budget, for example, has "made it possible for the vice president to develop an independent staff structure that largely paralleled the president's, including specialists in both domestic and foreign policy and assistants for scheduling, speech writing, congressional relations, and press relations."[30] But resources themselves do not tell even half of the story in terms of the development of the office. To complete the picture we must consider the vice president's access to the president.

Recall that in the traditional era, many vice presidents did not often meet with their presidents. Later in the transitional era this had begun to change. Johnson, for example, had fairly regular access to the president, attending meetings with the Cabinet, the National Security Council, with legislative leaders, and others regarding policy, at which he could sometimes exchange views with John Kennedy.[31] Johnson and Nixon were less generous with their vice presidents[32] (of course Nixon had also been treated poorly by Eisenhower during his own tenure as vice president).

However when Ford asked Rockefeller to be his vice president he told the nation that he wanted a vice president who was a "full partner." It is hard to believe that Rockefeller would have taken the job under other circumstances. Indeed, Rockefeller "never want[ed] to be vice president of anything."[33] He had personally known every vice president since Henry Wallace and knew that they all left the job unhappy men.[34] He took office believing he could and would be the architect of the administration's domestic agenda. His resume suggested he was capable, but from the start he was frustrated. The major obstacle he faced was being locked out

BOX. 5.1

Life at the Vice President's Residence

The large telescope at the Naval Observatory in Washington, D.C. attracted hundreds of visitors in 1910, including President Howard Taft and his wife, Helen. The stargazing Tafts drove up the hill past the superintendent's house to the Naval Observatory in their new automobile to look at Halley's Comet. The white 19th Century house overlooking Massachusetts Avenue in Washington D.C. was built in 1893 for the superintendent of the United States Naval Observatory. The house was so lovely that the chief of naval operations booted the superintendent and made the house his home in 1923.

The house was "taken over" again in 1974 when Congress turned "Number One Observatory Circle" into the official residence of the Vice President. Before 1974, vice presidents and their families lived in their own home, but the cost of securing these private homes had grown substantially over the years. After years of debate, Congress agreed to refurbish the house at the Naval Observatory as a home for the Vice President.

Over the years, the Naval Observatory has continued to operate. Scientists there make observations of the sun, moon, planets and selected stars, determine and distribute precise time, and publish astronomical data needed for accurate navigation.

From "Number One Observatory Circle: Life at the Vice President's Residence" (georgewbush-whitehouse.archives.gov/history/life/vpresidence.html).

of White House affairs by the president's staff, especially Chief of Staff Donald Rumsfeld. This was in part due to the fact that his confirmation took four months during, which time the Ford administration was being shaped and formed without him. Nonetheless, in his first few months in office, Rockefeller participated actively in the administration and throughout his term met privately with Ford once a week.

Carter made it clear he would make his vice president a partner and after the election met with Mondale to discuss his role in the administration.[35] Several key decisions were made at that point that enhanced his position in this regard. Carter made his commitment to include Mondale clear to his staff, telling them, "If you get a request from Fritz [Mondale's nickname], treat it as if from me."[36] Staff was repeatedly told that Mondale was to be included in everything. Mondale was included in the paper flow to and from the Oval Office, given access to any presidential meeting he wished, and kept Rockefeller's tradition of lunching privately with the president once a week. It was also decided that Carter's and Mondale's staff would work together, a decision facilitated by the fact that campaign aides had worked out of the same campaign headquarters.[37] All of this led to a situation whereby Mondale was in a position to regularly offer the president advice on the entire range of domestic and foreign policy issues facing the administration. Of course, the president did not always follow the advice,[38] but Mondale did have access to the president, setting the standard for future vice presidents.

Perhaps no other change in the institution of the vice presidency is more significant than the fact that vice presidents have become trusted advisers to their presidents. "Most recent vice presidents—Mondale, Gore, and Cheney—come closer than earlier vice presidents to being second in command in a president's administration."[39] This is why access is so important: Proximity to the president makes it more likely the vice president will be included in major decision making. In the modern era vice presidents have regular access to the president.

A final aspect in the emergence of the modern vice presidency that should be acknowledged is the role of precedent. "Practice and precedent have by far been the most important determinants of vice-presidential roles."[40] Almost all modern vice presidents have consulted previous vice presidents about what to expect from the job and how to do it more effectively. (Humphrey and Mondale seem to have been consulted most frequently, by both Democrats and Republicans).[41] This consultation crosses party lines. Mondale passed his experience along to George H. W. Bush, who took many of his lessons to heart. Gore spoke with both Mondale and Dan Quayle. Institutional memory, along with practice and precedents, have created higher expectations for the vice presidency and make it unlikely that the institution will ever revert back to its premodern status.

The point is that once one vice president was granted an office in the West Wing, a weekly meeting with the president, and so on, it became difficult for any subsequent presidents to deny *their* vice president the same. These things "now [constitute] a virtual 'litmus test' that observers apply to vice presidents."[42] To change the pattern of resource allocation or access would risk the vice president, and by extension, the administration, losing face, and thus credibility.

CONCLUSION

The rise of the modern vice presidency was the product of a confluence of factors occurring over a span of approximately fifty years. Increased concerns over presidential succession, which placed a greater focus on vice presidential competence and readiness, can be said to have been based the growth of the national government and the rise of the modern presidency. The emergence of the primary system of selecting presidential candidates means that those candidates can take their time in the selection of their own running mates, systematically examining qualifications, compatibility, and more. When the selection is made the two typically come to some sort of an agreement over what role the vice president will play in the administration, and in the modern era this role is not insignificant. Institutional factors, meaning increased resources and access to the president, are important as well, as is the fact that each new vice president takes office assuming the resources his (or her) predecessor enjoyed.

In the following chapters we look at the tenures of modern vice presidents, from Nelson Rockefeller through Joe Biden, in greater detail.

NOTES

1. Robert Higgs, *Crisis and Leviathan: Critical Episodes in the Growth of American Government* (New York: Oxford University, 1987).

2. Randall G. Holcombe, "The Growth of the Federal Government in the 1920s," *Cato Journal* 16 (1996): 175–99.

3. Higgs, *Crisis and Leviathan*; Michael S. Lewis-Beck and Tom W. Rice, "Government Growth in the United States," *The Journal of Politics* 47 (1985): 2–30.

4. Fred I. Greenstein, "Nine Presidents: In Search of a Modern Presidency," in *Leadership in the Modern Presidency*, ed. Fred I. Greenstein (Cambridge, MA: Harvard University Press, 1988), 297.

5. Theodore J. Lowi, *The "Personal" President: Power Invested, Promise Unfulfilled* (Ithaca: Cornell University, 1985).

6. Greenstein, "Nine Presidents."

7. Fred I. Greenstein, "Toward a Modern Presidency," in *Leadership in the Modern Presidency*, ed. Fred I. Greenstein (Cambridge, MA: Harvard University Press, 1988), 4.

8. Hatfield, *Vice Presidents of the United States*, 418.

9. Stephen Ambrose, *Eisenhower: (Vol. 2) The President (1952–1969)* (New York: Simon & Schuster, 1984).

10. "The Battle for the Democratic Party," *Time*, July 17, 1972.

11. Mayer, "A Brief History of Vice Presidential Selection," 348–51; Joel K. Goldstein, *The Modern American Vice Presidency: The Transformation of a Political Institution* (Princeton, NJ: Princeton University, 1982); Natoli, *American Prince, American Pauper*, 24.

12. See Wayne, *The Road to the White House*, 104–11, for a brief discussion of the shift from the convention to the primary system of delegate selection; see also Goldstein, *The Modern American Vice Presidency*, Chapter 3.

13. Natoli, *American Prince, American Pauper*, 39.

14. Michael Nelson, "The Election: Turbulence and Tranquility in Contemporary American Politics," in *The Elections of 1996*, ed. Michael Nelson (Washington, DC: Congress Quarterly, 1997), 68.

15. Mayer, "A Brief History of Vice Presidential Selection," 341; see also Goldstein, *The Modern American Vice Presidency*, 56–57, 61; Natoli, *American Prince, American Pauper*, 36; Miller Center Commission, "Report of the Commission on Choosing and Using Vice Presidents" (Miller Center of Public Affairs: University of Virginia, 1992); and Nelson, *A Heartbeat Away*, 45.

16. Frank Kessler, "Walter F. Mondale (b. 1928)," in *Vice Presidents: A Biographical Dictionary*, ed. L. Edward Purcell (New York: Checkmark Books, 2001), 380–82.

17. Bill Turque, *Inventing Al Gore: A Biography* (Boston: Houghton Mifflin, 2000).

18. David, "The Vice Presidency," 773.

19. Light, *Vice-Presidential Power*.

20. Mayer, "A Brief History of Vice Presidential Selection," 340, Table 9.1.

21. Pika, "The Vice Presidency," 524.

22. Executive Order 13594: "Adjustments of Certain Rates of Pay," signed December 19, 2011, Federal Register, Vol. 76, No. 247, p. 80191, December 23, 2011 (www.gpo.gov/fdsys/pkg/FR-2011-12-23/pdf/2011-33087.pdf).

23. 3 USC § 111, Expense allowance of Vice President (http://www.law.cornell.edu/uscode/text/3/111).

24. Jody C Baumgartner, *The American Vice Presidency Reconsidered* (Westport, CT: Praeger, 2006).

25. "The Vice President's Room" (S. Pub. 106-7), prepared under the direction of the U.S. Senate Commission on Art by the Office of Senate Curator. Washington, D.C.: Government Printing Office, 2002, (www.senate.gov/artandhistory/art/resources/pdf/Vice_President_s_Room.pdf.).

26. David, "The Vice Presidency," 773.

27. Pika, "The Vice Presidency," 498–99.

28. Broder and Bob Woodward, *The Man Who Would Be President Dan Quayle* (New York: Simon & Schuster, 1992), 156.

29. Hatfield, *Vice Presidents of the United States, 1789–1993*.

30. Pika, "The Vice Presidency," 498–99.

31. David, "The Vice Presidency," 739.

32. Cronin, "Rethinking the Vice-Presidency," 335; Hatfield, *Vice Presidents of the United States, 1789–1993*; Agnew, *Go Quietly . . . or Else*, 32; Cronin, "Rethinking the Vice-Presidency," 334; Hatfield, *Vice Presidents of the United States, 1789–1993*.

33. Michael S. Kramer, *I Never Wanted to Be Vice-President of Anything! An Investigative Biography of Nelson Rockefeller* (New York: Basic Books, 1976).

34. James Cannon, "Gerald R. Ford and Nelson A. Rockefeller: A Vice Presidential Memoir," in *At the President's Side: The Vice Presidency in the Twentieth Century*, ed. in Timothy Walch (Columbia: University of Missouri, 1997), 137.

35. Kessler, "Walter F. Mondale (b. 1928)," 380.

36. Ibid., 381.

37. Light, *Vice-Presidential Power*, 131.

38. Kessler, "Walter F. Mondale (b. 1928)," 381.

39. Polsby and Wildavsky, *Presidential Elections*, 84. The classic work on vice presidential influence is Light, *Vice-Presidential Power*.

40. Pika, "The Vice Presidency," 503.

41. Ibid., 499–500; Cronin, "Rethinking the Vice-Presidency," 339–40.

42. Pika, "The Vice Presidency," 514.

6

Vice Presidents in
the Modern Age

This chapter examines the vice presidency in the modern age, from 1974 forward. This period is distinguished from previous ones by the fact that vice presidents are now quite active players in our governmental system, acting as informal assistants to their presidents. Although the focus here is on all modern vice presidents, the tenures of Al Gore, Dick Cheney, and Joe Biden will be covered in greater detail in chapters 7 to 9.

According to procedure outlined the Twenty-Fifth Amendment, Nelson Rockefeller, the four-term governor from New York, was selected by Gerald Ford and confirmed by Congress as vice president in 1974 (box 6.1). He served through 1977 and was followed by Walter Mondale, a two-term senator from Minnesota, who served as Jimmy Carter's vice president (1977–1981). George H. W. Bush, in office from 1981 to 1989, was Ronald Reagan's vice president. Bush had a diverse political background and had challenged Reagan for the Republican presidential nomination in 1980. After Bush captured the Republican nomination for president in 1988 he selected Dan Quayle, the conservative junior senator from Indiana as his running mate. Quayle served as vice president from 1989 to 1993.

Following Quayle was Al Gore, the well-known senator from Tennessee. Gore served two terms with Bill Clinton, from 1993 to 2001. Washington insider Dick Cheney, elected with George W. Bush in 2000, served two terms as well (2001–2009), generating a fair amount of controversy while in office. Finally, Joe Biden, who had served Delaware for more than three decades in the Senate, was elected with Barack Obama in 2008. His term began in 2009 and continues today. See table 6.1.

BOX 6.1

Vice Presidential Selection: The Special Cases of Gerald Ford and Nelson Rockefeller

In 1973, after the resignation of Vice President Spiro Agnew, Gerald Ford became vice president under the provisions of the Twenty-Fifth Amendment to the Constitution. In 1974, Nelson Rockefeller became vice president under those same provisions after President Richard Nixon resigned and Gerald Ford assumed the presidency. How and why these men were selected for the vice presidency must be treated as different cases of vice presidential selection for several reasons.

The first, and perhaps most important, is that under the Twenty-Fifth Amendment, a different electorate—Congress, not the people—confirms the president's choice. Second, the political environment under which the vice presidential choice was ratified in these cases was extraordinary. Both Presidents Nixon and Ford were dealing with a Democratic Congress during, and immediately after, the Watergate scandal. In other words, in both cases Congress had the upper hand, so to speak, and the vice presidential choice was conditioned by this reality. The third difference is that both candidates, at the request of Congress, underwent extensive background checks by the FBI and were subjects of lengthy congressional hearings and debate. It took Congress almost two months to confirm Ford and almost four to confirm Rockefeller.[1]

Many, though not all, of the usual considerations driving vice presidential selection were not relevant in these two cases. One factor that did play into the selection of both men was their competence. Both had long and distinguished records of public service. It was widely agreed by Democrats and Republicans alike that both Ford and Rockefeller were qualified to be president in the event of a presidential vacancy. Many of the questions by members of Congress, especially to Ford, were oriented around what the nominee would do if he were president. In Ford's case this looked more likely with every passing week.

This said, Nixon had initially hoped to nominate Treasury Secretary John Connally. It was no secret that Nixon saw him as his chosen successor. However, congressional Democrats made it clear that Connally would not be confirmed. Rockefeller and Ronald Reagan were also purportedly considered as possible nominees by Nixon. Nixon settled on Ford primarily for three reasons. First, as the highly respected House Minority Leader, he was acceptable to Congress. Second, Ford had long been a Nixon supporter and had maintained a relationship with him since 1951. In other words, Nixon knew that Ford would be loyal.[2] A final consideration was that Ford claimed to have no presidential ambitions. Nixon still held to the hope that Connally would be able to run in 1976 and wanted the way to be clear for him to do that.

In the case of Rockefeller, similar considerations prevailed. President Ford's first choice, George H. W. Bush, was unacceptable to Congress because it was assumed he had presidential ambitions. This, of course, is a measure of how the office had evolved to this point. Members of Congress believed that whoever was vice president would have a good chance of eventually securing the presidential nomination and perhaps winning the presidency itself. The political consideration that was most important in Ford's choice of Rockefeller was to try and put Watergate behind the nation. Thus, he turned to Rockefeller, a nationally known and respected public figure.

[1]Nelson, *A Heartbeat Away*, 54.
[2]Hatfield, *Vice Presidents of the United States, 1789–1993*.

Table 6.1.   Modern-Era (1974–present) Vice Presidents

In Office	Vice President	President
1974–1977	Nelson Rockefeller*	Gerald Ford
1977–1981	Walter Mondale	James (Jimmy) Carter
1981–1989	George H. W. Bush	Ronald Reagan
1989–1993	J. Danforth (Dan) Quayle	George H. W. Bush
1993–2001	Albert (Al) Gore	William (Bill) Clinton
2001–2009	Richard (Dick) Cheney	George W. Bush
2009–present	Joseph (Joe) Biden	Barack Obama

*Assumed vice presidency Dec. 19, 1974, according to provisions of Twenty-Fifth Amendment.

SELECTING VICE PRESIDENTIAL NOMINEES IN THE MODERN ERA

By 1976, several differences in vice presidential selection between the traditional and modern eras were evident. First, in the modern era, presidential candidates are the sole decision makers in the process. Presidential candidates may consult with party leaders or others as a courtesy, but it is not a necessity. Second, whereas vice presidential selection was typically a haphazard process through 1972, an increasingly front-loaded primary system has given presidential nominees time to systematically examine possible vice presidential choices and deliberate on their selection. As a rule they take advantage of this, usually asking a trusted individual to head the search. This is the essence of the Carter model of vice presidential selection discussed in the previous chapter. In 1976, Ford asked Bryce Harlow and Melvin Laird to head his search. Using a scale of one to five, they ranked a total of fifteen individuals on twelve different dimensions of "qualification and performance."[1] In 1988 Michael Dukakis turned to his friend and advisor Paul Brountas to vet possible candidates.[2] In 2012 Mitt Romney turned to long-time aide Beth Myers.[3]

Third, with only one exception, no incumbent vice president has been replaced during a president's reelection bid in the modern era. Although observers often speculate that this may occur such a move would be interpreted as a sign of weakness and bad leadership on the part of the president. If the vice president should be replaced, why did the president select him in the first place? In other words it would be bad politics. Richard Nixon actively explored the possibility of replacing Spiro Agnew with Treasury Secretary (and former Democrat) John Connally but bowed to political expediency, retaining Agnew. In 1992 George H. W. Bush was under tremendous pressure to replace Quayle but did not. There was talk of Bush replacing Cheney in 2004 and Obama replacing Biden in 2012 as well. The exception was Rockefeller, dropped during Ford's reelection bid in 1976. However the circumstances in this case make it an anomaly. Ford was an unelected president with an unelected vice president and facing a strong challenge for the Republican nomination. Replacing Rockefeller seemed necessary for his political survival.[5]

Fourth, fewer individuals now seem to refuse the vice presidential nomination. This is because of the increased importance of the office and the fact that it is seen as a stepping stone to the presidency. In fact, in the modern era many potential vice presidential nominees are individuals who had previously aspired to the presidency or the vice presidency in the modern era. Prominent politicians now actively campaign for the vice presidency, though not in the conventional sense. The campaigns are not public and the only "vote" that matters is that of the presidential nominee.[6] Jack Kemp, the Republican vice presidential nominee in 1996, suggested that the road to the vice presidential nomination is one where you "keep your mouth shut, your head down, and don't act like you want it."[7] Public activity is designed to avoid the perception that it is an attempt to win the vice presidential nomination. Michigan Governor John Engler apparently was "an unabashed self-promoter for the job" in 1996, making constant trips to Washington, which is a prime example of what *not* to do.[8] Quayle launched a quiet and unofficial campaign to secure the second spot on the day after the 1988 New Hampshire primary. During the next few months he made more speeches in the Senate, wrote more op-ed pieces, issued more press releases, and increased his contact with then-Vice President Bush and his aides. Bush, Quayle claims, "noticed what we were doing and paid attention."[9]

A fifth difference is the heightened role of the news media. An increasingly front-loaded nomination season leaves more time between its end and the party national convention, during which time the news media has little actual campaign "news" to focus on. Their attention turns to what has become known as the "veepstakes."[10] Speculation runs rampant about possible vice presidential candidates, often—though not always—fueled by the presidential candidate's organization and convention organizers in an effort to hold the attention of the public. A final change in vice presidential selection is the timing of announcement of the selection itself. Most presidential candidates since 1984 have announced their vice presidential selections several days to one week before the convention. This helps to generate excitement about the convention and the ticket. Exceptions to this were Bush's selection of Quayle in 1988 and Bob Dole's selection of Kemp in 1996.

In short, the manner in which vice presidential candidates are selected in the modern era is dramatically different than in the tradition era. This has an effect on the type of individuals selected as well as the relationship between elected presidents and vice presidents.

GENERAL CHARACTERISTICS OF
MODERN-ERA VICE PRESIDENTIAL NOMINEES

After researching the range of possible choices, the presumptive presidential nominee has to select his or her running mate from the handful the list has been narrowed down to. In some years this so-called "short list" is longer than in others. In 1984, for example, Mondale was seriously considering eleven different individuals; in 2012 Romney considered only three. However, on average, the short list consists of about five or six people.[11] Most are highly thought of in party circles and thought to be able to bring something to the ticket by way of stature or electability. Table 6.2 lists nonincumbent vice presidential nominees from 1976 to 2012.

Most of these candidates were fairly well known, if not by the general public, then by political and media elite. One trend in the modern era is for presidential candidates to focus more on individuals who have been exposed to the national spotlight.[12] Selecting someone that the national press is not familiar with can lead to unexpected and negative outcomes because no one can be certain how the news media will frame the choice. "Two vice presidential nominees . . . who had not been previously exposed to the national media, [Geraldine] Ferraro in 1984 and Quayle in 1988, had far more of their share of turmoil during

Table 6.2. Modern-Era Nonincumbent Vice Presidential Candidates*

Year, Party	Vice Presidential Candidate (Presidential Candidate)
1976, Democrat	Walter Mondale (Jimmy Carter)
1976, Republican	Robert Dole (Gerald Ford)
1980, Republican	George H. W. Bush (Ronald Reagan)
1984, Democrat	Geraldine Ferraro (Walter Mondale)
1988, Republican	J. Danforth Quayle (George H. W. Bush)
1988, Democrat	Lloyd Bentsen, Jr. (Michael Dukakis)
1992, Democrat	Albert Gore (Bill Clinton)
1996, Republican	Jack Kemp (Robert Dole)
2000, Republican	Dick Cheney (George W. Bush)
2000, Democrat	Joe Lieberman (Albert Gore)
2004, Democrat	John Edwards (John Kerry)
2008, Democrat	Joe Biden (Barack Obama)
2008, Republican	Sarah Palin (John McCain)
2012, Republican	Paul Ryan (Mitt Romney)

*Winner is listed first.

their campaigns."[13] The selection of Sarah Palin in 2008 is obviously another example.

Several of these candidates harbored presidential or vice presidential ambitions. Mondale ran for president the same year he was selected as the vice presidential candidate. Bush ran for president in 1980 and had previously been considered for the vice presidency (in 1968, 1974, and 1976). Lloyd Bentsen ran for president in 1976 and was considered a vice presidential possibility in 1984. John Edwards ran for president in 2004, as did Biden in 1988 and 2008.

Presidential candidates in the modern era seem to pay more attention to the qualifications or experience of potential running mates.[14] Other factors are considered as well, but unless the vice presidential nominee is perceived to be qualified there is a risk that they will become a drag on the ticket. This dynamic was at work with the selection of Ferraro, Quayle, and Palin. Most vice presidential candidates have what can be considered a reasonable amount of experience in public office (see table 6.3). The fourteen modern era (nonincumbent) candidates had an average of 18.3 years of service in public office. This is similar to previous eras, but in the modern era we see a trend toward more experience in national government experience. In the modern era vice presidential candidates serve far fewer years in state or local government (3.3 years) compared with the traditional (5.4 years) and transitional (7.6 years) eras.

The least experienced vice presidential candidate was Bush, who served two terms in the U.S. House, was U.S. Ambassador to the United

Table 6.3. Political Offices Served by Modern-Era Vice Presidential Candidates

Candidate (Year, Party)	Local/State Government*	Governor	U.S. House	U.S. Senate	Other Nat. Gov.	Total
Walter Mondale (1976, Dem.)	4	0	0	12	4	20
Bob Dole (1976, Rep.)	10	0	8	7	0	25
George H. W. Bush (1980, Rep.)	0	0	4	0	5	9
Geraldine Ferraro (1984, Dem.)	4	0	6	0	0	10
Lloyd Bentsen (1988, Dem.)	2	0	7	17	0	26
Dan Quayle (1988, Rep.)	0	0	4	8	0	12
Al Gore (1992, Dem.)	0	0	8	8	0	16
Jack Kemp (1996, Rep.)	1	0	18	0	4	23
Joseph Lieberman (2000, Dem.)	13	0	0	12	0	25
Dick Cheney (2000, Rep.)	0	0	10	0	11	21
John Edwards (2004, Dem.)	0	0	0	5	0	5
Joe Biden (2008, Dem.)	2	0	0	36	0	38
Sarah Palin (2008, Rep.)	10	2	0	0	0	12
Paul Ryan (2012, Rep.)	0	0	14	0	0	14
Average Modern Era	*3.3*	*.3*	*8.8*	*13.1*	*6.0*	*18.3*
Average Traditional Era	*5.4*	*5.0*	*6.0*	*8.8*	*5.4*	*17.1*
Average Transitional Era	*7.6*	*6*	*12.7*	*12.1*	*7*	*17.9*

Average represents years only of those who served in the particular office.
*Does not include years served as governor (if any).

Nations for two years, Chief of the U.S. Liaison Office in the People's Republic of China,[15] and briefly as Director of Central Intelligence. Ferraro was Assistant District Attorney for Queens County, New York, before being elected to the U.S. House. Quayle served eight years in the U.S. Senate and four in the U.S. House. Biden was the most experienced, serving for thirty-six years in the U.S. Senate. Bentsen, Dole, and Joe Lieberman were also politically experienced before running for vice president.

There is a wide variation in the size of home states among these candidates (see table 6.4). Although the average percentage of Electoral College votes needed for victory (7.4) compares favorably to the average from the traditional and transitional eras, a few candidates came from small states (e.g., Cheney, Biden, Palin) and others from very large states (e.g., Bush, Ferraro, and Bentsen). There has been a clear decline in the number of Electoral College votes associated with vice presidential candidates' home states as the modern era has progressed. From 1976 to 1996 the average was 18.8 Electoral College votes, whereas from 2000 to 2012 it dropped to 6.4. Of the twenty tickets (incumbent and nonincumbent) in the modern age a total of fourteen won the vice presidential candidate's home state.[16]

Most discussion about possible vice presidential nominees centers on how well the individual "balances" the ticket. Does the individual add something to the ticket to broaden its electoral appeal? In previous eras this was almost exclusively a discussion of regional and ideological (or factional) balance. These factors continue to be important. In 1976, polls suggested that voters were concerned that Carter was out of touch with more liberal, non-Southern voters. His selection of Mondale, a Midwesterner, was partially a response to this. Bush, a moderate, tapped a more

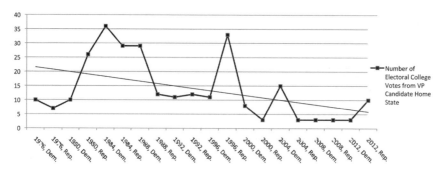

Figure 6.1.   Number of Electoral College Votes from Vice Presidential Candidates' Home States

Table 6.4.   Vice Presidential Candidate Home States in the Modern Era

Year	Vice Presidential Candidate	State	Number Electoral College Votes	Electoral College Votes (%)*	Won?
1976	Walter Mondale (D)	MN	10	3.7	Yes
	Robert Dole (R)	KS	7	2.6	Yes
1980	George H. W. Bush (R)	TX	26	9.6	Yes
	Walter Mondale (D)	MN	10	3.7	Yes
1984	George H. W. Bush (R)	TX	29	10.7	Yes
	Geraldine Ferraro (D)	NY	36	13.3	No
1988	J. Danforth Quayle (R)	IN	12	4.4	Yes
	Lloyd Bentsen, Jr. (D)	TX	29	10.7	No
1992	Albert Gore (D)	TN	11	4.1	No
	J. Danforth Quayle (R)	IN	12	4.4	Yes
1996	Albert Gore (D)	TN	11	4.1	Yes
	Jack Kemp (R)	NY	33	12.2	No
2000	Dick Cheney (R)	WY	3	1.1	Yes
	Joe Lieberman (D)	CT	8	3.0	Yes
2004	Dick Cheney (R)	WY	3	1.1	Yes
	John Edwards (D)	NC	15	5.6	No
2008	Joe Biden (D)	DE	3	1.1	Yes
	Sarah Palin (R)	AK	3	1.1	Yes
2012	Joe Biden (D)	DE	3	1.1	Yes
	Paul Ryan (R)	WI	10	3.7	No

*Represents the percentage of the 270 Electoral College votes needed for victory.

conservative Quayle in 1988. Northeastern liberal Democrat Michael Dukakis selected the more conservative Southerner Bentsen that same year. In some cases the selection is made to unite the party by appeasing a losing faction,[17] which helps explain Mondale's selection of Ferraro in 1984 and McCain's of Palin in 2012.[18]

Before their nomination, many vice presidential candidates hold issue positions that are at odds with those of the presidential candidate. However adopting the president's policy positions as their own is required if there is to be any meaningful relationship between the two subsequent to their election. In 1980 Bush (Reagan's main primary opponent) had been quite vocal in his criticism of Reagan's economic plan, which he referred to as "voodoo economics." After his nomination Bush explained, "I'm not going to say I haven't had differences at some point with Governor Reagan. . . . But what I will be doing is emphasizing common ground."[19]

Ideas about balancing presidential tickets have expanded to include other characteristics as well. Among these are religious, gender, racial, or ethnic diversity, typically meaning the selection of someone who is a woman, non-white, non-Protestant, or of non-Northwest European descent. A good example of a presidential candidate trying to diversify the ticket was Mondale's selection of Ferraro in 1984. Ferraro was somewhat lacking in terms of her experience, but most of the other people on Mondale's short list were also people "whose competence to be president was less obvious than their symbolic representation of the most vocal interests in the party, notably blacks, Hispanics, and women."[20] He gave serious consideration to two black mayors, Wilson Goode of Philadelphia and Tom Bradley of Los Angeles; San Antonio Mayor Henry Cisneros, a Hispanic; San Francisco Mayor Diane Feinstein (not only a woman, but Jewish as well); and Martha Layne Collins, Governor of Kentucky.

This case was exceptional. Mondale was influenced first by the fact that he was seriously challenged for the nomination by a black candidate (Jesse Jackson). In addition, another Democratic challenger, Gary Hart, had raised the issue of naming a woman vice presidential candidate and Mondale promised to do so if he won the nomination (in fact the National Organization for Women had threatened to oppose any male candidate). Finally, trailing in the polls, he hoped to exploit the gender gap that had formed in the electorate since the early Reagan years.[21]

Overall, however, the record of gender, race, ethnic, or religious balancing of presidential tickets in the modern era is mixed. There has never been, for example, a black or Hispanic major-party vice presidential candidate. Palin was only the second female vice presidential candidate and Protestants continue to dominate presidential politics: Lieberman was the first (and only) Jewish vice presidential candidate, and Paul Ryan joined Geraldine Ferraro (1984) and William Miller (1964) as the only Catholic vice presidential candidates.

Balancing can also mean the type of government experience the candidate brings to the ticket. A presidential candidate lacking in an area of policy expertise or other governmental experience can select a vice presidential candidate who fills the gap. In 1976 Carter had experience as a governor but none in national politics. All of his vice presidential possibilities were members of Congress and his eventual nominee was a prominent member of the U.S. Senate. In fact balancing the ticket by way of Washington insider–outsider status has become something of a norm in the modern era, particularly with so many presidential candidates being governors. Former California Governor Reagan selected Bush; Massachusetts Governor Dukakis selected long-time Senator Bentsen; Bill Clinton (governor of Arkansas) selected Senator Gore; Bush–Cheney and Romney–Ryan fit this pattern as well.[22]

Finally, the vice presidential candidate may have a personal characteristic or quality that the presidential candidate lacks or wants to emphasize.[23] One such characteristic is age. If a presidential candidate is perceived as being too old there may be concerns over his or her health. Reagan's selection of Bush and John McCain's of Palin were probably in part designed to alleviate these questions. Bush selected Quayle and John Kerry chose Edwards partly in the hope that their youth and charisma would attract younger voters and women.[24]

Balancing presidential tickets has always been driven by political considerations. Table 6.5 presents a summary of this discussion for the fourteen nonincumbent tickets in the modern era. There is some overlap in these categories, especially with regard to region, ideology, and party faction. All but three tickets were regionally balanced (Ford–Dole, Clinton-Gore, and Bush-Cheney being the exceptions) and all but two were ideologically balanced. Few were balanced in terms of diversity, and half had some form of government experience balance. Finally, the "personal characteristics" category becomes more important as we move through the modern era.

One final note with respect to the characteristics of vice presidential candidates: It may be tempting to believe that one of the presidential candidate's opponents in the primary will be selected as the vice presidential candidate. This is sometimes true, but only in cases when the opponent exits the nomination race relatively early and with a minimum amount of rancor toward the eventual nominee. This was the case, for example, with Bush in 1980, Edwards in 2004, and Biden in 2012. Those opponents who contest the nomination until late in the season and do so with vigor, meaning they are not reluctant to attack the nominee (Hillary Clinton in 2012), stand little chance. Too much depends on the two having a good relationship if elected.

Table 6.5. Balancing Presidential Tickets in the Modern Era

Ticket (Year)	Region	Ideology	Diversity	Experience	Personal/Other
Carter–Mondale (1976)	Yes	Yes	No	Yes	No
Ford–Dole (1976)	No	Yes	No	No	No
Reagan–Bush (1980)	Yes	Yes	No	Yes	Yes
Mondale–Ferraro (1984)	Yes	No	Yes	No	No
Dukakis–Bentsen (1988)	Yes	No	Yes*	Yes	No
Bush–Quayle (1988)	Yes	Yes	No	No	Yes
Clinton–Gore (1992)	No	No	No	Yes	Yes
Dole–Kemp (1996)	Yes	Yes	No	No	Yes
Bush–Cheney (2000)	No	Yes	No	Yes	No
Gore–Lieberman (2000)	Yes	No	Yes	No	Yes
Kerry–Edwards (2004)	Yes	Yes	Yes*	No	Yes
Obama–Biden (2008)	Yes	No	Yes*	Yes	Yes
McCain–Palin (2008)	Yes	No	Yes	Yes	Yes
Romney–Ryan (2012)	Yes	Yes	Yes	Yes	Yes

*These tickets are technically considered diversified because the presidential (as opposed the vice presidential) candidate was non-White, non-Protestant, or of non-Northwest European descent.

VICE PRESIDENTIAL CAMPAIGNING
IN THE MODERN ERA

The start of the vice presidential campaign is the announcement of the selection by the presidential candidate. This must be handled carefully. Unless the selection has been well vetted, all political aspects considered, and the media informed of the choices, the nominee may become the target of attack ads or negative press. The result? The candidate may become a drag on the ticket, or at minimum, an unwelcome distraction. There is potential that he or she may be perceived as unqualified to succeed to the presidency.

Quayle's selection by Bush was a good example. Bush kept his decision to select him so secret that even aides were surprised by the choice. Thus when questioned by the press after the announcement they were unprepared to answer questions about him.[25] As a result the press was free to suggest its own story line. His fairly pedestrian career in the Senate and House combined with his stumbling performance at the announcement conspired to suggest he was not to be taken seriously. Although Bush subsequently won, he did so despite image problems created by his choice. Quayle was not the only recent vice presidential candidate to suffer bad press. Mondale's 1984 selection of Ferraro by was initially well received, but revelations regarding her husband's wealth, allegations about his questionable business connections and tax returns, questions about the financing of her 1978 House campaign and the conflict between her views (as a Catholic) on abortion and those of the New York Archbishop, all created a stir in the press. The ticket was never able to shake the image problems created by these mini-scandals.[26] The Palin selection in 2012, although pleasing to many conservatives, generated a great deal of controversy and negative media coverage,[27] as well as several now-classic skits on *Saturday Night Live* (featuring Tina Fey as Palin).[28]

Vice presidential candidates, their wives, and frequently older children take to the stump throughout the campaign to enlist support for the ticket.[29] One function of the vice presidential candidate during the campaign may be to mobilize support from various interests and other groups. For example Mondale, well liked by traditional Democratic constituencies, worked with their leaders to secure their vote. One of the reasons Bush selected Quayle was because of his relationship with various conservative groups. Quayle attempted to convince these groups that Bush was the inheritor of the Reagan conservative movement, which was an idea many were skeptical of.

Vice presidential candidates can be more aggressive on the campaign trail than presidential candidates. Although Mondale criticized President Ford for his pardon of Nixon, Carter avoided the issue. In 1984 Ferraro implied that Reagan was to blame for the violence in Beirut.[30] In addition to attacking the opposition, vice presidential candidates sing the praises of their running mate. Initially this may be awkward if the two had differences in the past, but any differences are put aside. Although Carter and Mondale had differences over various issues, Mondale echoed Carter's positions on government and the economy, minimizing their differences. Before the 1980 Republican convention, many of Bush's stands on the economy differed dramatically from Reagan's, but Bush dutifully adopted Reagan's as his own.[31] Although Cheney disagreed with George W. Bush on the issue of gay marriage he avoided speaking about it.[32]

The first vice presidential debate was held in 1976 between Mondale and Dole.[33] There were no debates in 1980, but in 1984 Ferraro challenged Vice President Bush to a debate in the hope that it would give the Mondale–Ferraro campaign a boost.[34] Since then, each election cycle has featured a vice presidential debate in addition to the presidential debates. Although viewership accounts for only a fraction of the American public, the press build up and postdebate analysis all serve to put vice presidential candidates in the limelight for almost one full week. Moreover, the aftermath typically sees a story line emerge about the performance of one or both candidates that has some effect on the course of the campaign.

Table 6.6 details the dates, candidates, moderator, and television viewership for the nine vice presidential debates from 1976 to 2012. One point that stands out is that viewership of vice presidential debates has only once (in 2008) exceeded that of the presidential debates. This is hardly surprising: although vice presidential candidates and vice presidents are more visible than in previous times they are still less of a draw than their presidential running mates.

Planning for the debates is quite detailed and includes stipulating the size of the audience, who will select audience members, lighting, heights of the podiums, themes, how long candidates will speak, who the moderators and panelists (if any) will be, and more. Negotiations over these issues are often as intense as negotiations over the presidential debates.[35] Another important element of debate preparation is trying to control expectations of the candidate. Campaigns typically downplay either the ability of their candidate to debate or the importance of the debate, because if expectations are low and the candidate does poorly they can later claim that all went as expected. On the other hand, if the candidate does well they can claim an outright victory.

Debate preparation entails working out issue positions, anticipating and preparing for questions, likely themes and responses by the opponent and style and presentation of self. Candidates typically take several days off to study issues and practice with a debate partner. These mock debates are taped, studied, and critiqued by aides. Washington attorney

Table 6.6. Vice Presidential Debates, 1976–2012

Date and Location	Candidates	Moderator	Viewership*
Oct. 15, 1976, Alley Theatre, Houston, TX	Mondale, Dole	James Hoge, Chicago Sun Times	43.2 million (65.4)
Oct. 11, 1984, Pennsylvania Hall, Civic Center, Philadelphia, PA	Bush, Ferraro	Sander Vanocur, ABC	56.7 million (66.2)
Oct. 5, 1988, Omaha Civic Auditorium, Omaha, NE	Quayle, Bentsen	Judy Woodruff, PBS	46.9 million (66.2)
Oct. 13, 1992, Georgia Tech, Atlanta, GA	Gore, Quayle, Stockdale	Hal Bruno, ABC	51.2 million (66.4)
Oct. 9, 1996, Mahaffey Theater, St. Petersburg, FL	Gore, Kemp	Jim Lehrer, PBS	26.6 million (41.2)
Oct. 5, 2000, Centre College, Danville, KY	Cheney, Lieberman	Bernard Shaw, CNN	28.5 million (40.6)
Oct. 5, 2004, Case Western Reserve Univ., Cleveland, OH	Cheney, Edwards	Gwen Ifill, PBS	43.5 million (53.4)
Oct. 2, 2008, Washington Univ., St. Louis, MO	Biden, Palin	Gwen Ifill, PBS	66.9 million (57.4)
Oct. 11, 2012, Centre College, Danville, KY	Biden, Ryan	Martha Raddatz, ABC	51.4 million (64.0)

*Figures in parentheses are average viewership of presidential debates that year.
Source: Baumgartner, The America Vice Presidency Reconsidered, Table 5.1, p. 95, and the Commission on Presidential Debates (http://www.debates.org/).

Bob Barnet, who helped Mondale in 1976, headed Ferraro's debate team in 1984. The team

> included experts on domestic policy issues, foreign policy specialists, political consultants and her public speaking coach, Dayle Hardy. Their first task was the compilation of a briefing book. This eight-pound volume that included an analysis of all of Bush's public statements, Ferraro's voting record and major speeches, and the campaign's position on foreign and domestic issues, was given to Ferraro two weeks before the debate. She studied it in all her spare moments, especially while traveling. Six days before the debate . . . a hotel suite in New York became, according to the congresswoman, a "battle zone" where experts would "grill" her on the issues and critique her responses. Two days before, the operation was moved to a rented television studio where a replica of the Philadelphia set had been constructed (including a gently inclining ramp leading to the podium so that she would not look so much shorter than the vice president).[36]

Preparation also involves strategy. In 1984 Bush had to find a strategy for debating a woman. Although debates are typically confrontational the "stereotypical attitudes regarding women and the 'appropriate' or 'proper' treatment of them by men [meant that] Bush was prevented from employing those rhetorical behaviors typically associated with political debates. He could not appear to be attacking her." The problem was made worse by the fact that Ferraro had a "combative or feisty rhetorical style."[37] In 2008 Biden faced a similar dynamic in his debate with Palin, while in 2012 he was tasked with attempting to regain positive momentum for the campaign after Obama's lackluster performance in the first presidential debate. As the result he aggressively attacked Ryan.[38]

Postdebate news coverage is often supplemented or even overshadowed by a focus on a particular exchange between the candidates. This often translates into a story about how one candidate stumbled and their opponent seized the opportunity to score points. In some cases the exchange in question becomes, fairly or unfairly, the lasting story of the debate. For example in 1984 the exchange that was remembered after the debate related to Ferraro's gender and Bush's treatment of her. After a question about the Reagan administration's response to random terrorism in Lebanon and state-backed terrorism in Iran, Bush said to Ferraro, "Let me help you with the difference, Mrs. Ferraro, between Iran and Lebanon." She replied,

> let me just say, first of all, I almost resent, Vice President Bush, your patronizing attitude that you have to teach me about foreign policy. I've been a member of Congress for six years. I was there when the Embassy was held hostage in Iran, and I have been there and I've seen what has happened in the past several months of your administration.[39]

Bush had no response. This exchange, in addition to the fact that he addressed her throughout the debate as "Mrs. Ferraro" instead of "Congresswoman" (as had been agreed), was what the media focused on, and left the impression that Bush was patronizing and condescending.[40] Coupled with predebate headlines such as "Shoot-Out at Gender Gap" and the fact that Bush's mother had made a rather unflattering remark about Ferraro prior to the debate, this ensured that gender remained a focus in postdebate coverage.[41]

The classic example of a memorable exchange in a vice presidential debate occurred during the 1988 debate between Quayle and Bentsen. Quayle came into the debate having suffered weeks of negative publicity about his lack of competence, and one of Bentsen's goals in the debate was to highlight this. At one point Quayle correctly noted that he had as much government experience as John Kennedy had when he had run for president. Bentsen's response was, "Senator, I served with Jack Kennedy. I knew Jack Kennedy. Jack Kennedy was a friend of mine. Senator, you are no Jack Kennedy." The line drew laughter and applause from the audience.[42] This exchange, in part because it built on predebate expectations, was all that was remembered afterward and has become a part of presidential campaign debate lore.

A comment John Edwards made about the conservative Cheney's daughter in the 2004 debate created a minor stir as well. Cheney's youngest daughter Mary is a lesbian and some Democrats had attempted to make this an issue. During the debate, in response to a question about gay marriage, Edwards said, "I think the vice president and his wife love their daughter. I think they love her very much. And you can't have anything but respect for the fact that they're willing to talk about the fact that they have a gay daughter." The comment caused a minor stir and was compounded by remarks made by Kerry in the next presidential debate and by Edwards's wife Elizabeth, who suggested that the Cheney family's reaction to the issue being brought up demonstrated that the vice president was ashamed of her.[43]

The question of "who won" the debate is typically measured in public opinion polls. In 1976 one poll showed that 51 percent of those surveyed "thought favorably of Mondale as vice president, while only 33 percent considered Dole to have been helpful to his ticket."[44] The results of the 1988 debate were unambiguous. Even a majority of those who supported the Bush–Quayle ticket before the debate thought that Bentsen had won.[45] Similarly, in 1992, Quayle appeared to lose to Gore, as did third-party vice presidential candidate James Stockdale, in the only three-way vice presidential debate in history.

In 1996 Gore bested Kemp. One poll reported that 53 percent of viewers thought he had won, as opposed to 41 percent for Kemp.[46] Despite the fact that Joe Lieberman turned in an admirable performance in 2000,

ABC News declared Cheney the winner by 19 percentage points. Cheney "won" by a smaller margin in 2004 over Edwards, 43 to 35 percent (with 19 percent undecided).[47] Palin may have done better than expected in 2008, but this was because of low expectations, and virtually all polls suggested that Biden bested her.[48] However in 2012 Biden's aggressive strategy led many to perceive him as somewhat "unpresidential," with the result being that Ryan probably won, if only by a small margin.[49]

What effect do vice presidential debates have the campaign? Probably not much, except perhaps at the margins.[50] For example, some scholars suggest that Dole's performance in 1976 may have hurt the Ford ticket somewhat. Bentsen may have hurt his ticket in 1988 by making his presidential running mate, Dukakis, appear weak by comparison to him.[51] A more straightforward interpretation of the 1988 race might be to note that despite Quayle's poor debate performance Bush won the election. Similarly, despite the fact that Ferraro's rebuke of Vice President Bush in the 1984 debate drew loud applause from the audience, she and Mondale lost in one of the biggest landslides in U.S. history.

How does the vice presidential candidate affect presidential voting? Most research on this question is not empirically grounded.[52] Some political scientists have suggested that Quayle may have cost Bush as many as eight percentage points in the election of 1992.[53] Although it seems incontrovertible that Quayle was a drag on the Republican ticket, this number is hard to verify. The fundamental problem in examining whether or how the vice presidential candidate affects citizens' voting choice is that it is virtually impossible to disentangle presidential and vice presidential preferences in our system of presidential elections. Most research into the question suggests that the vice presidential candidate has—at most—a marginal effect on voters' choices.[54]

Although vice presidential candidates and vice presidents are more visible in the modern era the focus during the campaign is on presidential candidates. People cast their vote, in other words, based on the presidential candidate, not the vice presidential candidate. Nixon once suggested that "the Vice President can't help you . . . he can only hurt you."[55] In other words, the vice presidential candidate should not cost the ticket any votes. Virtually all scholars agree with some version of the Nixon doctrine that vice presidential candidates can hurt but not help their ticket.

FORMAL ROLES OF MODERN-ERA VICE PRESIDENTS

The constitutional roles of the vice president have not changed in the modern era. The vice president remains the constitutional successor to the president in the event of presidential vacancy and is the President of the Senate. No president in the modern era has been unable to complete his term, meaning that no vice president in the modern era has succeeded to the presidency. However there has been occasion for vice presidents to serve temporarily in that capacity.

On July 13, 1985, Reagan underwent surgery to remove cancerous polyps from his colon. Reagan did not, however, formally invoke the Twenty-Fifth Amendment. His letter to the Speaker of the House of Representatives and to the President pro tempore of the Senate indicated that he was turning over the power of the presidency to Vice President Bush. However he also indicated that he did not think the Twenty-Fifth Amendment applied in that type of situation.[56] Cheney became the first vice president to formally become "acting president" under the Twenty-Fifth Amendment, which George W. Bush invoked twice (on June 29, 2002, and July 21, 2007) to undergo a routine colonoscopy.[57] Box 6.2 is a copy of the text from Bush's letter to Congress transferring power to Cheney before the second procedure.

Cheney also unilaterally took steps to remedy a potential gap in the provisions of the Twenty-Fifth Amendment. By the time he took office he had suffered four heart attacks, the most recent during the recount controversy of the election of 2000. Shortly after he took office he drafted a letter of resignation, kept in his safe, to be used in the event he became incapacitated. He was motivated by the fact that although the Twenty-Fifth Amendment resolved a number of issues surrounding presidential and vice presidential vacancy, it did not specify provisions for the removal of a sitting but incapacitated vice president.[58]

Modern vice presidents spend little time presiding over the Senate. In fact "senators nowadays view vice-presidents as semi-intruders . . . as a member of the executive branch."[59] The situation is worse when vice presidents run afoul of established Senate customs. This happened to Rockefeller, who had no experience whatever in the Senate (indeed, in Washington) before becoming vice president. He was presiding over a Senate debate about whether rules governing filibusters could be changed by a simple majority vote or whether the rule change itself could be filibustered. Several previous vice presidents (Nixon, Johnson, Humphrey, and Agnew) had avoided taking a position on the issue out of deference to the Senate.[60] When a motion to change the rule was introduced Rockefeller, following the letter of Senate rules, allowed a vote on it. On another occasion he refused to recognize two senators who were attempting to prolong a filibuster. Both incidents earned him the ire of many senators.[61] Mondale ran into trouble in his role as presiding officer as well. In 1977 he used his power as chair to stop a filibuster on a bill to deregulate natural gas. The experience somewhat soured relations between Mondale and his former colleagues.[62]

BOX 6.2

Letter to Congressional Leaders from George W. Bush on the Temporary Transfer of the Powers and Duties of the President of the United States

July 21, 2007

Dear Madam Speaker: (Dear Mr. President:)

This morning I will undergo a routine medical procedure requiring sedation. In view of present circumstances, I have determined to transfer temporarily my Constitutional powers and duties to the Vice President during the brief period of the procedure and recovery.

In accordance with the provisions of Section 3 of the Twenty-Fifth Amendment to the United States Constitution, this letter shall constitute my written declaration that I am unable to discharge the Constitutional powers and duties of the office of the President of the United States. Pursuant to Section 3, the Vice President shall discharge those powers and duties as Acting President until I transmit to you a written declaration that I am able to resume the discharge of those powers and duties.

Sincerely,

GEORGE W. BUSH

Source: George W. Bush, "Letter to Congressional Leaders on the Temporary Transfer of the Powers and Duties of the President of the United States," July 21, 2007. Online by Gerhard Peters and John T. Woolley, The American Presidency Project. http://www.presidency.ucsb.edu/ws/?pid=75568.

*Identical letters were sent to Nancy Pelosi, Speaker of the House of Representatives, and Robert C. Byrd, President pro tempore of the Senate.

Another reason vice presidents since Mondale have generally avoided their job as presiding officer of the Senate is their growing responsibilities in the executive branch. Although Quayle initially viewed the job as a grave responsibility, he eventually came to understand that the power of the presiding officer was fairly hollow and focused his energy elsewhere. This is not to say vice presidents never preside over the Senate. Because the Senate was so closely divided during their tenures, both Cheney and Biden were present "during votes on legislation considered a priority for the White House."[63] Cheney was especially "attentive to business of the Senate through the 2002 mid-term elections (when Republicans regained a majority) in order to be on hand."[64] Biden took a similar approach, presiding over crucial votes on a tax bill in 2012 and gun control and immigration reform in 2013.[65]

The exercise of the constitutional duty of the vice president to break tie votes in the Senate has declined in the modern era, mainly because tie votes are less likely with one hundred members. Three of seven modern vice presidents did not cast a single tie vote (Rockefeller, Quayle, and Biden, as of 2014), and one (Mondale) did so only once. See table 6.7.

George H. W. Bush cast three separate tie-breaking votes to renew chemical weapons production ("most unpopular, those tie-breakers were," he once noted).[66] Gore broke four tie votes during his two terms. Because "the Senate was so closely divided during his first term, Cheney broke more tie votes than any VP since Richard Nixon."[67] In fact for a short time he was the potential tie-breaking vote in the Senate at any time by virtue of the fact that there were an equal number of Republican and Democratic senators. From inauguration until late May 2001, Cheney gave the Republicans a 51–50 edge. During this period he cast a vote that ended Democratic efforts to create a Medicare prescription drug benefit with funds from the budget surplus.[68]

Vice presidents also have statutory and appointive formal duties. The most important of these is membership in the National Security Council (NSC). The vice president attends all meetings of the NSC and often chairs in the president's absence.[69] An important statutory change came during Mondale's vice presidency when Carter signed an executive order making the vice president "second in the chain of command for the control of nuclear weapons" (since 1958 this had been the responsibility of the Secretary of State).[70]

Although appointive duties (line assignments) of the vice president have declined as the modern era has progressed, most have been formally charged by their president with at least one. Rockefeller was named chair of Ford's Domestic Policy Council, created by Nixon to be the domestic equivalent of the NSC. He initially hoped to direct domestic policy in the same way Henry Kissinger directed foreign policy, but "conflict with the White House staff and Ford's shift to budget austerity prevented Rock-

Table 6.7.   Number of Times Modern-Era Vice Presidents Broke Tie Votes in the Senate

Vice President	Number
Nelson Rockefeller (served partial term)	0
Walter Mondale (one term)	1
George H. W. Bush (two terms)	7
Dan Quayle (one term)	0
Al Gore (two terms)	4
Dick Cheney (two terms)	8
Joe Biden (two terms, second incomplete)	0

efeller" from doing so. He was also instrumental in the creation of an Energy Independence Authority to deal with the energy crisis of the 1970s, the establishment of the White House Office of Science and Technology Policy,[71] and headed a Commission on Central Intelligence Agency (CIA) Activities.[72]

Mondale was an exception. When he accepted the vice presidential nomination he and Carter agreed to discuss Mondale's role after the election. But based on conversations with Humphrey and Rockefeller he determined that line assignments were a waste of the vice president's time[73] and he avoided taking any. This freed him up for his advisory role, the signature development that marks the difference between the modern vice presidency and previous eras.

Bush also avoided most line assignments but did head "task forces to cut government paperwork (the Task Force on Regulatory Relief) and to combat drugs."[74] Quayle headed a newly reconstituted National Space Council and a Council on Competitiveness, charged with reviewing government regulations and their effect on the business environment.[75] Gore generally followed the Mondale model of line assignments, declining an early opportunity to head the president's task force on health care reform.[76] He did, however, agree to head the administration's high profile National Performance Review, charged with "re-inventing government" by "consolidating functions, changing personnel processes, and modernizing government work with the application of new technologies."[77]

Cheney headed the team charged with Bush's transition into office[78] and an energy task force (the National Energy Policy Development Group) in 2001. The group excited some controversy in part because former colleagues of Cheney's from Halliburton were included in the group and their work was kept from the public's eye, inviting charges of corruption. Generally, however, he avoided line assignments. Like Cheney, Biden has also avoided taking on line assignments although he did oversee the implementation of Obama's $787 billion stimulus bill (The American Recovery and Reinvestment Act of 2009), identifying and expediting funds toward appropriate projects.[79]

INFORMAL ROLES OF MODERN-ERA VICE PRESIDENTS

In addition to their formal duties, modern vice presidents are increasingly active in other informal roles. These include the vice president's *ceremonial* role, hosting state visits, attending various ceremonies, and other social events. The *diplomatic* role of the vice president includes traveling overseas and meeting with other state leaders, either on state business or otherwise. *Political* roles include campaigning for congressional candidates and helping his president get reelected and promoting his agenda. The final role, *advisory*, is new to the modern era. Vice presidents are increasingly included in presidential decision making and sometimes are solely responsible for the policies or appointments made by the administration.

The Ceremonial Vice Presidency

Modern vice presidents, like those in previous eras, are responsible for attending, hosting, or taking part in any number of official events. Although this is part of the vice president's job (indeed, part of the president's job as well), it can be frustrating. In 1975 Rockefeller paid to have the vice presidential seal redesigned (see chapter 4)[80] and claimed it was "the most important thing I've done all year,"[81] reflecting his own extreme vexation with the job.

Ceremonial tasks include attending the funerals of important individuals, either at home or abroad. Bush described this role succinctly when he said, "you die, I fly."[82] This is especially important because U.S. presidents (like most heads of state) are constrained by diplomatic protocol to attend only the funerals of other heads of state.[83] Mondale attended the funeral of Yugoslav President Josip Tito in 1980.[84] Bush had the distinction of attending the funerals of three Soviet leaders in twenty-eight months (Leonid Brezhnev in 1982, Yuri Andropov in 1984, and Konstantin Chernenko in 1985).[85] Gore attended a memorial in New York City for assassinated Israeli leader Yitzhak Rabin in December 1995, Cardinal Joseph Bernardin in Chicago in late 1996, and former Florida Governor Lawton Chiles in December of 1998, among others.[86]

Unusually for a modern vice president, Cheney made his first trip abroad after five years in office to attend the funeral of King Fahd of Saudi Arabia.[87] Biden attended the funerals of several prominent senators, including those of former Democratic presidential candidate George McGovern, Arlen Specter in 2012, and Frank Lautenberg in 2013.[88] In 2013 he took part in a memorial service for former South African President Nelson Mandela at the Washington National Cathedral[89] and in 2014 gave a eulogy for former Israeli Prime Minister Ariel Sharon.[90]

Vice presidents attend other official events in their ceremonial capacity as well. In 2003 Cheney commissioned the aircraft carrier U.S.S. *Ronald Reagan* and later marked the fiftieth anniversary of the Korean War armistice by laying a wreath at the Tomb of the Unknown Soldier in Arlington Cemetery.[91] Biden, with former Presidents Clinton and George W. Bush attended the dedication of the Flight 93 National Memorial in Pennsylvania in 2011[92] and led the presidential delegation to the inauguration mass of Pope Francis in 2013.[93]

Modern vice presidents are also frequently dispatched to the sites of natural disasters, or as Rockefeller once quipped, "I go to earthquakes."[94] Here the vice president expresses sympathy and in some cases facilitates relief efforts. Quayle, for example, "was dispatched as a trouble-shooter to Alaska in the wake of a catastrophic oil spill, to California after the 1989 San Francisco earthquake, and to Los Angeles following the 1992 riots."[95] Throughout his tenure Gore visited flooded areas in Minnesota, North and South Dakota, and the Pacific Northwest, earthquake-damaged areas in California, and tornado-ravaged areas in Kentucky, Ohio, and West Virginia.[96] In the wake of Hurricane Katrina in the fall of 2005, Bush sent Cheney to tour the devastated Gulf Coast areas.[97] Similarly, Biden visited flooded areas in Northeastern Pennsylvania in 2011 and Colorado in 2013.[98]

The Diplomatic Vice Presidency

Continuing a trend begun in the transitional era, modern vice presidents are increasingly expected to act as presidential envoys overseas. Some vice presidential trips abroad are purely ceremonial (e.g., for funerals, inaugurations), but even these are often mixed with official or unofficial or behind the scenes state business. Unlike in the transitional era, vice presidents are now sometimes sent by their presidents on state visits solely for diplomatic purposes. Using the vice president for various foreign policy missions has become something of a necessity for presidents given U.S. interests throughout the world. Vice presidents are now trusted presidential emissaries when they travel abroad. Vice presidential travel abroad is also used to burnish the foreign policy credentials of those who harbor presidential ambitions.

Mondale visited some thirty-six countries in fourteen trips, the first of which was within twenty-two hours after taking office.[99] On the ten-day trip he conferred with major allies of the United States on a range of issues and conveyed Carter's hope that Germany and France would join in a moratorium on the sale of nuclear breeder devices. The next year he visited Europe, acting as presidential point man in Carter's foreign policy emphasis on human rights.[100]

Bush was the consummate vice presidential traveler, making forty-one trips abroad—both state and ceremonial—during his two terms.[101] Among his accomplishments were ironing out differences with Chinese leader Deng Xiao Ping about arms sales with Taiwan and a trip to Europe in 1983 that paved the way for NATO deployment of theater-range nuclear weapons. Immediately after attending the funerals of each of the three Soviet leaders mentioned previously, Bush was one of the first Western leaders to meet their successors.[102] As president, Bush sent Quayle abroad nineteen times, to forty-two countries.[103] Rarely, however, did Quayle travel to areas where sensitive diplomacy was required. His main accomplishment in terms of foreign policy came when he "helped persuade the Japanese to direct hundreds of millions of dollars of" foreign aid to countries that were foreign policy priorities for the United States. "He also is credited with playing a significant role in persuading Japanese auto makers to buy billions of dollars more of American automobile parts each year."[104]

Gore was allowed to "set up an extensive foreign policy shop"[105] and by 1994 he was spending up to 25 percent of his time on foreign affairs. His first visit was to Mexico to discuss implementation of the North American Free Trade Agreement (NAFTA) with the Mexican president.[106] He established bilateral commissions responsible for working out trade, technology transfer, and economic development issues with South Africa, Egypt, the Ukraine, and Russia, as well as nuclear disarmament concerns in the case of the latter two countries.[107] He also made several visits to Russian Prime Minister Viktor Chernomyrdin, visits that were reciprocated. Their relationship proved so good that it allowed them to negotiate—without their respective presidents—the withdrawal of Russian troops from Kosovo.[108]

Cheney made fewer trips abroad than most of his immediate predecessors. The majority of his travel abroad was related to the war in Iraq, the Israeli–Palestinian conflict, Iran, or the war on terror.[109] For example he made three trips to Iraq from 2005 to 2008, visiting troops on each occasion.[110] Generally, however, Cheney preferred to stay at home, presumably to better stay abreast of both domestic and foreign policy developments.

Biden, on the other hand, "traveled to more than two dozen countries" during the first six years of his tenure. His travels took him to countries in most major regions of the world, including Central and South America, Western, Central, and Southern Europe, Africa, the Middle East, Russia, and Central and East Asia.[111] Shortly after he was inaugurated he traveled to Germany to represent the United States at the Forty-Fifth Munich Conference on Security Policy.[112] That same year he also made trips to Bosnia-Herzegovina,[113] Ukraine and Georgia,[114] and Poland, Romania, and the Czech Republic.[115] On each trip he was tasked with a substantive foreign policy mission.

The Political Vice Presidency

Vice presidents are also expected to actively help advance the president's political and policy objectives, which includes campaigning at midterm elections for their party, fund-raising, acting as congressional liaison, or otherwise promoting presidential policies. Vice presidents are able to help shape public debate and promote the president's policies by doing what the president cannot, either because of time or political constraints. For example presidents may not have time to campaign for congressional candidates. Vice presidents can also lead hard-hitting attacks that the president, by virtue of his position as national leader, cannot.

Ford's vice president, Rockefeller, spent most of his time attempting (and largely failing) to work inside the administration. Little if any of his vice presidency was spent working to advance the president's policies with Congress (he had few ties and no background) or with the public. Because he took office after the 1974 midterm elections he could not fulfill the role of party campaigner. However he was instrumental in helping Ford secure the party nomination in 1976, delivering the New York delegation to Ford, and raising more than three million dollars for the campaign, despite being dropped from the ticket.[116]

Mondale was a valuable political asset to the Carter administration. Neither Carter nor his staff had legislative experience or ties in Washington. Mondale, as a former senator, provided both. He was also active in supporting congressional candidates throughout the country and traveled to forty-eight states as an administration spokesperson.[117]

Bush did "tireless service" promoting his president's domestic policies on Capitol Hill. Like Mondale he was well-suited to this task. He had served in the House and had ties to the Senate as well. Bush "used his splendid office just off the Senate lobby, his airplanes, his residence, his appearances at fund-raisers, the telephone, the tennis court, and even the steam bath in the House gym to lobby on key votes."[118] He also campaigned vigorously for fellow Republicans in the congressional elections of 1982, 1984, and 1986. This is not surprising given that he was Chairman of the Republican National Committee in 1973 and had presidential ambitions.

Quayle made a "political trip somewhere around the country at least once or twice a week, usually returning the same night. [His job was] to touch the dozens of reelection bases that Bush [did] not have time to visit." Throughout his term he traveled to more than two hundred cities, raising more than $20 million for the party and its candidates. It was on one of these trips that Quayle made his infamous spelling error. During a spelling bee in Trenton, New Jersey, a student was given the word "potato." The student spelled the word correctly, but Quayle was given a card that misspelled it, and subsequently "corrected" the child the wrong way.[119] Needless to say this did not help Quayle's image. He was also active as a legislative liaison, typically spending two afternoons a week working on Capitol Hill.[120] For example, despite his opposition to it, he played a key role in securing the support of congressional conservatives in the budget battle of 1990 in which Bush reneged on his "read my lips" campaign promise not to raise taxes.[121]

Gore was an integral political player in the Clinton administration. His earliest and perhaps biggest policy contribution came in 1993. Clinton was facing opposition from his own party—especially labor—over passage of NAFTA. Gore debated Ross Perot on *Larry King Live* over the issue. His performance, combined with Perot's meltdown (claiming that NAFTA would produce a "giant sucking sound" as jobs left the country) changed the dynamics of public debate. Gore was also the administration's chief spokesperson for environmental and various science and technology issues, including further development of the Internet.[122] Another of Gore's political contributions to the administration was his prodigious fund-raising, especially for the 1996 reelection campaign. Gore was featured at some thirty-nine fund-raising events, raising almost $9 million.

Unlike other recent vice presidents Cheney took a "minimalist approach to public appearances."[123] He rarely spoke in public and granted few interviews, although he became more vocal during his second term. For example in 2005 he set out on a month-long tour, holding town hall meetings to promote social security reform.[124] He was also the point man for the president's policies on Capitol Hill, instrumental in getting President Bush's third tax cut through the Senate in 2003.[125] In 2005 he lobbied hard for passage of the Central American Free Trade Agreement.[126] Cheney was also an active campaigner. In 2000 he pushed himself so hard in the postelection campaign he suffered a mild heart attack (his fourth). Cheney was also quite active in the 2002 congressional campaign in which the Republican Party was able to reverse historical trends by gaining seats in both houses of Congress. His goal that summer was to raise $10 million for some sixty Republican candidates.[127] In the last week of the 2004 campaign he visited more than thirty cities.[128] In 2006 he "held 114 campaign events across the country and raised more than $40 million for the G.O.P. cause."[129]

Biden has been a whirlwind of activity for Obama on the political front throughout his tenure. He had been a senator for more than three decades, developing "a network of alliances," and frequently interacts with the Democratic caucuses of both chambers.[130] Therefore, it was natural for the president to look to him to lead important legislative initiatives. "In 2010, he worked with Senate leaders to secure their approval of the New START nuclear arms reduction treaty with Russia."[131] In 2011 Obama asked him to take the lead in working with both houses of Congress to set spending levels for the remainder of the year and avoid shutting down the government. Biden's work with Senator Mitch McConnell was central to breaking the impasses and "bringing about a bipartisan deal . . . in the form of the Budget Control Act of 2011."[132] His "relationship with McConnell once more proved important as the two negotiated a deal that led to the American Taxpayer Relief Act of 2012 being passed at the start of 2013."[133]

In the midterm election of 2010 Biden was seemingly indefatigable helping congressional Democrats try (unsuccessfully) to retain their majority in both houses. One report suggested that by the end of the campaign he had attended "149 campaign events in more than 30 states."[134] He "crisscrossed the country stumping for Democratic governors and senators to congressman and congressional hopefuls," and in the last month of the campaign alone he appeared at "36 events, 11 in the last week."[135] After being named to head the Gun Violence Task Force in the aftermath of the Sandy Hook shootings in December of 2012, Biden took to the road again, publicly promoting stricter gun control measures.[136]

The Advisory Vice Presidency

Perhaps no other change in the institution of the vice presidency is more significant than the fact that vice presidents have become trusted advisors to their presidents. "Most recent vice presidents . . . come closer than earlier vice presidents to being second in command in a president's administration."[137] As the modern era has worn on, vice presidents have been increasingly included in presidential decision making and sometimes are solely responsible for the policies or appointments made by the administration.

This change in the vice presidency has come about incrementally and is the result of several factors. Some of these are physical in nature. For example, having a West Wing office gives vice presidents proximity to the president. A full-time staff and a regular budget give the vice president the resources needed to develop policy proposals.[138] The fact that presidential candidates now choose their own running mates helps ensure that vice presidents are compatible with their presidents. Equally important is the emergent norm that vice presidents are loyal to—and serve—their presidents. In addition, most vice presidents have to some degree prearranged their role in the administration with the president.

The advisory role of the modern vice presidency traces its origins to Mondale. Most of the factors listed previously that contribute to vice presidential influence prevailed during his tenure. Mondale had consulted with Humphrey before taking office, and taking his advice, declined any line assignments. Carter and Mondale agreed that their staff would work together, a decision facilitated by the fact that campaign aides had worked out of the same campaign headquarters.[139] This ensured that rival "camps" or factions did not emerge within the administration. Mondale's experience in the capitol made him a valued asset to Carter and he regularly promoted Carter's programs, even when he disagreed with them.[140] This helped further build trust between the two men.

All of this led to a situation whereby Mondale was in a position to regularly offer the president advice on the entire range of domestic and foreign policy issues facing the administration. Of course, the president did not always follow it.[141] Mondale was successful in getting some cabinet members appointed, but was less successful, for example, in promoting more liberal domestic policies, especially as the economy worsened. But even when not successful, he was well-positioned to try, setting the standard for future vice presidents.

Mondale passed his experience along to Bush, who took many of his lessons to heart. Like Mondale, he eschewed most line assignments; he occupied a White House office; he had a weekly lunch meeting with President Reagan; he had access to the entire White House document flow; and his campaign manager, James Baker III, was appointed Reagan's Chief of Staff. Because Bush had attacked Reagan during the primaries the president and his staff were initially wary of Bush. Over time however, Bush built a strong personal relationship with Reagan, established himself as a loyal soldier, and the president came to appreciate him.[142] Bush eventually came to be a trusted adviser to Reagan.

One incident that helped establish Bush's loyalty came after the assassination attempt on Reagan on March 3, 1981. Bush was aboard Air Force Two when he received word of the attempt. Landing at Andrews Air Force Base he was encouraged to take Marine One (the president's helicopter) directly to the White House. Instead, he flew to the vice presidential mansion, and from there took a limousine to the White House. He later claimed, "only the president lands on the South Lawn" of the White House.[143]

Quayle was not fully trusted by the president's staff, but did enjoy all of the access that Bush did as vice president, including the weekly lunch and an open invitation to all meetings. On a daily basis he was exposed to and immersed in "discussions and decisions on vital national and international issues" in the Oval Office.[144] He took part in the daily national security briefing and often meetings with the president's chief of staff.[145] Although not a first-tier adviser, Bush valued his input, especially when it was in line with his own thinking. This was especially true on matters of politics and the administration's dealings with Congress. He has been described as Bush's "legislative counselor," and in this respect, may have been more influential than Bush was as vice president.[146]

Gore was the "second most important figure in the eight-year Clinton-Gore administration."[147] Clinton and Gore were fairly compatible in terms of their politics and both were policy-oriented individuals, which helped their personal relationship. Thus, Gore "succeeded in bucking the dismal tradition of his office to become the president's closest adviser. . . . Rarely did Bill Clinton reach a major decision without consulting Gore. 'I want to talk to Al' became a common presidential refrain heard by staff members."[148] Gore was one of President Clinton's main advisers on presidential appointments, foreign affairs, and also figured prominently in the administration's policies on such domestic concerns as the environment, communications technology, tobacco, and disarmament in the former Soviet Union.[149]

However, the relationship (both personal and professional) between Gore and Clinton had its ups and downs. Until 1994, Gore was the image of a second-in-command, but Bob Woodward's publication detailing passage of Clinton's 1993 economic plan portrayed Gore as a tough taskmaster to a sometimes dithering Clinton.[150] After this both seemed to become more cautious around each other when others were present.[151] As Clinton's second term began, Gore became even more influential as a result of the departure of top Clinton aides Dick Morris, George Stephanopoulos, and Leon Panetta. However, when the Monica Lewinsky scandal broke Gore began to distance himself from the president. He understood the danger to his upcoming presidential campaign and felt personally betrayed as well. Weekly lunches became less frequent, in part because Gore seemed to be away from Washington more. The relationship never recovered,[152] but Gore remained loyal and said nothing to publicly betray his president.

Cheney surpassed Gore in terms of his advisory role and influence on the president, at least in his first term. Bush's reliance on Cheney began by asking him to head the search for a running mate and this dependence continued immediately after Election Day (before the election had been officially decided) when Cheney was charged with funding and heading a private transition office.[153] He also exercised considerable influence in the selection of top administration officials.

Cheney met with the president several times a day, making weekly lunches with the president a formality. They jointly presided over domestic and foreign policy meetings, and Cheney met weekly with top administration officials.[154] Cheney reportedly was behind Bush's decision early on to renege on his campaign promise to lower carbon-dioxide emissions.[155] Woodward (and others) have suggested that it was Cheney who was in the lead in pushing for the 2003 invasion of Iraq.[156] In short, the Bush–Cheney relationship during the first term came close to the model that was being touted in 1980 for Reagan and Ford, that of a presidency/copresidency. In fact, early on, members of Cheney's staff were suggesting "that the model for the new administration would be 'a corporate one: Bush as the nation's chairman of the board, Cheney as America's chief executive.'"[157] This was not without a grain of truth.

However during their second term, Bush became less reliant on Cheney. In part this was as a result of Bush's having grown into the job, so to speak, as well as his desire to distance himself from some of Cheney's more controversial positions.[158]

Biden once suggested that as the result of Cheney's presumed influence over Bush, he may have been "the most dangerous vice president we've had."[159] However, by all accounts Biden and Obama enjoy a relationship just as intimate, if not more, as any of their predecessors. "Aides to both men say that Obama has found Biden to be an indispensable advisor."[160] Before agreeing to run as vice president Biden asked Obama to agree to what were essentially two conditions: any assignment he took should have a specific timeline attached to it and he "wanted to be the last guy in the room after meetings."[161] He understood that the advisory role of the office was his primary opportunity to play a part in governance.

This is not to say that the relationship between the two men has been without problems. Biden has a well-known penchant for speaking his mind, which can sometimes lead to ill-timed or poorly worded remarks. During the 2008 campaign he suggested that if elected Obama would be faced with a crisis early in his tenure as the result of some world leaders testing him. At the signing ceremony of the Affordable Care Act in 2010 Biden, unaware that the microphones were on, leaned over to the president, remarking that "this is a big f***ing deal."[162] In 2012 he publicly came out in support of gay marriage, despite the fact that Obama had been largely silent on the issue in hopes that the campaign could avoid becoming engaged in a divisive culture war.[163]

Despite these gaffes Biden remains one of the president's most trusted advisers. This is the result of several factors, the first of which was the pre-election agreement. Beyond this, Biden and the president are close, both professionally and personally. In addition, Biden and "the president see eye to eye on [most all] policy issues."[164] Biden has suggested that he and the president are "totally simpatico."[165] Biden has also proven to be both loyal to the president and a "forceful advocate on behalf of the president [and] his policies."[166] The relationship is further enhanced by the fact that their staff and aides are so closely integrated with each other. "Theirs is by all accounts a conjoined administration."[167] At minimum this prevents infighting within the administration and allows for both men and their assistants to work more closely together. The top advisers of each man gather together almost every day to discuss and set the agenda for the day.[168] There is little room for dissension to grow between the two men with regard to strategy and messaging.

Finally, like Cheney, Biden frequently interacts with the president. All this has led to a situation in which Biden has been able to exert a good amount of influence in the Obama administration. He has been directly involved with or affected decision making on the "stimulus, health care reform, the 2010 lame-duck session, the salvaged debt ceiling breakdown and the withdrawals from Iraq and Afghanistan,"[169] and the confirmations of Supreme Court nominees Sonia Sotomayor and Elena Kagan. "On financial reform, it was Biden who prodded an indecisive Obama to embrace, at long last, Paul Volcker's idea of barring banks from risky trading."[170] Biden, in other words, has easily matched, if not surpassed, the amount of influence Cheney had in the Bush administration.

CONCLUSION

The noted historian Arthur Schlesinger once claimed that "history had shown the American Vice Presidency to be a job of spectacular and, I believe, incurable frustration."[171] Before the modern era, this was understandable. Vice presidents did very little of any substance and were cast aside in the president's reelection effort. This is not the case in the modern era. Modern vice presidents are now given a wide array of responsibilities, many of which are important to the business of government. Most presidents in the modern era have included their vice presidents in the business of the administration, if for no other reason than to better prepare them to take over in the event of a presidential vacancy. The following chapters explore the vice presidencies of Gore, Cheney, and Biden in more detail.

NOTES

1. Miller Center Commission, "Report of the Commission on Choosing and Using Vice Presidents."
2. Nelson, "Choosing the Vice President," 863–64.
3. Jody C Baumgartner, "The Post-Palin Calculus: The 2012 Republican Veepstakes," *PS: Politics and Political Science* 45 (2012): 605–9.
4. Natoli, *American Prince, American Pauper*, 39.
5. Interestingly, Ford later claimed that this was the most cowardly political move he ever made.
6. Michael Nelson, "The Election: Turbulence and Tranquility in Contemporary American Politics," 68.
7. Richard L. Berke, "The Second Spot: Invisible, Subtle Race to Become No. 2," *New York Times*, May 3, 2000, www.nytimes.com/library/politics/camp/050300 vp-prospects.html.

8. Berke, "The Second Spot: Invisible, Subtle Race to Become No. 2."

9. Broder and Woodward, *The Man Who Would Be President: Dan Quayle*, 15–25.

10. S. Robert Lichter and Linda S. Lichter, "Covering the Convention Coverage," *Public Opinion*, September/October: 41–44.

11. See Jody C Baumgartner, "The Veepstakes: Forecasting Vice Presidential Selection in 2008," *PS: Politics and Political Science* 41 (2008):765–72; Baumgartner, "The Post-Palin Calculus; Jody C Baumgartner, "Vice Presidential Selection in the Convention Era: Experience or Electoral Advantage?" *Congress and the Presidency* 39 (2012): 297–315; Mark Hiller and Douglas Kriner, "Institutional Change and the Dynamic of Vice Presidential Selection," *Presidential Studies Quarterly* 38 (2008): 401–21; Lee Sigelman and Paul J. Wahlbeck, "The "Veepstakes": Strategic Choice in Presidential Running Mate Selection," 855–64.

12. Other names on the short lists were similarly well known. For example, New York Governor Mario Cuomo was a favorite among Democrats for his stirring speech at the 1984 Democratic Convention, making him a possibility for the vice presidency in 1992.

13. Polsby and Wildavsky, *Presidential Elections*, 132.

14. Baumgartner, "The Veepstakes."

15. At the time the United States did not have official relations with the People's Republic of China so this position was analogous to ambassador.

16. One previous study suggests that vice presidential candidates bring, on average, about a 0.3 percent electoral advantage from their home state. See Robert L. Dudley and Ronald B. Rappaport, "Vice-Presidential Candidates and the Home-State Advantage: Playing Second Banana at Home and on the Road," *American Journal of Political Science* 33(1989): 537–40. See also Christopher J. Devine, "The Vice Presidential Home State Advantage Reconsidered: Analyzing the Interactive Effect of Home State Population and Political Experience, 1884–2008," *Presidential Studies Quarterly* 41(2010):1–16; Christopher J. Devine and Kyle C. Kopco, "Presidential Versus Vice Presidential Home State Advantage: A Comparative Analysis of Electoral Significance, Causes, and Process, 1884–2008," *Presidential Studies Quarterly* (2013) 43: 814–34; Carl, D. Tubbesing, "Vice Presidential Candidates and the Home State Advantage: Or, 'Tom Who?' Was Tom Eagleton in Missouri," *Western Political Quarterly* 26 (1973): 702–16.

17. Natoli, *American Prince, American Pauper*, 21.

18. Polsby and Wildavsky, *Presidential Elections*, 85; Natoli, *American Prince, American Pauper*, 21–22.

19. Natoli, *American Prince, American Pauper*, 41.

20. Nelson, "Choosing the Vice President," 863.

21. Nelson, "The Election," 68; Polsby and Wildavsky, *Presidential Elections*, 130; Natoli, *American Prince, American Pauper*, 46–49.

22. Polsby and Wildavsky, *Presidential Elections*, 130; Natoli, *American Prince, American Pauper*, 43.

23. Polsby and Wildavsky, *Presidential Elections*, 129.

24. Ibid., 130.

25. Broder and Woodward, *The Man Who Would Be President*, 60–63; Pika, "The Vice Presidency," 512.

26. Southwick, *Presidential Also-Rans and Running Mates, 1788–1996*; Natoli, *American Prince, American Pauper*, 48.

27. For more on press coverage of vice presidential candidates, see Ulbig, *Vice Presidents, Presidential Elections, and the Media: Second Fiddles in the Spotlight.*

28. Jody C Baumgartner, Jonathan S. Morris, and Natasha L. Walth, "The Fey Effect: Young Adults, Political Humor, and Perceptions of Sarah Palin in the 2008 Presidential Election Campaign," *Public Opinion Quarterly* 76 (2012): 95–104.

29. Goldstein, *The Modern American Vice Presidency,* 91.

30. Jack Germond and Jules Witcover, *Wake Us When It's Over: Presidential Politics of 1984* (New York: Macmillan Publishing, 1985), 488–89.

31. Goldstein, *The Modern American Vice Presidency,* 99.

32. Pater Baker, *Days of Fire: Bush and Cheney in the White House* (New York: Doubleday, 2013).

33. Kevin Sauter, "The 1976 Mondale-Ford Vice Presidential Debate," in *Rhetorical Studies of National Political Debates—1992,* ed. Robert V. Friedenberg. 2nd ed. (Westport, CT: Praeger, 1994), 45.

34. Judith S. Trent, "The 1984 Bush-Ferraro Vice Presidential Debate," in *Rhetorical Studies of National Political Debates—1992,* ed. Robert V. Friedenberg. 2nd ed. (Westport, CT: Praeger, 1994), 122.

35. Sauter, "The 1976 Mondale-Ford Vice Presidential Debate," 50.

36. Trent, "The 1984 Bush-Ferraro Vice Presidential Debate," 136.

37. Trent, "The 1984 Bush-Ferraro Vice Presidential Debate," 122–26, 128, 135.

38. Jody Baumgartner, "Biden, Ryan, Both Accomplish Goals," *USA Today,* October 12, 2012, www.usatoday.com/story/opinion/2012/10/12/vice-president-debate-romney-biden-baumgartner/1626609/.

39. Trent, "The 1984 Bush-Ferraro Vice Presidential Debate,"132–33.

40. Ibid.

41. Trent, "The 1984 Bush-Ferraro Vice Presidential Debate," 121, 133, 138, 140.

42. Warren D. Decker, "The 1988 Quayle-Bentsen Vice Presidential Debate," in *Rhetorical Studies of National Political Debates—1992,* ed. Robert V. Friedenberg. 2nd ed. (Westport, CT: Praeger, 1994).

43. James W. Ceaser and Andrew E. Busch, *Red Over Blue: The 2004 Elections and American Politics* (Lanham, MD: Rowman & Littlefield, 2005), 131.

44. Sauter, "The 1976 Mondale-Ford Vice Presidential Debate," 46, 64.

45. Decker, "The 1988 Quayle-Bentsen Vice Presidential Debate," 182.

46. Gaut Ragsdale, "The 1996 Gore-Kemp Vice Presidential Debates," in *Rhetorical Studies of National Political Debates—1996,* Robert V. Friedenberg, ed. (Westport, CT: Praeger, 1997), 54, 57.

47. Gary Langer and Dalia Sussman, "A Debate Win: Cheney Gains with Help from His Friends," *ABCNews.Com,* October 6, 2004, abcnews.go.com/sections/politics/Vote2004/vp_debate_poll_041006.html.

48. Avi Zenilman, "CBS News/Knowledge Networks Insta-poll: Biden Wins Big," *Politico,* October 2, 2008, www.politico.com/blogs/michaelcalderone/1008/CBS_NewsKnowledge_Networks_instapoll_Biden_wins_big.html?showall; Jon Swaine, "Who Won the VP Debate: Palin or Joe Biden?"; *The Telegraph,* October 3, 2008, www.telegraph.co.uk/news/newstopics/uselection2008/presidential debates/3129259/Who-won-the-VP-debate-Palin-or-Joe-Biden.html.

49. Jesse Merkel, "Who Won the VP Debate 2012: Paul Ryan Wins the Polls against Laughing Joe Biden," *PolicyMic,* October 12, 2012, www.policymic.com/

articles/16407/who-won-the-vp-debate-2012-paul-ryan-wins-the-polls-against-laughing-joe-biden.

50. One scholar suggests that the vice presidential debates do affect public opinion. See Thomas M. Holbrook, "The Behavioral Consequences of Vice Presidential Debates: Does the Undercard Have Any Punch?" *American Politics Quarterly* 22(4) (1994): 469–82.

51. Ragsdale, "The 1996 Gore-Kemp Vice Presidential Debates," 54.

52. David, "The Vice Presidency," 736.

53. Nelson, "The Election," 68.

54. See Danny M. Atkinson, "The Electoral Significance of the Vice Presidency," *Presidential Studies Quarterly* 12(3) (1992): 330–36; David W. Romero, "Requiem for a Lightweight: Vice Presidential Candidate Evaluations and the Presidential Vote," *Presidential Studies Quarterly* 31(3) (2001): 454–63; Thomas M. Holbrook, "The Behavioral Consequences of Vice Presidential Debates: Does the Undercard Have Any Punch?"; Brian J. Brox and Madison L Cassels, "The Contemporary Effects of Vice-Presidential Nominees: Sarah Palin and the 2008 Presidential Campaign," *Journal of Political Marketing* 8 (2009): 349–63; Edward M. Burmilla and Josh M. Ryan, "Reconsidering the "Palin Effect" in the 2008 Presidential Election," *Political Research Quarterly* 66 (2013): 952–59; Jonathan Knuckey, "Comments on "Reconsidering the 'Palin Effect,'" *Political Research Quarterly*, 66 (2013): 960–63; and Jonathan Knuckey, "The "Palin Effect' in the 2008 U.S. Presidential Election,'" *Political Research Quarterly* 20 (2008): 1–15.

55. Natoli, *American Prince, American Pauper*, 43.

56. History News Network Staff, "What Is the 25th Amendment and When Has It Been Invoked?" History News Network, http://hnn.us/articles/812.html.

57. Tamara Lipper, "President Cheney?" *Newsweek*, July 8, 2002, 140 (2): 8; Peter Baker, "Bush Will Temporarily Hand Reins to Cheney," *Washington Post*, July 21, 2007, www.washingtonpost.com/wp-dyn/content/article/2007/07/20/AR2007072001790.html.

58. Dick Cheney, *In My Time: A Personal and Political Memoir Hardcover* (New York: Threshold Editions, 2011).

59. Cronin, "Rethinking the Vice-Presidency," 328.

60. Humphrey actually inserted himself into the fray, ruling from the chair in favor of the liberals in 1969 but was reversed by the Senate; Goldstein, *The Modern American Vice Presidency*, 143–45.

61. Hatfield, *Vice Presidents of the United States, 1789–1993*, 510.

62. Hatfield, *Vice Presidents of the United States, 1789–1993*, 523.

63. Ed O'Keefe, "Biden to Preside Over Senate During Immigration Bill Vote," *Washington Post*, June 27, 2013, www.washingtonpost.com/blogs/post-politics/wp/2013/06/27/biden-to-preside-over-senate-during-immigration-bill-vote/.

64. Baumgartner, "Scoundrel or Über-Lieutenant?" 242.

65. O'Keefe, "Biden to Preside Over Senate"; Sunlen Miller, "With VP Biden Presiding, Senate Passes Democrats' Tax Cut Plan," *ABC News*, July 25, 2012, abcnews.go.com/blogs/politics/2012/07/with-vp-biden-presiding-senate-passes-democrats-tax-cut-plan/; Reid J. Epstein, "Biden to Preside Over Senate Gun Control Votes," *Politico*, April 17, 2013, www.politico.com/politico44/2013/04/biden-to-preside-over-senate-gun-control-votes-161928.html.

66. "Address by President George H. W. Bush, "The Leader's Lecture Series 1998–2002," www.senate.gov/artandhistory/history/common/generic/Leaders_Lecture_Series_Bush.htm.

67. Baumgartner, "Scoundrel or Über-Lieutenant?" 242.

68. "Cheney Casts Tie-breaker as Senate Debates Budget," *CNN*, April 3, 2001, http://cgi.cnn.com/2001/ALLPOLITICS/04/03/senate.budget.02/.

69. U.S. Department of State, "History of the National Security Council, 1947–1997," Office of the Historian, August, 1997, www.whitehouse.gov/nsc/history.html#summary.

70. Steven M. Gillon, "A New Framework: Walter Mondale as Vice President," in *At the President's Side: The Vice Presidency in the Twentieth Century*, ed. Timothy Walch (Columbia: University of Missouri, 1997), 146.

71. Pika, "The Vice Presidency," 498–99.

72. Hatfield, *Vice Presidents of the United States, 1789–1993*.

73. Frank Kessler, "Walter F. Mondale (b. 1928)," 380–82.

74. L. Edward Purcell, "George Herbert Walker Bush (b. 1924)," in *Vice Presidents: A Biographical Dictionary*, ed. L. Edward Purcell (New York: Checkmark Books, 2001), 390.

75. Shirley Anne Warshaw, "J. Danforth Quayle (b. 1947)," in *Vice Presidents: A Biographical Dictionary*, ed. L. Edward Purcell (New York: Checkmark Books, 2001); Pika, "The Vice Presidency," 516.

76. Turque, *Inventing Al Gore*, 266.

77. Pika, "The Vice Presidency," 523.

78. Edward L. Purcell, "Richard Bruce Cheney (b. 1941)," in *Vice Presidents: A Biographical Dictionary*, ed. L. Edward Purcell (New York: Checkmark Books, 2001).

79. Michael Scherer, "What Happened to the Stimulus?" *Time*, July 1, 2009, http://content.time.com/time/magazine/article/0,9171,1908417,00.html.

80. See Executive Order 11884.

81. Hatfield, *Vice Presidents of the United States, 1789–1993*, 510.

82. Purcell, "George Herbert Walker Bush (b. 1924)," 390.

83. Kamal Ahmed, "The Death of Diana: Mandela and Clinton to Miss Funeral," *The Guardian*, September 3, 1997: 2.

84. Hatfield, *Vice Presidents of the United States, 1789–1993*, 522.

85. Chase Untermeyer, "Looking Forward: George Bush as Vice President," in *At the President's Side: The Vice Presidency in the Twentieth Century*, ed. Timothy Walch (Columbia: University of Missouri, 1997).

86. John M. Goshko, "Thousands Crowd Madison Square Garden to Remember Rabin," *The Washington Post*, December 11, 1995, A4; Irv Kupcinet, "Kup's Column" *Chicago Sun Times*, November 22, 1996, 48; "Gore, MacKay to Speak at Funeral," *St. Petersburg Times*, December 16, 1998, 12A.

87. "Washington Wire," *Wall Street Journal*, August 5, 2005, A4.

88. Maryclaire Dale, "Arlen Specter Funeral Draws Vice President Joe Biden, Hundreds More," *HuffingtonPost*, October 16, 2012, www.huffingtonpost.com/2012/10/16/arlen-specter-funeral_n_1970318.html; Jonathan Ellis, "Biden on McGovern: 'Your Father Was a Genuine Hero'" *ArgusLeader*, October 26, 2012, www.argusleader.com/article/20121026/NEWS/310260044/Biden-McGovern-Your-father-genuine-hero-; Jill Colvin, "Joe Biden Jokes about Always Being One

-Upped by Frank Lautenberg at Senator's Funeral," *Politicker*, June 5, 2013 http://politicker.com/2013/06/joe-biden-jokes-about-always-being-one-upped-by-frank-lautenberg-at-senators-funeral/.

89. Justin Sink, "Biden to Lead Mandela Memorial in DC," *The Hill*, December 9, 2013, http://thehill.com/homenews/administration/192471-biden-to-lead-mandela-memorial-at-national-cathedral.

90. Dave Boyer, "Biden to Lead Delegation to Sharon Funeral," *The Washington Times*, January 12, 2014, www.washingtontimes.com/news/2014/jan/12/biden-lead-delegation-sharon-funeral/.

91. Dick Cheney, "Remarks by the Vice President at the Ronald Reagan Presidential Library and Museum," *Whitehouse.gov*. March, 2004, http://whitehouse.gov/news/releases/2004/03/200403173.html; The Associated Press, "Cheney Marks Anniversary with Wreath at Arlington," *St. Petersburg Times*, July 27, 2003, www.sptimes.com/2003/07/27/Korea/Cheney_marks_annivers.shtml.

92. Katharine Q. Seelye, "In Shanksville, Thousands Gather to Honor Flight 93 Victims," *New York Times*, September 10, 2011, www.nytimes.com/2011/09/11/us/11shanksville.html=.

93. Stephanie Condon, "Biden Taking Pelosi, N.M. Governor to Papal Inauguration," *CBS News*, March 15, 2013, www.cbsnews.com/news/biden-taking-pelosi-nm-governor-to-papal-inauguration/.

94. Hatfield, *Vice Presidents of the United States, 1789–1993*, 510.

95. Pika, "The Vice Presidency," 516.

96. Brian Bakst, "Gore, FEMA Director to Tour Minnesota, Dakota Flood Areas," *Star Tribune*, April 10, 1997, A20.

97. Jodi Wilgoren, "'Going to Get it Done,' Cheney Vows on Gulf Tour," *The New York Times*, September 9, 2005, A21.

98. Borys Krawczeniuk, "Biden Calls Flooding 'An American Problem,'" *CitizensVoice*, September 17, 2011, http://citizensvoice.com/news/biden-calls-flooding-an-american-problem-1.1204562; Bruce Finley, "Biden, Hickenlooper Give Flooded Areas High-Level Attention," *Denver Post*, September 23, 2013, www.denverpost.com/environment/ci_24157137/vp-joe-biden-hickenlooper-aerial-survey-flood-ravaged.

99. Light, *Vice-Presidential Power*, 166; Goldstein, *The Modern American Vice Presidency*, 161.

100. Goldstein, *The Modern American Vice Presidency*, 161–62.

101. Pika, "The Vice Presidency," 504.

102. Untermeyer, "Looking Forward: George Bush as Vice President," 164.

103. Pika, "The Vice Presidency," 504; Broder and Woodward, *The Man Who Would Be President*, 90.

104. Broder and Woodward, *The Man Who Would Be President*, 98.

105. Turque, *Inventing Al Gore*, 277.

106. Scott W. Rager, "Albert Arnold Gore, Jr. (b. 1948)," in *Vice Presidents: A Biographical Dictionary*, ed. L. Edward Purcell (New York: Checkmark Books, 2001), 405–6.

107. Stephen Singular, *Joe Lieberman: The Historic Choice* (New York: Pinnacle, 2000), 95; Turque, *Inventing Al Gore*, 277.

108. Turque, *Inventing Al Gore*, 277.

109. Howard LaFranchi, "Cheney's Mideast Reality Check," *Christian Science Monitor*, March 20, 2002, 94(80): 1; Brian Knowlton, "Cheney's Davos Trip Is Just 2nd Appearance Overseas," *International Herald Tribune*, January 23, 2004, 3; Aryn Baker, "Cheney in the War Zone," *Time*, March 12, 2007, 19; Nick Squires, "Cheney Visits an Australia Roiled by Guantanamo, Iraq," *Christian Science Monitor* 99(60) (2007): 4–10.

110. Daniel Dombey and Andrew Ward, "Oil tops Cheney's Middle East Tour Agenda," *Financial Times*, March 16, 2008, http://ft.com/cms/s/0/d132d1e2f3a211 dcb6bc0000779fd2ac.html?nclick_check=1; Richard W. Stevenson, "Cheney, in Surprise Visit, Hails Iraq Efforts," *The New York Times*, December 19, 2005, A12; "Cheney Urges Political Unity in Iraq Visit," *USA Today*, March 17, 2008, www .usatoday.com/news/world/iraq/20080317iraquscheney_N.htm.

111. "Vice President Joe Biden," http://www.whitehouse.gov/administration/vice-president-biden.

112. Mark Memmott, "Biden Departs Today on First Foreign Trip as VP," *USA Today*, February 06, 2009, http://content.usatoday.com/communities/theoval/post/2009/02/62475523/1.

113. Lionel Beehner, "Biden the Embellisher Heads to Bosnia," *The Guardian*, May 20, 2009, www.theguardian.com/commentisfree/cifamerica/2009/may/19/joe-biden-bosnia-serbia.

114. Ariel Cohen, "Joe Biden's Trip to Ukraine and Georgia," *The Heritage Foundation*, July 27, 2009, www.heritage.org/research/reports/2009/07/joe-bidens -trip-to-ukraine-and-georgia.

115. Clive Leviev-Sawyer, "US Vice President Biden Departs for Central Europe Trip," *Sofia Echo*, October 20, 2009, http://sofiaecho.com/2009/10/20/802087_us -vice-president-biden-departs-for-central-europe-trip.

116. Goldstein, *The Modern American Vice Presidency*, 189.

117. Ibid., 189, 196.

118. Untermeyer, "Looking Forward: George Bush as Vice President," 163.

119. Hatfield, *Vice Presidents of the United States, 1789–1993*.

120. Broder and Woodward, *The Man Who Would Be President*, 91, 99, 103.

121. Warshaw, "J. Danforth Quayle (b. 1947)," 398.

122. Rager, "Albert Arnold Gore, Jr. (b. 1948)," 406.

123. Richard W. Stevens and Elisabeth Bumiller, "Cheney Exercising Muscle on Domestic Policies," *The New York Times*, January 18, 2005, A1.

124. Tim Funk, "Cheney Sees Need to Educate Nation on Social Security Plan," *Charlotte Observer*, March 12, 2005, A4.

125. Ibid.

126. Lawrence M. O'Rourke, "CAFTA Unsettled in House," *Sacramento Bee*, July 28, 2005, D1.

127. Marc Sandalow, "Cheney's Disappearing Act: Vice President to Surface— and Give Speech—in S.F.," *San Francisco Chronicle*, August 4, 2002, A1.

128. David Hume Kennerly, "Dick Cheney's Final Assault across America," *The Digital Journalist*, November, 2004, http://dirckhalstead.org/issue0411/dis_ kennerly.html.

129. Mike Allen and James Carney, "Exclusive Interview: Cheney on Elections and Iraq," *Time*, Oct. 19, 2006, www.time.com/time/printout/0,8816,1548061,00 .html.

130. Hite, *Second Best*, 212.

131. "About Joe Biden," http://1.barackobama.com/about/joe-biden/.

132. Glenn Thrush, Carrie Budoff Brown, Manu Raju, and John Bresnahan, "Joe Biden, Mitch McConnell and the Making of a Debt Deal," *Politico*, August 2, 2011, www.politico.com/news/stories/0811/60463.html; Tim Reid, "Q+A: Debt and Deficit Talks in Early Stages," Reuters, May 16, 2011, http://www.reuters.com/article/2011/05/16/us-usa-debt-talks-idUSTRE74F26V20110516.

133. Karoun Demirjian, "It's Over: House Passes 'Fiscal Cliff' Deal," *Las Vegas Sun*, January 1, 2013, www.lasvegassun.com/news/2013/jan/01/its-over-house-passes-fiscal-cliff-deal/.

134. Patrick O'Connor, "Joe the Fighter: Biden Logs 149 Campaign Events," *Washington Wire*, November 2, 2010, http://blogs.wsj.com/washwire/2010/11/02/joe-the-fighter-biden-logs-149-campaign-events/.

135. Ibid.

136. Leigh Ann Caldwell, "Obama Sets Up Gun Violence Task Force," *CBS News*, December 19, 2012, www.cbsnews.com/news/obama-sets-up-gun-violence-task-force/.

137. Polsby and Wildavsky, *Presidential Elections*, 84. The classic work on vice presidential influence is Light, *Vice-Presidential Power*.

138. Light, *Vice-Presidential Power*, 135.

139. Light, *Vice-Presidential Power*, 131.

140. Kessler, "Walter F. Mondale (b. 1928)," 381; Hatfield, *Vice Presidents of the United States, 1789–1993*.

141. Ibid., 381.

142. Pika, "The Vice Presidency," 508; Purcell, "George Herbert Walker Bush (b. 1924)," 390.

143. Purcell, "George Herbert Walker Bush (b. 1924)," 390.

144. Broder and Woodward, *The Man Who Would Be President*, 18.

145. Ibid., 94–95.

146. Ibid., 99.

147. Charles Babington, "Campaigns Matter: The Proof of 2000," in *Overtime: The Election 2000 Thriller*, ed. Larry J. Sabato (New York: Longman, 2002), 46.

148. Turque, *Inventing Al Gore*, 268.

149. Rager, "Albert Arnold Gore, Jr. (b. 1948)"; Singular, *Joe Lieberman*, 95; Turque, *Inventing Al Gore*, 267.

150. Bob Woodward, *The Agenda: Inside the Clinton White House* (New York, Simon & Schuster, 1994).

151. Turque, *Inventing Al Gore*, 288.

152. Ibid., 321, 359.

153. Dan Freedman, "Cheney Opens Office as Base for Transition," *Milwaukee Journal Sentinel*, November 30, 2000, A16; Ben White, "White House Transition" *Washington Post*, December 15, 2000, A39.

154. "Richard B. Cheney, 46th Vice President (2001–2009)," *The United States Senate (Art & History)*, N.D., www.senate.gov/artandhistory/history/common/generic/VP_Richard_Cheney.htm.

155. Nicholas Lemann, "The Quiet Man: Dick Cheney's Discreet Rise to Unprecedented Power," *The New Yorker*, May 7, 2001.

156. Bob Woodward, *Plan of Attack* (New York: Simon & Schuster, 2004).

157. Dana Milbank, "The Chairman and the CEO," *Washington Post*, December 24, 2000, A1.

158. Baker, *Days of Fire*.

159. Michael Hirsh, "Biden May Be the Most Influential Vice President Ever," *National Journal*, December 31, 2012, www.nationaljournal.com/whitehouse/biden-may-be-the-most-influential-vice-president-ever-2012123.

160. Michael A. Memoli, "Biden Forged Bond with Obama Through His Loyalty," *Los Angeles Times*, September 6, 2012, http://articles.latimes.com/print/2012/sep/06/nation/la-na-biden-20120906.

161. Mario Trujillo, "Biden: VP Has No Inherent Power," *The Hill*, February 10, 2014, http://thehill.com/blogs/blog-briefing-room/197921-biden-vp-has-no-inherent-power.

162. Glenn Thrush, "What Did Biden say?" *Politico*, March 23, 2010, www.politico.com/politico44/perm/0310/what_did_biden_say_522d0179-66c9-479e-ba2b-5c4e79aba3be.html.

163. Edward-Isaac Dovere and Darren Samuelsohn, "The Joe Biden Factor," *Politico*, September 5, 2012, http://dyn.politico.com/printstory.cfm?uuid=27E45D34-99F6-4A2A-84E2-8B57E7AFFD2C.

164. Douglas Brinkley, "Joe Biden: The Rolling Stone Interview," *Rolling Stone*, May 23, 2013, http://www.rollingstone.com/politics/news/joe-biden-the-rolling-stone-interview-20130509.

165. Kevin Bohn, "Biden on Obama at Start of Second Term: 'Totally Simpatico'," *CNN*, Jan. 22, 2013, www.cnn.com/2013/01/21/politics/borger-biden-intv/.

166. Michael A. Memoli, "Biden Forged Bond with Obama Through His Loyalty," *Los Angeles Times*, Sept. 6, 2012, Available at http://articles.latimes.com/2012/sep/06/nation/la-na-biden-20120906.

167. Jeanne Marie Laskas, "Have You Heard the One about President Joe Biden?" *GC*, July, 2013, http://www.gq.com/news-politics/newsmakers/201308/joe-biden-presidential-campaign-2016-2013.

168. Ibid.

169. Edward-Isaac Dovere and Darren Samuelsohn, "The Joe Biden factor," *Politico*, September 5, 2012. Available at http://Dyn.politico.com/printstory.cfm?uuid=27E45D34-99F6-4A2A-84E2-8B57E7AFFD2c.

170. Michael Hirsh, "Biden May Be the Most Influential Vice President Ever," *National Journal*, Dec. 31, 2012. Available at www.nationaljournal.com/whitehouse/biden-may-be-the-most-influential-vice-president-ever-20121231.

171. Schlesinger, "On the Presidential Succession," 478.

7

Al Gore and the
Gore–Clinton Partnership

Building on the themes introduced in previous chapters, this chapter examines the vice presidency of Al Gore. Gore was selected because of his similarities to Bill Clinton, particularly their shared centrist ideologies. From the start Clinton insisted that Gore would be a partner in his presidency. Gore subsequently headed a well-publicized task force to streamline government, was associated with the administration's environmental and technology initiatives, and to facilitate relations with Russia, was encouraged to develop a relationship with Russian Prime Minister Viktor Chernomyrdin. Gore was also, famously, deceived by the president about the Monica Lewinsky matter, which somewhat soured relations between the two. This said, Gore was easily the most active and visible vice president since Walter Mondale. And, because each of the past three vice presidents has been quite active, it could be argued that Clinton and Gore were at least partially responsible for helping cement the new role of the vice president.

SELECTION AND THE CAMPAIGN OF 1992

The 1992 presidential campaign saw the incumbent Republican President (former Vice President) George H. W. Bush facing off against the Democrat Bill Clinton, a six-term governor from Arkansas. Bush had a fair amount of foreign policy success to his credit, including presiding over the disintegration of the Soviet Union and the end of the Cold War as well as the first Gulf War in 1991. His approval ratings in spring 1991 were extremely high. However, as 1992 opened it began to look as if the country was going deeper into an economic recession, which made him electorally vulnerable.

Clinton, who had risen to national prominence during the 1988 Democratic National Convention, faced a relatively weak field in his battle for the Democratic nomination. In part this was the result of the president's high approval ratings in 1991, which likely scared off several worthy opponents, including the well-known governor of New York, Mario Cuomo. His main challenger, Senator Paul Tsongas, proved to be a minor threat. The Clinton campaign managed to survive allegations of an extramarital affair that emerged immediately before the New Hampshire primary and he secured his party's nomination by early March.[1]

Clinton charged a three-person search committee, headed by Warren Christopher to head his vice presidential search committee.[2] His "short list" was actually longer than some others in the modern era and included several names that had been mentioned as possible presidential candidates (Cuomo, Dick Gephardt, Jay Rockefeller, and Al Gore) and one primary opponent (Bob Kerrey) in 1992. During his first meeting with Gore, Clinton discovered a rapport that reportedly played a large part in his selection of the senator from Tennessee. However Gore was initially reluctant to accept Clinton's offer, despite the fact that his father had once aspired to the vice presidency himself. He eventually agreed and the announcement of the selection came in early July, well received by all but a minority of Democratic Party notables.

A major reason for this minority dissent was that of all major-party presidential tickets in recent memory, the Clinton–Gore ticket was arguably the least balanced. Both Clinton and Gore were in their forties, Southern Baptists, and came from the moderate wing of the party. The two were close on almost all issues. Clinton's selection was designed to emphasize his baby boomer image and appeal to that same demographic in the general election. In other words Clinton was attempting to accentuate rather than offset his own characteristics.[3] It is also likely that Gore's reputation as a family man played a role as well, an attempt on Clinton's part to deflect attention from scandals revolving around his alleged extramarital affairs. Finally, Gore brought a wealth of experience in Washington politics that Clinton, as a long-term governor, did not possess.

The troubles of Gore's counterpart, the incumbent Vice President Dan Quayle, have been detailed in previous chapters. By 1992 he had become something of laughing stock, the butt of any number of jokes by late-night comedians.[4] Although there was sentiment within the Republican Party and among Bush's chief advisers to replace Quayle on the ticket, Bush stuck by his vice president.

The Democratic campaign of 1992 was unique in how the presidential and vice presidential candidates divided their time. Because both Clinton and Gore were from the South they shared the same regional strength. Therefore, there was little point in crafting different regional strategies. Moreover the two got along well. Immediately after the Democratic convention the two—with their families—embarked on an eight-state bus tour of the Northeast. This mini-tour went so well that they campaigned together often throughout the fall, although part of the reason for this was the fact that Gore insisted on it.[5]

Both vice presidential candidates played their attack roles well. Quayle conducted a war on the nation's "cultural elites" that was reminiscent of Spiro Agnew's war on the press. Although the target of his attacks was originally the television character Murphy Brown (who claimed that bearing a child out of wedlock was a "lifestyle choice"), the moral theme of these speeches reminded listeners of character issues being raised about Clinton. Quayle went further by suggesting that Gore was chosen as vice presidential candidate "because he went to Vietnam" (in contrast to Clinton).[6] Gore did his part by charging that President Bush and his administration had helped Saddam Hussein buy more than one billion dollars in weapons with money from loan guarantees that were originally meant for U.S. farm products.[7]

The vice presidential debate in 1992 was a bit more complex than in previous years because the debate featured not only the Democratic and Republican candidates but James Stockdale, independent presidential candidate Ross Perot's running mate, as well. A three-candidate debate meant, among other things, that a more complex question order had to be negotiated. One aspect of the format negotiated by Gore's team to his favor was that a total of nine minutes was allotted for each topic in the hope that Quayle would display a certain shallowness if given enough time. Gore's overall strategy was to drive home the central theme of the Clinton campaign, namely, the economy. Quayle's goals included focusing on Clinton's character and to project an image of Clinton as a "traditional" tax-and-spend Democrat. He also wanted to portray Gore as pompous and out of touch.[8] The most memorable moment came from Stockdale, who in his opening statement asked, rhetorically, "Who am I? Why am I here?" However the rhetoric was lost on the audience, who found the statement somewhat amusing and a bit odd. This story line crowded out most stories about the major party candidates, neither of whom suffered terribly from their debate appearances.

IN OFFICE: THE FORMAL VICE PRESIDENCY

There were no typical (e.g., health scares, assasination attempts) succession crises during the eight years Gore was vice president. However, in

1998 President Clinton was impeached by the House of Representatives. This set up the potential for Gore to assume the presidency in the event Clinton was removed by the Senate. The possibility of this happening was considered to be remote, even by the president's most ardent detractors.

Like other modern vice presidents Gore spent little time presiding over the Senate in his role as president of that body. Shortly after taking office he presided over a vote on a Republican-led effort to codify the "strict anti-gay policy that the military practiced before Clinton." The president campaigned on liberalizing that policy and had ordered the military to begin taking steps to do so the previous week. Gore's presence for the vote was symbolic, inasmuch as the measure was defeated by a vote of 62 to 37.[9] In February 2000 he made a similarly symbolic appearance, abruptly returning to Washington in the midst of his presidential campaign to preside over a vote "on an abortion-rights amendment being considered by the Senate." Gore claimed he was there in the event there was a tie vote. However, the fact that it passed, 82 to 17, suggests that he may have been grandstanding.[10]

Leading up to Clinton's impeachment trial there were some questions regarding a potential conflict of interest for Gore, who had stated that he might exercise his constitutional right to cast tie-breaking votes on procedural questions guiding the Senate impeachment trial.[11] However this was not necessary. In fact the Constitution safeguards against any potential conflict of interest in the vice president's role (an ambitious vice president might like to see his president removed, or a loyal vice president would likely try and protect his president) in an impeachment trial by stipulating that the Chief Justice of the Supreme Court preside over the proceedings.

In his role as President of the Senate the vice president is also responsible for presiding over, certifying, and announcing the winner of the Electoral College vote. Richard Nixon announced his own defeat in 1961, but Hubert Humphrey declined to fulfill his duty to do so in 1969.[12] Gore had the distinction of being the first vice president since Nixon to officially announce his own defeat in the Electoral College to Congress in 2001. This he did in the face of more than a dozen objections from Democratic members of the House who claimed that the results from Florida were compromised. Although he ruled the objections out of order, at one point he responded to one of the protest leaders, stating, "We did all we could. . . . The chair thanks the gentleman."[13]

Gore cast four tie-breaking votes during his two-term tenure as vice president, slightly more than half the number (seven) that Bush cast. The first, in 1993, was on the budget bill that was President Clinton's legislative priority that year.[14] During the first presidential debate in 2000 Gore said of this vote, "I had the honor of casting the tie-breaking vote to end the old economic plan here at home and put into place a new economic plan that has helped us to make some progress: 22 million new jobs and the greatest prosperity ever."[15] A second vote in his first year in office dealt with Clinton's deficit reduction plan. In 1994 he cast a tie-breaking vote in favor of a measure preserving ethanol tax subsidies, and in 1999 he broke a tie over a bitterly debated amendment to a bill that closed the so-called "gun-show loophole" on gun sales at gun shows.[16]

In the modern era only one vice president (Mondale) took on fewer line assignments than did Gore. Clinton asked, and Gore agreed, to head the National Performance Review, or the "reinventing government" initiative inspired by a book of the same name by political scientist David Osborne. His focus was "waste, fraud, and abuse in the federal government," and he "advocated trimming the size of the bureaucracy and the number of regulations." Meeting with federal employees, cabinet secretaries, and even talking to late-night talk shows ("wearing safety goggles and smashing an ash tray with a hammer to poke fun at the Pentagon's requirement for an expensive 'ash receiver, tobacco, desk type'"), he devoted six months to the effort. His report, titled "From Red Tape to Results: Creating a Government that Works Better and Costs Less," was unveiled

> on the South Lawn on September 7, against a backdrop of two forklifts piled high with government rules and regulations . . . [it] made 284 recommendations for streamlining and energizing the bureaucracy and promised $108 billion in savings and a 12 percent cut in the federal workforce—252,000 jobs—by1998.[17]

As a result, more than 100,000 federal government jobs, sixteen thousand pages from the Federal Register, and ten thousand pages from federal employee manuals were eliminated.[18]

IN OFFICE: THE INFORMAL VICE PRESIDENCY

Bush and Dan Quayle are included among modern vice presidents. However, it was the vice presidency of Gore that truly continued the precedent set by Mondale of the vice president as active governing partner. This was not an accident. Gore had listened to his father's suggestion that he and Clinton have a clear understanding of Gore's place in the administration before taking office. Clinton and Gore met after the election and forged a two-page document outlining Gore's role. The result was the most active vice presidency in the twentieth century.

This is not to imply that Gore was able to shun and shirk ceremonial and symbolic aspects of the job. Like other vice presidents Gore attended his share of funerals and memorial services during his eight years in office. In December 1995 he was present at a memorial service held in Madison Square Garden in New York City for slain Israeli Prime Minister Yitzhak Rabin,[19] and two months later, the funeral of two-term French President François Mitterrand held in the Notre Dame Cathedral in Paris. In 1996 he was in Chicago to honor the passing of Joseph Cardinal Bernardin,[20] and in early 1997 he attended a memorial service for the noted scientist Carl Sagan.[21] Gore was also present at the 1999 memorial service for the twelve students and one teacher killed in the Columbine high school massacre in Littleton, Colorado.[22]

He attended a number of funerals for prominent politicians as well. In 1994 he was in Cambridge, Massachusetts, for the funeral of former Democratic Speaker of the House Thomas ("Tip") O'Neill.[23] The following year saw him at services for former Defense Secretary and member of the House Les Aspin.[24] When former five-term mayor of Los Angeles, Tom Bradley died in 1998 Gore honored him as well.[25] In a few cases Gore's *non*-attendance at the funeral of well-known politicians' was notable. In 1998, feminist, antiwar activist, and former Congresswoman Bella Abzug died, and Gore's wife Tipper represented the president and the vice president at her private service.[26] Finally, in his role as a son, he attended services for his father, former Tennessee Senator Albert Gore Sr., who passed away at the age of ninety in 1998.[27]

In his ceremonial role Gore also visited his share of natural disaster sites. For example in 1993 he toured the Mississippi River watershed after floods in the Midwest.[28] In 1997 he visited the Ohio River Valley after "one of the biggest floods of the century" from that river,[29] and later the upper Midwest, where "North Dakota, South Dakota, and 21 counties in Minnesota [had] been declared Federal disaster areas" from flooding.[30] Gore visited areas of Florida in 1998, where severe drought had caused numerous wildfires.[31] After tornadoes ravaged parts of Alabama, Mississippi, and Georgia in 1998, killing dozens and leaving hundreds homeless the vice president toured damaged regions by helicopter, promising the locals that the federal government would do all it could to help in the recovery and rebuilding efforts.[32] In 1999 Gore visited Madison County, Tennessee, where tornadoes had touched down and his mother and other relatives lived.[33]

Of course there were the "standard" ceremonies that Gore, like all politicians (including the president), was obligated to attend. This included a ceremony marking the end of the U.S., French, and British military presence in Berlin in 1994.[35] In 1995 he "honored victims and survivors of the Holocaust during a commencement speech yesterday at the Jewish Theological Seminary of America" in New York City[36] and with fifty other world leaders a banquet held by Queen Elizabeth II saluting all those who helped defeat fascism in World War II.[37] In 1997 Gore spoke at the annual awards ceremony of the National Gay and Lesbian Task Force[38] and broke ground on a memorial to the victims of the Oklahoma City bombing in that city in 1998.[39]

In his diplomatic role Gore's predecessor Quayle had largely been confined to ceremonial contributions. This was not the case for Gore, who played an active and significant role in the crafting of foreign policy for the Clinton administration. In part this was the result of President Clinton's focus on domestic policy and Secretary of State Warren Christopher's focus on the Middle East. Clinton also seemed to be allowing Gore to burnish his foreign policy record in preparation for a presidential bid of his own.

Gore made his first major trip abroad after only three months in office, when he traveled to Poland on the occasion of the fiftieth anniversary of the Warsaw ghetto uprising. His two-day visit included a meeting with Polish President Lech Walesa, addressing the Polish Parliament, talking with environmental leaders, and joining "Israeli Prime Minister, Yitzhak Rabin, and Mr. Walesa at a ceremony attended by thousands of foreigners and hundreds of Holocaust survivors at the ghetto monument."[40] Later that year he was in Mexico to discuss the implementation of the recently passed North American Free Trade Agreement (NAFTA).[41] Foreign travel in 1994 included attending the inauguration of South African President Nelson Mandela[42] and addressing government leaders on the occasion of a 109-nation trade agreement reached in the Uruguay Round of negotiations under the General Agreement on Tariffs and Trade (GATT) in Morocco.[43]

In subsequent years Gore was responsible for handling bilateral relations with a number of countries (e.g., South Africa, Egypt, the Ukraine) on issues ranging from trade, technology transfer, and economic development.[44] In 1997 he was in Beijing to "underscore Washington's enthusiasm for expanding trade with China" by appearing at the signing of two deals between the Chinese government and American firms, "including a purchase by the Chinese of five Boeing 777 jetliners for $685 million."[45] He also made a last-minute appearance in Japan that year to help push through an agreement on the Kyoto Protocols, despite the fact that he and Clinton knew the treaty had no chance of passing in the Senate.[46] In 1998 Gore excited controversy among Asian nations by using a speech at the annual Asia-Pacific Economic Cooperation summit "to urge democratic reforms in the wake of the arrest and jailing two months [previous of Malaysian prime minister Mahathir Mohamad's] longtime second-in-command, Anwar Ibrahim."[47]

Most of Gore's diplomatic activity throughout his tenure was devoted to relations with Russia. During President Clinton's first meeting with Russian President Boris Yeltsin in spring 1993 he gave Gore responsibility for managing relations between the two countries. To this end the two presidents established a "U.S.-Russia Commission on Economic and Technical Cooperation" which was to be "co-chaired by Gore and Russian Prime Minister Viktor Chernomyrdin." The group, which came to be known as the "Gore-Chernomyrdin Commission," was originally tasked with promoting "cooperation between Russia and the United States on issues of space exploration, energy, trade and business development, defense conversion, science and technology, health, agriculture, and [the] environment." However their agenda soon came to include the full range of issues included in U.S.–Russia relations.[48]

In total the commission met eleven times, often twice a year, including several times under the various prime ministers Yeltsin appointed after Chernomyrdin (Sergei Kirienko, Yenvgeny Primakov, and Sergei Stepashin).[49] Meetings alternated between Washington and Russia,[50] and Gore also met with Yeltsin himself on occasion.[51] The meetings with Chernomyrdin included agreements on partnership in the international space station program, the expansion of the North Atlantic Treaty Organization (NATO),[52] nuclear disarmament concerns, religious freedom, plutonium production, the withdrawal of Russian troops from Kosovo, and more.[53]

On the political front Gore was no less valuable. One of the reasons Clinton selected Gore was because of his experience in Washington. Eight years in the House of Representative and eight years in the Senate made Gore a good choice to help the president navigate his way through the corridors of power in the capitol, especially in Congress. Like many vice presidents, Gore served as Clinton's main liaison to party leaders (especially Democratic Party leaders) in each chamber. In this he was assisted by his long-time legislative aide from his days in the Senate, Goody Marshall, the son former Supreme Court Justice Thurgood Marshall. As "deputy counsel and legislative director" for the vice president, Goody worked as "Gore's personal lobbyist, assisting the White House in the care and feeding of Congress."[54] His assistance was invaluable and included helping the administration persuade Congress to pass NAFTA.

In 1994, congressional Republicans experienced a historic triumph in the midterm elections, regaining control of both houses of Congress for the first time in decades. Republicans, led by House Speaker Newt Gingrich, were quite public with their own policy prescriptions, at times threatening to overshadow the president's. It was in this context that Clinton relied on Gore to help build public support for his various policy proposals. Gore was quite vocal in pushing the president's agenda throughout his tenure. For example while the administration tried to build congressional support (from both parties) for NAFTA, Gore took to the airwaves to debate 1992 independent presidential candidate Perot on *Larry King Live* about the issue. Most agree that his performance helped change the dynamics of the public debate about the issue.[55]

Gore also spoke publicly in favor of the administration's 1994 proposed version of a federal "three strikes and you're out" crime bill, designed for "serious repeat offenders for whom life sentences make sense."[56] In some cases his public rhetoric was leveled at Republican proposals. In 1995 Gore "leveled a blistering attack on" the Republican push to pass the Telecommunications Act by suggesting that it promoted the interests of corporations rather than average citizens.[57] In other cases his attacks were more generic. In one speech in 1995 he railed against right-wing extremism, claiming that "House Speaker, Newt Gingrich, was controlled by right-wing extremists and that he and Senator Bob Dole were directing a Congress that pandered to environmental polluters and was trying to cut antidrug programs in the crime bill and Federal money for college loans as well as billions from Medicare to underwrite tax cuts for the wealthy."[58] In the wake of mass shootings in Seattle and Honolulu in 1999 he challenged Republicans to approve a tougher gun control bill.[59]

It should be noted that some of Gore's public political activity was likely designed and executed with an eye toward a run for the presidency in 2000. Gore became, among other things, the chief spokesperson for the administration on his signature issues such as the environment and science and technology.[60] In a speech at the Massachusetts Institute of Technology in 1998 he introduced his vision of a satellite that would "beam back sun-washed images of the whole Earth . . . that would show storm systems and forest fires and cloud formations in real time, a channel devoted to all Earth, all the time.[61] That same year he announced an "Electronic Bill of Rights" that would "help insure the privacy of consumers' medical records, Internet transactions and other computerized personal data."[62] Gore also (famously) pushed for the continued development of the Internet.

Of course Gore was also an integral part of the 1996 Clinton–Gore reelection effort. A significant part of his contribution was fund-raising. In total he raised almost nine million dollars and held better than three dozen different fund-raising events. Unfortunately he became embroiled in two separate controversies surrounding his fund-raising activity. The first concerned allegations that he and his former chief of staff placed phone calls soliciting funds from his office in the White House. The calls, made to potential $25,000 or more donors, were made at the request of the Democratic National Committee.[63] Technically this was a violation of the 1882 Pendleton Act making it illegal for federal employees to raise or accept funds inside a federal building.[64] A second allegation concerned a trip to a Buddhist temple in California where illegal campaign contributions were made. The Justice Department eventually determined Gore was not culpable in either case. But combined with accusations from various sources that Gore "had been heavy-handed in his pitches for money," the overall impression created was not favorable. A cloud hung over Clinton's reelection effort—and Gore's 2000 presidential election campaign—as a result.[65]

Gore's vice presidential opponent in 1996 was Jack Kemp, a former member of the House, and Secretary of Housing and Urban Development under President George H. W. Bush. Kemp had criticized presidential nominee Bob Dole's economic policies and had previously endorsed another candidate during the Republican primaries. However, he agreed to run with Dole and subsequently played down their policy differences.[66] Dole, a moderate-conservative, looked to Kemp as a more conservative candidate in part to avert an insurgency by the religious right. In addition Kemp balanced Dole's style. "Kemp . . . was energetic and visionary where Dole was laconic and pragmatic, smiling and articulate where Dole was dour and cryptic."[67] However, Kemp seemed less than enthusiastic on the campaign trail, disappointing Dole as well as party leaders.[68] This likely had something to do with his reported reluctance to act as Dole's "Agnew," a reference to one of the penultimate vice presidential hit men.[69]

Both candidates appeared to take debate preparation seriously. Gore arrived in St. Petersburg, Florida, five days before the vice presidential debate. He conducted four 90-minute mock debates with former House Representative Thomas Downey. Kemp arrived a day later and held three mock debates with the Republican Senator Judd Gregg.[70] The debate itself was hardly memorable, especially considering that Clinton held a comfortable lead over Dole. The consensus was that Gore bested Kemp, and public opinion agreed. One poll reported that 53 percent of viewers thought Gore won as opposed to 41 percent for Kemp.[71]

Perhaps the most important political activity Gore engaged in during his time in office was his steadfast support of the president during the Lewinsky scandal and Clinton's subsequent impeachment. Gore repeatedly attested to Clinton's veracity and urged a "do-nothing" Congress and the American people to focus on "issues more important to the American people."[72] This support was often expressed as Gore energetically campaigned for fellow Democrats for the 1998 midterm elections.[73]

Finally, Gore played an important advisory role in major policy and key appointment decisions in the Clinton administration. Before taking office the vice president secured a formal, written agreement from Clinton defining his duties and responsibilities.[74] The terms of this agreement established that Gore and Clinton would meet weekly for lunch, that Gore would have a say in key presidential appointments, and more. It also helped that Gore and Clinton got along well with each other and were simpatico with respect to most policy issues. Accounts of the Gore vice presidency suggest that he was integral to the Clinton administration and was included in most major decisions made by the White House during his tenure.[75]

One illustration of the influence Gore had was the appointment of various friends, supporters, and staffers to cabinet positions, White House posts, and chairs of other executive agencies.[76] In spring 1993, after several missteps and public relations blunders by the administration, Gore was responsible for bringing David Gergen, Washington insider and former adviser to Presidents Nixon, Gerald Ford, and Ronald Reagan, into the administration.[77] Shortly after the Clinton administration took over, Gore, along with others, successfully pushed for deficit cutting as a necessary economic policy.[78] The vice president's influence on policy was reflected in the independence Clinton gave him with respect to foreign policy (and relations with Russia, in particular). It was Gore that persuaded Clinton to allow former President Jimmy Carter to go to North Korea in 1994 (albeit as a private citizen) to try and ease tensions with Kim Il Sung over their nuclear program and to Haiti in an attempt to further a regime change.[79] Gore's influence was also evident in the adoption of environmental and science and technology policies and projects that he held dear.

Often Gore's contributions came in the form of quiet advice that helped shaped debate, reinforce the president's position, or support him when he seemed to vacillate. In 1995 the NATO response to the violence in Bosnia-Herzegovina was stymied by Serbian use of United Nations' peacekeepers as human shields during bombing raids. As the president's advisors debated a vigorous response it was Gore who framed the discussion in terms of human tragedy. His narrative resulted in an outcome that integrated military bombings with diplomatic discussions that included all parties.[80] During the 1995–1996 budget battle, Gore helped Clinton remain steadfast, and at one point contacted the major TV networks to arrange for Clinton to appear during prime time and explain that his own budget plan was a superior alternative to that of his Republican congressional opponents.[81] Gore was also instrumental in helping the president overcome personal misgivings about the welfare reform act of 1996.[82]

This is not to say that the relationship between Gore and Clinton was without problems. As noted in chapter 6, public accounts of Gore prodding Clinton during times of indecision caused the two to be more circumspect with each other when in the company of others. Subsequent to the 1994 election, when Republicans took control of Congress, Gore's star seemed to rise, at least relative to Clinton's. Rumors began circulating that Gore would replace Clinton as the nominee in 1996. To protect his position as valued adviser, Gore quickly dispelled these rumors.[83] As the second term began Gore was relied on more heavily, at least in part because of Clinton's loss of close adviser Dick Morris. And, although their professional relationship remained solid through the end of their terms, their personal relationship suffered enormously as the result of the fact that Gore (like others) felt betrayed by Clinton with regard to the Lewinsky affair.

EVALUATING THE GORE VICE PRESIDENCY

Martin Van Buren and George H. W. Bush are the only two sitting vice presidents in the post-Twelfth Amendment era to have sought and won the presidency. The problems associated with assuming that the vice presidency is a natural stepping stone to the presidency are so well known that it has a name: the "Van Buren Jinx."[84]

This said, Gore seemed to have been better positioned than any incumbent vice president in recent memory to win the presidency. By 2000 he was a two-term vice president, selected because he was ideologically similar to his president. In addition, President Clinton continued to enjoy approval ratings in the low-60 percent range throughout his term, this despite his impeachment. On top of this, the economy was enjoying a period of almost unprecedented growth. All of this was Gore's to capitalize on, especially because it was understood from the beginning of his term that he was Clinton's chosen "successor." And, unlike many past presidents, Clinton enthusiastically endorsed Gore's candidacy. Finally, Gore had been actively building his campaign organization for several years.

The vice president faced a surprisingly strong early primary challenge from Senator Bill Bradley but prevailed fairly easily. His campaign suffered from some organizational difficulties, and as it progressed, image problems as well. In particular, he seemed to have some difficulty finding "which" Gore to present to the public. Was he, for example, a policy wonk extraordinaire or a populist man of the people? He attempted to instill some warmth into his sometimes wooden image with his on-stage kiss of wife Tipper during the Democratic convention. His aggressive style in the first debate was parodied in *Saturday Night Live,* and in the second debate he seemed to be a different (more laid back) Gore. His image problems, in fact, are well illustrated by the title of one of his biographies: *Inventing Al Gore.*[85] But his biggest difficulty probably lay in defining himself in relation to the president.

This, in truth, is the major problem all vice presidents face in their campaign for the White House. An incumbent vice president is well positioned to be rewarded for the success of the administration. This forces a vice president to run, to some degree, on the record of the administration. However there is a down side to this strategy. To align oneself too closely with the administration risks creating the perception that it was the president, not the vice president, who should receive credit. Moreover, with the credit that comes with success comes blame for failure. In other words, incumbent vice presidents face an excruciatingly fine balancing act: to align oneself close enough to get a boost from the administration's success without being tainted with its failures.[86] Alternatively, in the case of an unpopular administration, one can attempt to distance oneself from the president, but this runs the risk of appearing disloyal, a violation of the cardinal rule of the modern vice presidency.

Thus, in 1968, Humphrey found it impossible to disentangle himself from Lyndon Johnson's Vietnam policy. In 1988, Bush had to work hard to establish himself as his own man, and not just a Reagan lackey. In 2000, the Lewinsky scandal was the elephant in the living room, so to speak, of the Gore campaign. One of the main reasons Gore chose Joe Lieberman as his running mate was to distance himself from Clinton's character problems. Gore also tried to establish himself as his own man. The result, in the eyes of most observers, was that he put too much distance between himself and Clinton, and thus could not fully reap the electoral rewards of the popular president's administration. In fact, he refused to let Clinton become actively involved in the campaign. In the end, Gore won the popular vote but lost the Electoral College vote (271 to 266) after a thirty-seven-day postelection struggle that ended up in the U.S. Supreme Court.[87]

His eventual loss of the presidency notwithstanding, the fact remains that Gore won the popular vote in the national election totals. This suggests that minor image problems during the campaign aside, he remained a fairly popular figure. His loss of the presidency should not detract from an evaluation of how he performed as vice president.

Gore was, in a real sense, a true governing partner as vice president. Perhaps more than any other vice president in history (including his two successors) he was granted autonomy for the direction of various public policies. This can be seen most clearly in foreign affairs in his working relationship with Russian prime ministers and in environmental and science and technology policy. Although Clinton retained the final say, it seems to have largely been Gore setting the tone in these policy areas. More than this Gore contributed advice in other policy areas as well, in addition to acting as a sounding board and source of support for the president.

Of course in retrospect it is easy to see that many of his actions were designed to better position himself for a run for the presidency in 2000. This does not detract from the fact that up to that point he was the most active and influential vice president ever. He had a large and impressive staff working to develop ideas and who were answerable only to him. Gore truly was a governing partner with Clinton. And in a real sense, his vice presidency helped make the Dick Cheney vice presidency possible.

NOTES

1. James Ceaser and Andrew Busch, *Upside Down and Inside Out the 1992 Elections and American Politics* (Lanham, MD: Rowman & Littlefield, 1993).

2. Bill Turque, *Inventing Al Gore: A Biography* (Boston: Houghton Mifflin, 2000), 245–46.

3. Natoli, *American Prince, American Pauper*, 22, 30, 44–45; Goldstein, *The Modern American Vice Presidency*, 82; Polsby and Wildavsky, *Presidential Elections*, 131; Turque, *Inventing Al Gore*, 248.

4. S. Robert Lichter, Jody C Baumgartner, and Jonathan S. Morris, *Politics Is a Joke! How TV Comedians Are Remaking Political Life* (Boulder: Westview, 2014).

5. Richard E. Neustadt," "Vice Presidents as National Leaders: Past, Present, and Future," in *At the President's Side: The Vice Presidency in the Twentieth Century*, Timothy Walch, ed. (Columbia: University of Missouri, 1997), 186; Pika, "The Vice Presidency," 507; Turque, *Inventing Al Gore*, 254.

6. Jack Germond and Jules Witcover, *Mad as Hell: Revolt at the Ballot Box* (New York: Warner Books, 1993), 398, 419.

7. Turque, *Inventing Al Gore*, 258–59.

8. L. Patrick Devlin, "The 1992 Gore-Quayle-Stockdale Vice Presidential Debate," in *Rhetorical Studies of National Political Debates—1992*, Robert V. Friedenberg, ed. 2nd ed. (Westport, CT: Praeger, 1994), 212–15.

9. Elaine S. Povich, "Senate Backs Clinton on Gays," *Chicago Tribune*, February 5, 1993. Available at http://articles.chicagotribune.com/1993-02-05/news/930317 5856_1_standby-reserve-status-avowed-homosexuals-two-democrats.

10. Newsweek Staff, "The Record: Gore as a Tie Breaker," *Newsweek.Com*, October 31, 2000. Available at www.newsweek.com/record-gore-tie-breaker-157071.

11. "Gore Consults Democrats on Role in Impeachment Trial," BaltimoreSun.com, December 26, 1998. Available at http://articles.baltimoresun.com/1998-12-26/news/1998360011_1_gore-senate-impeachment-trial.

12. James Kuhnhenn, "Gore Presides over Official Confirmation of Bush's Win," *Philly.Com*, January 7, 2001. Available at http://articles.philly.com/2001-01-07/news/25311670_1_electoral-votes-al-gore-electoral-college.

13. Ibid.

14. Pika, "The Vice Presidency," 502.

15. Newsweek Staff, "The Record: Gore as a Tie Breaker," *Newsweek.Com*, October 31, 2000. Available at www.newsweek.com/record-gore-tie-breaker-157071.

16. Bob Franken, "Senate Passes Juvenile Crime Bill", CNN. Com, May 21, 1999 www.cnn.com/ALLPOLITICS/stories/1999/05/20/gun.control/.

17. "Albert Arnold Gore, Jr. 45th Vice President: 1993–2001" (Senate Historical Office, available at www.senate.gov, no date); Turque, *Inventing Al Gore*, 278.

18. Hite, *Second Best*, 160.

19. Carey Goldberg, "Thousands Pay Tribute to Rabin and Listen to Appeals for Unity," *New York Times*, December 11, 1995. Available at www.nytimes.com/1995/12/11/nyregion/thousands-pay-tribute-to-rabin-and-listen-to-appeals-for-unity.html.

20. Peter Steinfels, "Chicago, Joined by an Array of Dignitaries, Bids Farewell to Cardinal Bernardin," *New York Times*, November 21, 1996. Available at www.nytimes.com/1996/11/21/us/chicago-joined-by-an-array-of-dignitaries-bids-farewell-to-cardinal-bernardin.html.

21. Warren Allen Smith, "The Carl Sagan Memorial Service," *Skeptical Inquirer*, Volume 21(4), July/August 1997. Available at www.csicop.org/si/show/carl_sagan_memorial_service/.

22. James Brooke, "Terror in Littleton: The Service," *New York Times*, April 26, 1999. Available at www.nytimes.com/1999/04/26/us/terror-in-littleton-the-service-70000-mourn-in-quiet-tears-song-and-rain.html.

23. Andrew L. Wright, "Politicians, Friends Attend Funeral for 'Tip' O'Neill," *Harvard Crimson*, January 12, 1994. Available at www.thecrimson.com/article/1994/1/12/politicians-friends-attend-funeral-for-tip/.

24. "Funeral for Les Aspin," *New York Times*, May 27, 1995. Available at www.nytimes.com/1995/05/27/us/funeral-for-les-aspin.html.

25. Don Terry, "Los Angeles Honors Legacy of Tom Bradley," *New York Times*, October 6, 1998. Available at www.nytimes.com/1998/10/06/us/los-angeles-honors-legacy-of-tom-bradley.html.

26. "Abzug Memorial Service," *New York Times*, April 2, 1998. Available at www.nytimes.com/1998/04/02/nyregion/abzug-memorial-service.html.

27. "Funeral Tuesday for Al Gore's Father," *CNN.Com*, December 7, 1998. Available at www.cnn.com/ALLPOLITICS/stories/1998/12/07/gore.senior/.

28. "The Midwest Flooding," *New York Times*, July 12, 1993. Available at www.nytimes.com/1993/07/12/us/the-midwest-flooding-gore-plans-visit-to-flood-area.html.

29. Robyn Meredith, "In Ohio River Valley, the Water's Edge Is Now Its Middle," *New York Times*, March 6, 1997. Available at www.nytimes.com/1997/03/06/us/in-ohio-river-valley-the-water-s-edge-is-now-its-middle.html.

30. Dirk Johnson, "In Fight against the River, A Victory in North Dakota," *New York Times*, April 12, 1997. Available at www.nytimes.com/1997/04/12/us/in-fight-against-the-river-a-victory-in-north-dakota.html.

31. Pam Belluck, "23 Dead or Missing as Storms Rage in East and the Midwest," *New York Times*, June 30, 1998. Available at www.nytimes.com/1998/06/30/us/23-dead-or-missing-as-storms-rage-in-east-and-the-midwest.html.

32. Rick Bragg, "Siren Was the Same but Not the Storm," *New York Times*, April 11, 1998. Available at www.nytimes.com/1998/04/11/us/siren-was-the-same-but-not-the-storm.html.

33. Emily Yellin, "Tornadoes Hit Tennessee, Killing 8 and Injuring 105," *New York Times*, January 19, 1999. Available at www.nytimes.com/1999/01/19/us/tornadoes-hit-tennessee-killing-8-and-injuring-105.html.

34. Jacques Steinberg, "In Ceremony of Remembrance, Reminders of Human Courage," *New York Times*, April 19, 1993. Available at www.nytimes.com/1993/04/19/nyregion/in-ceremony-of-remembrance-reminders-of-human-courage.html.

35. Stephen Kinzer, "Allied Soldiers March to Say Farewell to Berlin," *New York Times*, June 19, 1994. Available at www.nytimes.com/1994/06/19/world/allied-soldiers-march-to-say-farewell-to-berlin.html.

36. "Commencements," *New York Times*, May 19, 1995. Available at www.nytimes.com/1995/05/19/nyregion/commencements-words-to-live-by-music-to-dance-by.html.

37. "In V-E Day Ceremony, British Monarch Calls for Reconciliation," *New York Times*, May 7, 1995. Available at www.nytimes.com/1995/05/07/world/in-v-e-day-ceremony-british-monarch-calls-for-reconciliation.html.

38. "Vice President Vows to Support Gay Issues," *New York Times*, September 16, 1997. Available at www.nytimes.com/1997/09/16/us/vice-president-vows-to-support-gay-issues.html.

39. Michael Janofsky, "Breaking Ground for a Memorial in Oklahoma," *New York Times*, October 26, 1998. Available at www.nytimes.com/1998/10/26/us/breaking-ground-for-a-memorial-in-oklahoma.html.

40. Jane Perlez, "Gore Congratulates Poland on Its Democracy," *New York Times*, April 21, 1993. Available at www.nytimes.com/1993/04/21/world/gore-congratulates-poland-on-its-democracy.html.

41. Scott W. Rager, "Albert Arnold Gore, Jr. (b. 1948)," in *Vice Presidents: A Biographical Dictionary*, ed. L. Edward Purcell (New York: Checkmark Books, 2001), 405–6.

42. Paul Kengor. *Wealth Layer or Policy Player? The Vice President's Role in Foreign Policy*. (Lanham, MD: Lexington Books, 2000).

43. Alan Riding, "109 Nations Sign Trade Agreement," *New York Times*, April 16, 1994. Available at www.nytimes.com/1994/04/16/business/109-nations-sign-trade-agreement.html.

44. Singular, *Joe Lieberman*, 95; Turque, *Inventing Al Gore*, 277.

45. James Bennet, "Gore Witnesses Boeing-China Deal," *New York Times*, March 25, 1997. Available at www.nytimes.com/1997/03/25/world/gore-witnesses-boeing-china-deal.html.

46. "Albert A. Gore, Jr., 45th Vice President (1993–2001)," Senate.Gov, no date. Available at www.senate.gov/artandhistory/history/common/generic/VP_Albert_Gore.htm.

47. Bob Drogin, "Gore Gets Scolding from APEC, Business Leaders," *Los Angeles Times*, November 18, 1998. Available at http://articles.latimes.com/1998/nov/18/news/mn-44145.

48. Members of the Speaker's Advisory Group on Russia, United States House of Representatives 106th Congress. "Russia's Road to Corruption: How the Clinton Administration Exported Government Instead of Free Enterprise and Failed

the Russian People," Federation of American Scientists, September, 2000. Available at http://fas.org/news/russia/2000/russia/part05.htm. Chapter 5.

49. Members of the Speaker's Advisory Group on Russia, "Russia's Road to Corruption."

50. Turque, *Inventing Al Gore*, 277.

51. Reuters, "Al Gore Meets in Moscow with Russian Premier," *New York Times*, July 15, 1996. Available at www.nytimes.com/1996/07/15/world/world-news-briefs-al-gore-meets-in-moscow-with-russian-premier.html.

52. Reuters, "Al Gore Meets in Moscow with Russian Premier," *New York Times*, July 15, 1996. Available at www.nytimes.com/1996/07/15/world/world-news-briefs-al-gore-meets-in-moscow-with-russian-premier.html.

53. Michael R. Gordon, "Gore in Russia, Hoping to Be Cast in a Different Light," *New York Times*, September 22, 1997. Available at www.nytimes.com/1997/09/22/world/gore-in-russia-hoping-to-be-cast-in-a-different-light.html; Members of the Speaker's Advisory Group on Russia, "Russia's Road to Corruption."

54. Paul F. Horvitz, "Schmoozing His Way through the Corridors of Power," *New York Times*, November 15, 1993. Available at www.nytimes.com/1993/11/15/news/15iht-horup.html.

55. Rager, "Albert Arnold Gore, Jr. (b. 1948)," 406.

56. Gwen Ifill, "White House Offers Version of Three-Strikes Crime Bill," *New York Times*, March 2, 1994. Available at www.nytimes.com/1994/03/02/us/white-house-offers-version-of-three-strikes-crime-bill.html.

57. Mark Landler, "Gore Assails Bill to Revise Telecommunications Laws," *New York Times*, September 13, 1995. Available at www.nytimes.com/1995/09/13/business/gore-assails-bill-to-revise-telecommunications-laws.html.

58. Robert Hanley, "In Hudson County, Gore Calls Republican Congress Extreme," *New York Times*, October 18, 1995. Available at www.nytimes.com/1995/10/18/nyregion/in-hudson-county-gore-calls-republican-congress-extreme.html.

59. Eric Schmitt, "Gore Calls on Republicans To Pass a Gun Control Bill," *New York Times*, November 5, 1999. Available at www.nytimes.com/1999/11/05/us/gore-calls-on-republicans-to-pass-a-gun-control-bill.html.

60. Rager, "Albert Arnold Gore, Jr. (b. 1948)," 406.

61. Katharine Q. Seelye, "Gore Proposes Video Channel to Show Earth, All the Time," *New York Times*, March 14, 1998. Available at www.nytimes.com/1998/03/14/us/gore-proposes-video-channel-to-show-earth-all-the-time.html.

62. John M. Broder, "Gore to Announce 'Electronic Bill of Rights' Aimed at Privacy," *New York Times*, May 14, 1998. Available at www.nytimes.com/1998/05/14/us/gore-to-announce-electronic-bill-of-rights-aimed-at-privacy.html.

63. Leslie Wayne, "Gore's Calls to Big Donors Number 86, Papers Show," *New York Times*, August 27, 1997. Available at www.nytimes.com/1997/08/27/us/gore-s-calls-to-big-donors-number-86-papers-show.html.

64. Turque, *Inventing Al Gore*, 299, 319, 322.

65. Ibid.

66. Larry J. Sabato, "The Conventions: One Festival of Hope, One Celebration of Impending Victory," in *Toward the Millennium: The Elections of 1996*, Larry J. Sabata, ed. (Needham Heights, MA: Allyn & Bacon, 1997), 31.

67. Michael Nelson, "The Election: Turbulence and Tranquility in Contemporary American Politics," in *The Elections of 1996*, Michael Nelson, ed. (Washington, D.C.: Congress Quarterly, 1997), 68–69.

68. Nelson, "The Election," 69; Southwick, *Presidential Also-Rans and Running Mates, 1788–1996*.

69. Gaut Ragsdale, "The 1996 Gore-Kemp Vice Presidential Debates," in *Rhetorical Studies of National Political Debates—1996*, Robert V. Friedenberg, ed. (Westport, CT: Praeger, 1997), 49.

70. Ragsdale, "The 1996 Gore-Kemp Vice Presidential Debates," 32–33.

71. Ragsdale, "The 1996 Gore-Kemp Vice Presidential Debates," 54, 57.

72. Michael Janofsky, "Gore Attacks Republicans on Impeachment Steps," *New York Times*, October 13, 1998. Available at www.nytimes.com/1998/10/13/us/gore-attacks-republicans-on-impeachment-steps.html.

73. Michael Janofsky, "Necessity Bridges Gulf between Gore and Gephardt," *New York Times*, October 17, 1998. Available at www.nytimes.com/1998/10/17/us/necessity-bridges-gulf-between-gore-and-gephardt.html.

74. Turque, *Inventing Al Gore*, 266–67

75. Troy Gipson, *From Carthage to Oslo,* (Mr. Troy Gipson, 2012), 109.

76. Rager, "Albert Arnold Gore, Jr. (b. 1948)," 405; Singular, *Joe Lieberman*, 97; Turque, *Inventing Al Gore*, 267–68.

77. Turque, *Inventing Al Gore*, 274.

78. Ibid., 270.

79. Ibid., 275–76.

80. Ibid., 300–301.

81. Ibid., 292–94.

82. Ibid., 306–308.

83. Turque, Ibid., 290–91.

84. See George S. Sirgiovanni, "The "Van Buren Jinx": Vice Presidents Need Not Beware," *Presidential Studies Quarterly* (1988) 18: 61–77; Marie D. Natoli, "The Vice Presidency: Stepping Stone or Stumbling Block?" *Presidential Studies Quarterly* (1988) 18: 77–79.

85. Turque, *Inventing Al Gore*.

86. Polsby and Wildavsky, *Presidential Elections*, 81.

87. Ceaser and Busch, *The Perfect Tie*.

8

Dick Cheney:
George W. Bush's
Loyal Lieutenant

The vice presidency of Richard "Dick" Cheney (2001–2009) was easily the most controversial in recent memory. He was criticized by many for the various policies he advocated, his secretive manner, his penchant to go around standard bureaucratic procedures, and for presumably exercising undue influence over the president. Ignoring for the moment any normative considerations, this chapter attempts to cut through some of this criticism, suggesting that Cheney was fulfilling a modern vice president's most basic function, that of loyal lieutenant.

The discussion will be organized similar to those in previous chapters, focusing first on Cheney's selection as vice presidential nominee and the campaign of 2000. Next, we will examine his tenure in office, looking at both formal and informal duties. Although Cheney was one of the most influential vice presidents in history, his influence seemed to wane during his second term.

SELECTION AND THE CAMPAIGN OF 2000

George W. Bush's selection of Washington D.C. veteran Cheney was applauded by many as a way to add some needed experience to the presidential ticket. Before becoming vice president Cheney had been an accomplished career politician who had served as a member of the White House staff under Presidents Richard Nixon and Gerald Ford, and for a time as Ford's Chief of Staff. In 1978 he was elected to the U.S. House of Representatives, where he served a total of five terms. Subsequently,

Cheney was Secretary of Defense under George H. W. Bush (1989–1993). In 1995, following his career in public life he became chairman and CEO of the Halliburton Corporation. And although he briefly flirted with the idea of running for president in 1996, he seemed content to remain in the private sector. It was certainly not his intention to become vice president. Like many veteran politicians Cheney viewed the vice presidency as a political black hole and had no interest in being trapped there.

When George W. Bush decided to run for president he began consulting with several of his father's former advisers, including Cheney, about various policy issues. The two had known each other since Cheney's time as the elder Bush's Secretary of Defense. Although they were not close, Cheney had donated to the younger Bush's campaign for governor of Texas in 1994. After Bush's election the two "met occasionally at the governor's mansion, discussing a wide range of subjects. These meetings made business sense for Cheney, whose political insights benefitted the ambitious but less experienced Bush. After Bush's reelection in 1998 Cheney (working in Texas) was invited to Austin with other experts to discuss national security policy. Their visits became more frequent as Bush ramped up his presidential bid."[1] It is safe to assume that it was during these meetings that Bush's trust of Cheney developed and grew.

Cheney became involved in Bush's presidential campaign effort early on. After Bush secured the nomination he probed Cheney about his interest in possibly becoming his running mate. Cheney expressed no interest but did agree to head the search for a running mate.[2] Several people had begun to position themselves for the nomination. Elizabeth Dole, for example, was quite active in stumping for Bush after her own bid for the presidential nomination ended. Her husband, Bob Dole, sang her praises and made it known she was available as a running mate. Pennsylvania Governor Tom Ridge campaigned for Bush and was also able to bring the Republican national convention to Philadelphia in 2000, presumably helping his chances of being selected.[3]

It is a matter of speculation as to whether Cheney used his position to "campaign" for the nomination. According to critics, Bush was led to the decision to pick Cheney by the latter's elimination of others. If this was the case Cheney's "method" of campaigning for the job was the epitome of subtlety. Both Bush and Cheney were present in interviews with potential candidates (e.g., John McCain, John Danforth, Fred Thompson, Ridge) where Cheney naturally challenged each. Moreover, it is likely that Cheney's presence interfered with Bush's ability to test how well he might personally work other potential individuals.

It should be noted that at the time, Cheney was registered to vote in Texas, the same state as Bush. This meant that he was not eligible to be on the ticket with Bush because the Constitution stipulates that the presidential and vice presidential candidate must come from different states. Therefore, he changed his voter registration to Wyoming, which made him eligible. In late July, Bush announced that while meeting with Cheney "it dawned on him that 'the best candidate might be sitting next to me.'"[4]

In one sense, the selection of Cheney went against the grain. He was from the same ideological wing of the party as Bush, and selecting him would only bring Wyoming's three Electoral College votes (which Bush could undoubtedly have won on his own) to the ticket. However selecting him helped blunt criticism about Bush's lack of national governing experience.[5] In the end Bush asked him to be on the ticket and Cheney accepted, but not without some stipulations.[6] It was agreed in advance that if elected, Cheney would have a meaningful role in the administration, although specifics in this regard were not discussed.

The choice of Cheney was a bit problematic at first. Although he had a good record in government service, when the spotlight was turned on other aspects of his background a few troublesome facts came to light. He had a DWI in the 1960s, had not voted in many years, and had passed bad checks through the Capital bank in the 1980s. Moreover, the severance package he received from his former employer (the energy giant Halliburton) was quite generous, raising questions about a potential conflict of interest. He also seemed less than prepared for scrutiny of his ultraconservative congressional voting record. He subsequently decided to give up the severance package, and none of the other issues seemed to have any durability after the initial flurry of attention they received.[7]

On the Democratic side, Energy Secretary Bill Richardson seemed to be to positioning himself for the vice presidential nomination as early as October 1999. This he did by traveling to New Hampshire to help Vice President Al Gore prepare to debate Bill Bradley, his only challenger for the Democratic presidential nomination. What made this conspicuous was the fact that Richardson flew around the globe on two different occasions (from India and London) to do so. Senator John Kerry was also fairly aggressive in his attempt to secure the vice presidential nomination by stumping for Gore in the early primary states and making policy-oriented speeches to get noticed by Gore.[8]

In the end Gore chose "the upright and conspicuously pious" Joseph Lieberman. A two-term senator from Connecticut who had previously served thirteen years in the Connecticut State Senate, Lieberman had been the first Democratic senator to publicly and strongly criticize President Bill Clinton for his behavior with Monica Lewinsky. His selection was made in part to distance Gore from the Clinton–Lewinsky scandals as well as deflect attention from questions about his unethical fund-raising practices.[9] Lieberman, the first Jewish candidate nominated for the vice presidency, was also selected in part to appeal to Jewish voters (another traditionally solid block of Democratic voters) in South Florida in the hopes it would make that state more competitive for Gore.[10]

Gore announced his selection of Lieberman roughly a week before the Democratic convention began, and press response was one of widespread approval. In fact Lieberman was considered by many to be a better strategic choice than Bush's choice of Cheney. Pundits reasoned that other Republicans could have added as much or more to the Bush campaign effort as Cheney, but few Democrats could have brought what Lieberman did to the Gore ticket.[11]

Cheney was quite energetic on the campaign trail in 2000, pushing so hard in the thirty-seven-day postelection period that on November 22 he suffered a mild heart attack. Both of Cheney's daughters (Liz Perry Cheney and Mary Cheney) were active in the campaign as well. One of the main tasks assigned to Lieberman was to court the high concentration of Jewish voters in South Florida. This is "precisely what he did, stalking the condominium precincts from Miami Beach to West Palm Beach while Jewish Democrats—sometimes weeping with joy at seeing one of their faith vying for the nation's second-highest office—treated him like a rock star."[12]

Cheney spent the days before the vice presidential debate in the congressional district of his debate partner, Republican Rob Portman.[13] Lieberman spent close to a week in rural Kentucky staging mock sessions with prominent Democratic lawyer Bob Barnett. The debate itself was rather subdued. "The two candidates engaged in a mild and friendly vice presidential debate. Sitting side by side it turned out to be more of a conversation than a debate." The lasting image was one of "two reasonable, concerned candidates enjoying a friendly and uncontentious discussion of their differences,"[14] although Lieberman may have expected a more aggressive Cheney and thus seemed slightly unprepared.[15] An ABC News poll showed that almost two-thirds of those surveyed had a favorable opinion of both candidates, but a majority also indicated that the vice presidential choice would not affect their vote.[16]

As Election Day went on, it became apparent that neither ticket had won the 270 Electoral College votes required to win. Attention turned to Florida, whose results were too close to call and whose twenty-five votes would tip the balance. After thirty-seven days of recounts in several counties and various court battles, the U.S. Supreme Court effectively ruled that the results, which had been previously certified by the Florida Secretary of State and awarded Bush all of Florida's Electoral College votes, should stand.[17] Thus, although the ticket of Gore–Lieberman won the popular vote, Bush and Cheney won 271 Electoral College votes. Cheney took office on January 20, 2001.

IN OFFICE: THE FORMAL VICE PRESIDENCY

Cheney was the first vice president to become temporary "acting president" under the provisions of the Twenty-Fifth Amendment. On June 29, 2002, President Bush temporarily transferred power to his vice president before undergoing a routine colonoscopy.[18] Bush did so again approximately five years later, in 2007.

To the delight of late-night comics and others who enjoy poking fun at vice presidents, Cheney was for a time at the center of another succession-related issue. Immediately following the attacks on the World Trade Center and the Pentagon on September 11, 2001, Bush and Cheney became concerned about the crisis that would result from the simultaneous deaths of the president, the vice president, the Speaker of the House of Representatives, and so on, in another attack. While there are clear-cut constitutional provisions for replacing the president and ensuring continuity of government, the fear was that in such an event the shock and grief would lead to a certain paralysis that was unacceptable in times of crisis. The president and vice president therefore concluded that when possible they should not be in the same place at the same time, and when they were together it was to be arranged discreetly. For a time Cheney was reported to be in a "secure undisclosed location," a phrase that political humorists and others seemed to enjoy tremendously. In reality this location alternated between Camp David, a bunker beneath the vice presidential residence, and his home in Wyoming. In addition, his schedule was distributed via secure methods and staff were not allowed to use his name or title when speaking on the phone and were to be ready to travel at a moment's notice in case it became necessary to evacuate the capital.[19]

Cheney was no exception to the modern era trend of vice presidents absenting themselves from the day-to-day business of the Senate. He rarely presided over the Senate. He did, however, cause a minor stir in this capacity. During a photo opportunity following a session of the Senate, Cheney got into a heated exchange with Vermont Senator Patrick Leahy over the former's ties to Halliburton and Bush's judicial nominees. Cheney ended the exchange with a well-publicized profanity.[20] Cheney also broke with tradition by inserting himself into Senate business in 2005 over the issue of judicial appointments and confirmations to the federal bench. The Democratic minority was refusing to bring a number of Bush's judicial selections to a vote, leading the Republican majority to begin discussions about amending Senate procedures by banning filibusters in such cases. Cheney publicly broke with Senate norms by announcing that he supported this move, referred to as the "nuclear option." As it happened, a compromise was reached and the action was unnecessary.[21]

Cheney took another action in his capacity as President of the Senate that was not only a bit controversial, but also broke the recent tradition of vice presidents backing the policies of their presidents. In 2008, the Court of Appeals for the District of Columbia Circuit ruled against a ban on handguns that was passed by the city of Washington, D.C. The case was subsequently brought before the Supreme Court, and the Court agreed to hear it. Bush's Justice Department filed an *amicus* brief asking the Supreme Court to send the case back to the lower courts on the basis that the Court of Appeals decision was too broad. However a majority of members of both houses (fifty-five senators, 250 members of the House) of Congress sent a brief supporting the lower court's decision and asking the Court to uphold it. Cheney also signed this brief, invoking his title as "President of the United States Senate." [22] Cheney's break with the administration drew some attention in the press, although Bush appears to have had no prior knowledge about it. And despite the fact that Bush aides questioned him about it, the "president never said a word" to him.[23] It did not, in other words, appear to create a rift between the two men.

Cheney presided over a closely divided Senate during his first term. In fact during his first four months in office the partisan makeup of the Senate was 50–50. However "in May of 2001 Vermont Republican Senator James Jeffords switched his party affiliation from Republican to independent and announced he would caucus with the Democrats. This [effectively] gave the Democrats a 51-49 majority."[24] Throughout the remainder of his first term neither party enjoyed more than a one or two seat advantage, meaning that Cheney's tie-breaking vote might have been necessary at any time. In the end he broke more tie votes than any vice president since Nixon, a total of eight during his time in office, with six during his first term. See table 8.1. Of the six that occurred in his first term, five concerned budget and tax matters that were considered to be important to the Bush administration.

Controversy also found Cheney with regard to his statutory membership in the National Security Council (NSC). Shorty after he and Bush took office there was a push, presumably headed by close Cheney aides, to have the vice president chair meetings of the Principals Committee (the statutory core group) of the NSC in Bush's absence. Although Dwight Eisenhower had established a precedent for such a practice, allowing Nixon to chair in his absence, in the past several decades this role has been reserved for the National Security Adviser, (in this case Condoleezza Rice). The push to allow Cheney to chair was presumably based on his previous experience as Secretary of Defense and the expectation that he would play a significant role in foreign policy for the new administration. Rice, however, objected, and took the issue to Bush, who agreed that she was the appropriate choice for the job. The move was seen as early

Table 8.1. Tie Votes Broken in the Senate by Dick Cheney, 2001–2008

Date	Legislation
April 3, 2001	Grassley Amendment 173 on bill for prescription drugs for seniors
April 5, 2001	Hutchison Amendment 347 on marriage penalty tax break
May 21, 2002	Motion to table Allen Amendment 3406 to provide mortgage assistance for employees who are separated from employment
April 11, 2003	Agreeing to House Budget Resolution 95 Conference report
May 15, 2003	Nickles Amendment 664 to modify the dividend exclusion provision
May 23, 2003	Jobs and economic growth H.R.2, to provide for reconciliation pursuant to section 201 of the concurrent resolution on the budget for fiscal year 2004
Dec. 21, 2005	Motion to concur in House Amendment with an amendment to S.1932 to provide for reconciliation of the concurrent resolution on the budget for fiscal year 2006
March 13, 2008	Motion to reconsider Senate Amendment 4189 to Senate Con. Res. 70, to repeal section 13203 of Omnibus Budget Reconciliation Act of 1993 by restoring Alternative Minimum Tax rates in effect before that time

From: "Votes to Break Ties in the Senate." The U.S Senate. Available at http://senate.gov/pagelayout/reference/four_column_table/Tie_Votes.htm.

evidence that Cheney was attempting to exert undue influence in the administration.[25]

Another source of controversy was that while being present at all NSC meetings (like modern-era vice presidents before him), Cheney may have been responsible for a certain dysfunction in the body. One possible reason given for this was his close relationship with Donald Rumsfeld, who had given Cheney his first job in Washington while the latter was still a student studying for his Ph.D. (a degree he never finished). In addition, "while Gore had a national security adviser . . . Cheney informally assembled what some have referred to as a rather large 'shadow NSC.'"[26] Cheney's people were often at odds with the NSC itself, and although they were kept apprised of the doings of the NSC, it was not necessarily the case that the opposite was true. At least one person familiar with the process suggested that this may have accounted for Cheney's influence in foreign and security policy matters.[27]

Cheney, like his immediate predecessors, avoided most line assignments. However shortly after taking office Bush asked him to head a task force to address energy problems that were affecting the country.[28] Especially hard hit was California, experiencing high costs for electricity and natural gas[29] and brownouts that were the product of insufficient energy production in the state.[30] Cheney's National Energy Policy Development Group concluded its work in about four months, releasing their report in May. The report included recommendations on how to "modernize conservation, modernize our energy infrastructure, increase energy supplies, accelerate the protection and improvement of our environment, and increase our nation's energy security."[31]

Cheney "came under immediate and intense criticism by Democrats for his secretive conduct of [these] meetings."[32] Opponents criticized him because the group met with many energy industry executives while excluding other groups (e.g., the environmental lobby). Perhaps most damning, according to critics, was the fact that Cheney's former employer, Halliburton, was included in the process. Despite the fact that the vice president had resigned from the company in order to run for office, he received a retirement package (placed in a blind trust for the duration of his tenure in office) that included several million dollars in stock options. This led, perhaps naturally, to the perception that the company was able to exert undue influence in the formation of the new energy policy. What made things worse was Cheney's unwillingness to make the composition of the group public, "believing that confidentiality of those involved is necessary for candid advice to be offered to the executive."[33]

Bush also gave Cheney the task of leading White House efforts to review and revise intelligence and terrorism policies.[34] Cheney was perhaps a natural choice, given that he strongly believed that a "'very robust intelligence capability'" was necessary to identify and stop any threats to the United States.[35] His efforts resulted in a report that included recommendations on how to improve response to an attack with weapons of mass destruction (WMD). It also had a strategy for preparation, response and better intelligence regarding bioterror attacks, WMD deployment and attack, and a better understanding of differing responsibilities between various levels of government. The report helped facilitate and establish policies and procedures that were implemented in the post–9/11 period.

IN OFFICE: THE INFORMAL VICE PRESIDENCY

The main story with respect to Cheney's informal roles throughout his vice presidency deals with his advisory role. He generally stayed in the nation's capital to remain close to the executive decision-making apparatus. Therefore, fulfillment of his ceremonial duties was somewhat limited. Even then controversy seemed to find him. In late October 2002 the Democratic Senator from Minnesota, Paul Wellstone, his family, and several campaign aides were killed when their chartered plane crashed. That same fall Cheney had been campaigning against Wellstone on behalf of his opponent, St. Paul Mayor Norm Coleman. The White House announced that Cheney would be attending the funeral on behalf of the president, but the vice president was asked by the family to stay away. The story that was given was that security measures for the vice president would have been too difficult to accommodate, but sources close to the Wellstone family quietly confirmed that the family considered the vice president's presence inappropriate.[36] In 2005, Cheney was asked by Bush to lead a presidential task force to lead recovery efforts in the aftermath of Hurricane Katrina. Although the vice president agreed, he did not relish or embrace the opportunity.[37]

Cheney's diplomatic activities were similarly constrained, at least with respect to foreign travel. He made several trips overseas but most of his time abroad was spent in the Middle East or East Asia, or (as in 2002) with allies discussing the situation in Afghanistan and Iraq. A trip to Switzerland for the Davos economic conference in early 2004 was only his second while in office.[38] In 2004 he visited China, South Korea, and Japan. Although the stop in Japan was ceremonial, the trip was actually made in an attempt to secure cooperation from the Chinese with regard to North Korea's nuclear weapon program.[39] In Washington, Cheney regularly met with foreign dignitaries. When, for example, British Prime Minister Tony Blair came to the White House for a meeting with Bush, he met with Cheney for an hour beforehand (the two had previously met in London).[40]

Given the controversial nature of his tenure one might expect that Cheney was limited in what he could offer politically to the administration. This was not the case. Like previous vice presidents in the modern era Cheney was quite active—and effective—as legislative liaison between the administration and Congress. Because he was formerly a member of the House, "he was the first vice president to have an office in the House of Representatives (during his first term)," as well as in the Senate. He also "attended meetings of the House leadership" to facilitate his legislative liaison work.[41] In all, "his knowledge of Washington and his experience as Minority Whip in the House were extremely helpful in promoting the president's agenda."[42]

Relative to his immediate predecessors Cheney made few public appearances to promote his president's policies. In summer 2003 he addressed a conservative think tank, defending the administration's decision to invade Iraq and its subsequent handling of the war effort.[43] This public defense continued throughout his tenure and he became "perhaps appropriately, a lightning rod of sorts in that regard."[44] He appeared on the Sunday talk shows to sell the administration's (largely his) energy policy.[45] He granted interviews to NBC and PBS to discuss and explain the response to the 9/11 terror attacks. But in general he granted few interviews, and those that he did agree to were often with reporters that were less confrontational to him. He appeared with some regularity, for example, on Fox News's "Hannity and Colmes" and Sean Hannity's radio program.

Cheney's tendency to avoid the media and the public eye was perhaps nowhere more evident than in the aftermath of an incident that occurred in February 2006. The vice president and several friends and acquaintances were hunting quail on the large Texas ranch of Republican supporter Anne Armstrong, when Cheney accidentally shot a fellow member of the party. News of the incident was not reported to the national press, and it was not until the following day that it was reported to a local newspaper (in fact the president was not informed for a full thirty-six hours). Four days later Cheney sat down for an exclusive interview with Fox News's Brit Hume to discuss the accident. Tellingly, despite the fact that other members of the national news media were outraged by his silence and in the face of ridicule by commentators and late-night talk show hosts (see box 8.1) nothing more was said publicly by the vice president about the incident.[46]

Cheney was not blind to criticism from his detractors. Knowing how controversial he had become he offered to withdraw from the ticket on three separate occasions in the run-up to the 2004 campaign. Bush declined his offer, and Cheney was indefatigable throughout the campaign.[47] As the incumbent, he faced John Edwards, a former trial lawyer and first-term senator from North Carolina. Edwards had begun his vice presidential bid hours after he withdrew from the presidential primary race, telling friends and close associates that he "was going to wage a 'full-fledged campaign' to ensure he got" the vice presidential nomination. This was risky because John Kerry, the presidential candidate, considered Edwards to be too ambitious.[48] In the end his efforts to secure the second spot paid off. Edwards brought a certain charisma to the ticket that Kerry lacked, and it was thought he might be able to attract southern voters as well.

Edwards's eldest daughter Cate, then twenty-one years old, was active on the campaign trail, making campaign stops with the family and on her own. Both of Cheney's daughters, Liz Perry Cheney and Mary Cheney, stumped for their father as well. However Edwards, whose image and appeal were based on a "sunny optimism," seemed to avoid overly aggressive partisan attacks throughout the campaign, probably because he had future presidential aspirations.[49] Cheney, on the other hand, had no qualms about attacking Kerry. He continually asserted Kerry was "weak and vacillating on issues of national security" and went so far as to suggest that if Kerry were elected, terrorists would be encouraged to again attack the nation.[50] He also questioned Kerry's patriotism.

Cheney again enlisted the aid of Rob Portman for debate preparation, practicing at his home near Jackson, Wyoming. Edwards, was "cloistered"

BOX 8.1

Late-Night Talk Show Hosts' Reaction to Cheney's Hunting Accident

"Hillary Clinton blasted the vice president today for failing to disclose all the facts. She wants Dick Cheney to give exact details. You know like, 'How do you shoot someone and make it look like an accident?'" (Jay Leno)

"Cheney also admitted that he'd been drinking. He said he had one beer. Okay, it was a 40-ounce Colt .45, but just one." (Jay Leno)

"They were in a car, they drive along, they get out of the car, he shoots his friend in the face, then they get back in the car and they go hide for 18 hours. That's not hunting . . . that's an episode of 'The Sopranos'" (Jay Leno)

"See, this is why Republicans have to commit white collar crimes to steal money. They're just not good with guns; they don't know how to handle them." (Jay Leno)

"President Bush says he is standing behind the vice president. Way behind him." (Jay Leno)

"The real question now is, is this a one-time thing, or will the vice president try to kill again?" (David Letterman)

"What a nightmare I had last night. I dreamed I was at a Washington party and I had to choose between Dick Cheney taking me on a hunting trip or Ted Kennedy driving me home." (Jay Leno)

"[Cheney] sat down for a one-on-one with Fox News. Very bold choice. Dick Cheney sitting down with Fox News is like Mrs. Butterworth sitting down with the Pancake Channel." (Jimmy Kimmel)

"I think Cheney is starting to lose it. After he shot the guy he screamed, 'Anyone else want to call domestic wiretapping illegal?'" (Jay Leno)

"Remember when the most embarrassing thing to happen to a vice-president was misspelling the word potato?" (Jimmy Kimmel)

"Police are still investigating. They want to know why Cheney was unable to see the hunter at the time of the accident. And, they also want to know how Cheney wound up with his wallet." (Jimmy Kimmel)

"This is a great story. You've got the Vice President, a shotgun, a bunch of rich guys hunting tiny little birds. The only thing that could possibly make this story better is if he shot Michael Jackson." (Jimmy Kimmel) in a historic nineteenth-century resort in Chautauqua, New York, sparring with Democratic lawyer Bob Barnett.[51] During the debate itself Cheney was less harsh than he typically appeared on the campaign trail. He methodically and steadfastly defended the Bush administration's record. He also spent some time sounding the theme of the campaign, that Kerry was not fit to wage the War on Terror. Edwards had been advised to attack but was also rather subdued. One report claimed that he "had practiced saying [to Cheney], 'You're lying to the American people,'" but what he actually said was "You are not being straight with the American people." There were no memorable moments with the exception of a comment Edwards made about the Bush administration's position on gay marriage and the fact that the Cheneys have a daughter who is gay.[52]

During the final week of the campaign, Cheney visited more than thirty cities in eight states. During one 24-hour period he "made stops in Toledo, OH, Romulus, MI, Fort Dodge, IA, Los Lunas, NM, and Honolulu, HI, and ended up in Jackson, WY. During this 24-hour period, he traveled almost 11,000 miles, spending approximately 18 and a half hours in the air."[53] He was also quite active in campaigning for Republican candidates in midterm elections. In 2002, he raised $10 million for approximately sixty Republican candidates, and in 2006 he "held 114 campaign events across the country and raised more than $40 million for the G.O.P. cause."[54]

It was in his capacity of "advising" the president that Cheney generated the most controversy. He held "an unrivaled portfolio across the executive branch," dependent in the first instance on the fact that Bush trusted him.[55] There is no question that a number of the decisions made and policies implemented by Bush were consistent with those advocated by Cheney.[56] This was especially true during their first term. And although Bush was the final decision maker, there also seems to be little doubt that Cheney exercised some amount of influence in this regard. For example, "he vetted numerous policy options before they reached the president and steered lower-level policy discussions around options he favored. . . . and was almost always the last person that Bush talked to before a major decision was made."[57] Former Vice President Dan Quayle described Cheney's role as that of a "surrogate chief of staff."[58] At one point during his first term, Bush went so far as to inform one Republican senator that "when you're talking to Dick Cheney, you're talking to me. When Dick Cheney's talking, it's me talking."[59] It was not uncommon for visitors to the White House who were "expecting to meet with the president" to meet with Cheney instead.[60]

Bush's trust in Cheney was evident before the two took office. Before the election results were even finalized, Bush tasked his vice president-to-be with starting and administering a privately funded transition team (they could not receive office space from the government until the election was decided).[61] As court challenges to the outcome of the election continued, Cheney began to assist Bush in assembling a cabinet by traveling to Austin for press conferences or meetings with Bush.[62] Cheney's influence on Cabinet selections was evident when some of these appointments were made, as he had worked closely with several of the individuals in the past: Donald Rumsfeld (his colleague and friend from the Ford administration) as Secretary of Defense, Colin Powell (from the first Bush administration) as Secretary of State, and Paul O'Neill as Secretary of the Treasury.[63]

Like his immediate predecessors in the modern era Cheney sat down with Bush for lunch on a weekly basis to discuss policy, but in reality these meetings were a formality.[64] As a rule the two met each morning at meetings of the NSC and several times throughout the day.[65] In addition, like most vice presidents since Walter Mondale, Cheney had "carte blanche" access "to all domestic and foreign policy meetings."[66] In fact during his first term he "met with Colin Powell, Donald Rumsfeld, and Condoleezza Rice on a weekly basis" and often with other cabinet secretaries.[67]

In other words, not only did Cheney have unlimited access to the policy process and players, he took advantage of it. In an effort to better access available intelligence Cheney visited Secret Service Headquarters and spent time at the Central Intelligence Agency (CIA), Federal Bureau of Investigation (FBI), and National Security Administration (NSA) facilities, among others.[68] Although much of his focus was on security-related issues, his portfolio, as he saw it, was far reaching. And it is hard to deny that he had some real influence on public policy, at least during his first term. His influence, however, was largely "exercised behind the scenes. . . . Some administration officials deferred to Cheney's position out of respect, others, out of fear," and "Cheney was almost always the last person that Bush talked to before a major decision was made."[69]

Cheney was reportedly instrumental in persuading Bush to renege on a campaign promise to lower carbon dioxide emissions.[70] The Bush administration adopted most of the recommendations of the vice president's energy task force. Cheney was likely influential in an early decision to cut special education funding, which in turn led Republican Senator Jim Jeffords to defect from the Republican Party.[71] He was chair of the review board responsible for the 2001 tax cuts, "served as gatekeeper for Supreme Court nominees, [and] referee of Cabinet turf disputes."[72]

Perhaps most infamously, "through his advocacy and his efforts in obtaining and interpreting data from the CIA about weapons of mass destruction [he] led the push to invade Iraq in 2003,"[73] the administration's warrantless wiretapping efforts, and more.[74] Bush's vice president was instrumental in the effort, known as the Terrorist Surveillance Program, designed to allow the NSA to monitor communications that originated or terminated in the United States.[75] Although the United States had been successful in removing Saddam Hussein from power in Iraq, by 2006 insurgents had been successful in destabilizing the country. As part of a strategy shift, Cheney helped develop a strategy to stabilize the situation by sending more troops to the region and ultimately helped convince the president to do so.[76]

As noted, during his second term, Cheney's influence with Bush began to wane. One example of this was the administration's policy with respect to North Korea. In early 2008 Cheney expressed concern over North Korea's desire to develop nuclear weapons. Despite this Bush announced that the country would no longer be on the list of countries that were considered state sponsors of terror.[77] Bush also parted ways with Cheney in "permitting courts to review the wiretapping of terrorism suspects, and [made] 'rhetorical nods to issues such as global warming and income inequality'."[78] Although it was commonplace to accuse Cheney of manipulating Bush, the fact remains that vice presidents have only as much power and influence as their presidents grant them.

Cheney's declining influence was the result of a few factors, all of which illustrate a fundamental fact about vice presidential power and influence. First, many of the policies Cheney advocated, especially the Iraq War, were clearly unpopular. His hunting accident and the very public trial of his top aide Scooter Libby likely contributed to the lack of public approval of Cheney himself as well. This all reflected poorly on Bush. Second, Bush himself had accumulated some understanding of foreign and security policy issues by the time his second term started. At the start of his presidency he had much less, and his tendency to (seemingly) rely on Cheney's expertise was therefore more pronounced. Bush, in other words, had less of a need for Cheney's guidance as time went on. Finally, perhaps Bush was more concerned about his legacy during his second term, which meant that he relied on less on his vice president and more on Secretary of State Condoleezza Rice, who typically took a less confrontational and ideological approach to foreign and security policy issues than did the vice president.[79]

EVALUATING THE CHENEY VICE PRESIDENCY

Two aspects of the Cheney vice presidency stand out immediately. He was clearly the most active and influential vice president to that point in our history, in addition to being one of the most controversial. His alleged policy "sins" are numerous, starting with his presumably having favored energy interests in the crafting Bush's energy policy, while at the same time refusing to allow access to information dealing with the process. He is "credited" with having played a central role in the push to invade Iraq in 2003, helping his former employer Halliburton win no-bid contracts during the war, and justifying and facilitating the use of torture in the War on Terror.

Cheney's chief of staff, Lewis "Scooter" Libby Jr., was convicted in the spring of 2007 of "perjury, obstruction of justice, and lying to the FBI in an investigation regarding the leak of CIA officer Valerie Plame's identity in the summer of 2003."[80] More damning was the fact that Libby was believed to have been acting at the behest of (and covering for) Cheney in an alleged leak of classified CIA reports in an effort to "undermine the credibility" of Joseph Wilson, a critic of the Iraq War and Plame's husband. At times Cheney went outside of normal bureaucratic procedure to achieve his ends. For example when helping plan the administration's policy on foreign terrorists' access to the judicial process, he bypassed virtually all high-ranking administration officials and went directly to Bush. Critics also charged Cheney with being secretive, and there seems to be little doubt that this was the case. "During his tenure the work of the office of the vice presidency . . . was stored in large safes, talking points were often labeled as "Treated as: Top Secret/SCI" (sensitive compartmented information), and he . . . refused to disclose the names or size of his staff; refused to hand over [then] newly de-classified documents to the National Archives and Records Administration."[81]

According to many critics Cheney's worst transgression was the amount of influence he presumably exercised over Bush. The popular image of Cheney for most of his tenure was that of a puppet master, controlling the president. An editorial cartoon titled "George W. Bush and puppet master Dick Cheney, 2004" from the well-known artist David Levine, sums up this view well. In 2007 Mondale publicly suggested that Cheney "stepped way over the line" in pushing for the invasion of Iraq.[82] That same year a proposal was introduced in the House of Representatives to impeach the vice president on the grounds that he had manipulated intelligence leading up to the invasion of Iraq.[83] Others have gone so far as to suggest that the vice president acted in a criminal or unconstitutional manner in refusing to turn over declassified documents.[84] Finally, Cheney—like Bush—left office with historically low public approval ratings. Most polls showed that the percentage of the public who thought he was doing a good or excellent job was less than 20 percent.[85] On the face of things, in other words, Cheney appears to have been a poor vice president.

On the other hand, there is little indication that Bush was incapable of or unwilling to make decisions independent of his vice president. On the contrary, on the policies and issues that Cheney is most reviled for, Bush was in agreement. In addition, when the two differed, as they frequently did during their second term, Bush's view prevailed. It seems less than likely, based on accounts of the administration and the relationship between the two men, that Cheney was a "stealthily ambitious" individual who wanted to be able to "manipulate" a "more malleable president."[86]

Moreover, even when Cheney differed with the president he did not make their disagreement public.[87] In other words, despite the fact that Cheney was the target of much criticism, he served his president well, and nothing in the public record suggests that Bush himself was unhappy with his performance.

At the heart of much of the controversy surrounding his vice presidency was his "expansive view of executive branch power, especially with regard to foreign policy. This is the result of his experience serving as President Gerald Ford's chief of staff" during a time when Congress was attempting to roll back the "imperial" use of presidential power. Moreover, his experience in Washington (in particular working in the White House as a Secretary of Defense) made him unusually proficient in how to navigate the bureaucracy. He often prevailed because he understood the rules of the game better than others around him—and was willing in some cases to circumvent them. Finally, from a substantive perspective, most of what Cheney did while in office was in response to the attacks of September 11, 2001. The vice president, who was predisposed to focus on foreign and security policy, became even more focused on these issues in the months and years following.[88]

Throughout his vice presidency Cheney made it clear he had no interest in running for president. Although many observers doubted the veracity of these claims, he was true to his word. While Cheney has been a frequent and public critic of Barack Obama's administration, he retired from public office after leaving the vice presidency.

NOTES

1. Baumgartner, "Scoundrel or Über-Lieutenant?" 246.
2. Stephen F. Hayes, *Cheney* (New York: Harper Collins, 2007), 277.
3. Richard L. Berke, "The Second Spot: Invisible, Subtle Race to Become No. 2," *The New York Times*, May 3, 2000, www.nytimes.com/library/politics/camp/050300vp-prospects.html.
4. John Nichols, *Dick: The Man Who Is President* (New York: The New Press, 2004), 169–72.
5. Larry J. Sabato and Joshua J. Scott, "The Long Road to a Cliffhanger: Primaries and Conventions," in *Overtime: The Election 2000 Thriller*, Larry J. Sabato, ed. (New York: Longman, 2002), 27.
6. Hayes, *Cheney*, 277.

7. Purcell, *Vice Presidents*; William Crotty, "The Election of 2004: Close, Chaotic, and Unforgettable," in *America's Choice 2000*, William Crotty, ed. (Boulder: Westview, 2001); Ceaser and Busch, *The Perfect Tie*, 139.

8. Berke, "The Second Spot."

9. Polsby and Wildavsky, *Presidential Elections*, 130–31.

10. James W. Ceaser and Andrew E. Busch, *The Perfect Tie: The True Story of the 2000 Presidential Election* (Lanham, MD: Rowman & Littlefield, 2001), 139.

11. Ceaser and Busch, *The Perfect Tie*, 139.

12. Tom Fiedler, "Introduction: The Encore of *Key Largo*," in *Overtime: The Election 2000 Thriller*, Larry J. Sabato, ed. (New York: Longman, 2002), 7.

13. Ian Christopher McCaleb and Mike Ferullo, "Cheney Blisters Clinton-Gore Administration in Acceptance Speech," *CNN*, August 3, 2000, http://archives .cnn.com/2000/ALLPOLITICS/stories/08/03/conv.wrap/.

14. Crotty, "The Election of 2004: Close, Chaotic, and Unforgettable."

15. Mike Allen and John F. Harris, "Debate Assumes New Importance," *The Washington Post*, October 4, 2004. Available at www.washingtonpost.com/wp -dyn/articles/A4587-2004Oct3.html.

16. William Crotty, "The Presidential Primaries: Triumph of the Frontrunners," in *America's Choice 2000*, William Crotty, ed. (Boulder: Westview, 2001), 111.

17. Ceaser and Busch, *The Perfect Tie*.

18. Tamara Lipper, "'President Cheney?" *Newsweek*, July 8, 2002, 140(2), 8.

19. Hayes, *Cheney*, 336, 349.

20. Helen Dewar and Dana Milbank, "Cheney Dismisses Critic with Obscenity, Clash with Leahy about Halliburton," *Washington Post*. June 25, 2004, 4.

21. Charles Hurt, "Cheney Pledges Filibuster Override," *The Washington Times*, April 23, 2005, www.washingtontimes.com/national/20050422 114701 8401r.htm.

22. Hayes, *Cheney*, 495.

23. Ibid., 495.

24. Baumgartner, "Scoundrel or Über-Lieutenant?" 235–52.

25. Peter Baker, *Days of Fire: Bush and Cheney in the White House* (New York, Doubleday, 2013), 87.

26. Baumgartner, "Scoundrel or Über-Lieutenant?" 243.

27. Robert Dreyfuss, "Vice Squad." *The American Prospect*, April 17, 2006.

28. Hayes, *Cheney*, 311, 315.

29. Ibid., 311.

30. Ibid., 315.

31. Ibid., 316.

32. Baumgartner, "Scoundrel or Über-Lieutenant?" 244.

33. Ibid.

34. Barton Gellman, *Angler: The Cheney Vice Presidency*, (The Penguin Press, 2008), 110; Hayes, *Cheney*, 319.

35. Hayes, *Cheney*, 319.

36. Thomas M. DeFrank and Kenneth R. Bazinet, "Cheney not Welcome at Wellstone Memorial," *Daily News*, October 30, 2002, 26.

37. Hayes, *Cheney*, 430.

38. Brian Knowlton, "Cheney's Davos Trip is just 2nd Appearance Overseas." *The New York Times*, January 23, 2004, www.nytimes.com/2004/01/23/news/23iht-cheney_ed3_.html.

39. Hayes, *Cheney*, 433.

40. "The Vice President Visits the Middle East: March 10–16, 2002," The White House: President George W. Bush, http://georgewbush-whitehouse.archives.gov/vicepresident/vpphotoessay/part1/.

41. Baumgartner, "Scoundrel or Über-Lieutenant?" 245.

42. Ibid.

43. Eric Schmitt, "After the War: The Administration," *The New York Times*, July 25, 2005, A10.

44. Baumgartner, "Scoundrel or Über-Lieutenant?" 245.

45. Hayes, *Cheney*, 313.

46. Evan Thomas, "The Shot Heard Round the World," *Newsweek*, February 26, 2006, www.newsweek.com/shot-heard-round-world-113499.

47. Hayes, *Cheney*, 461, 423.

48. Evan Thomas, *Election 2004: How Bush Won and What You Can Expect in the Future* (New York: Public Affairs, 2004), 81–82.

49. Thomas, *Election 2004*, 117–18, 157.

50. Ibid., 99; Gerald Pomper, "The Presidential Election: The Ills of American Politics after 9/11," in *The Elections of 2004*, Michael Nelson, ed. (Washington, D.C.: CQ Press, 2005), 56.

51. Mike Allen and John F. Harris, "Debate Assumes New Importance," *The Washington Post*, October 4, 2004, www.washingtonpost.com/wp-dyn/articles/A4587-2004Oct3.html.

52. Thomas, *Election 2004*, 158.

53. David Hume Kennerly, "Dick Cheney's Final Assault Across America," *The Digital Journalist*, November, 2004, http://dirckhalstead.org/issue0411/dis_kennerly.html.

54. Baumgartner, "Scoundrel or Über-Lieutenant?" 245.

55. Ibid., 246.

56. Barton Gellman and Jo Becker, "A Different Understanding with the President," *Washington Post*, June 24, 2007, A1.

57. Baumgartner, "Scoundrel or Über-Lieutenant?" 247.

58. Gellman and Becker, "A Different Understanding with the President."

59. Nicholas Lemann, "The Quiet Man," *The New Yorker*, May 7, 2001, 56.

60. Baumgartner, "Scoundrel or Über-Lieutenant?" 247.

61. Hayes, *Cheney*, 299; Barton Gellman, *Angler: The Cheney Vice Presidency* (New York: Penguin Press, 2008), 32.

62. Hayes, *Cheney*, 299.

63. Ibid., 301; Gellman, *Angler*, 35.

64. Gellman and Becker, "A Different Understanding with the President."

65. Baumgartner, *The American Vice Presidency Reconsidered*, 132.

66. Baumgartner, "Scoundrel or Über-Lieutenant?" 247.

67. Ibid.

68. Hayes, *Cheney*, 363–64.

69. Ibid.

70. Lemann, "The Quiet Man."

71. Jo Becker and Barton Gellman," Leaving No Tracks," *Washington Post*, June 27, 2007, A1,

72. Gellman and Becker, "A Different Understanding with the President."

73. Baumgartner, "Scoundrel or Über-Lieutenant?" 238.

74. Charlie Savage, *Takeover: The Return of the Imperial Presidency and the Subversion of American Democracy* (New York: Back Bay Books, 2007).

75. Hayes, *Cheney*, 348.

76. Ibid., 451.

77. Ibid., 486.

78. Baumgartner, "Scoundrel or Über-Lieutenant?" 239.

79. Baker, *Days of Fire*.

80. Baumgartner, "Scoundrel or Über-Lieutenant?" 238.

81. Ibid., 237.

82. Daniel Yee, "Mondale: Cheney Is Out of Line." *StarTribune*, January 19, 2007, www.startribune.com/587/story/947072.html.

83. Jim Abrams, "Debate on Cheney Impeachment Averted," *Washington Post*, November 6, 2007, www.washingtonpost.com/wpdyn/content/article/2007/11/06/AR2007110601451.html.

84. Glenn Harlan Reynolds, "Is Dick Cheney Unconstitutional?" (*Northwestern University Law Review Colloquy*, 2007, 102: 110–16).

85. "Vice President Dick Cheney: Job Ratings," The Polling Report, December 31, 2006, http://web.archive.org/web/20080705231247/; www.pollingreport.com/C.htm.

86. Quoted in Hite, *Second Best*, 1, 183; see Baker, *Days of Fire* for a more nuanced account of the relationship between the two men.

87. Baker, *Days of Fire*.

88. Gellman, *Angler*, 139.

9

+

Joe Biden:
Barack Obama's Handyman

Likely selected for much the same reason as his predecessor, Joe Biden brought a wealth of experience in the Senate, in particular in the area of foreign policy, to the Barack Obama ticket in 2008. Interestingly, a common refrain on the campaign trail for Biden was that if elected, he would adopt a much lower profile than did Cheney. Of course this would have reversed developments in the institution throughout the past several decades. In fact, Biden has been quite active during the past six years, essentially acting as the president's all-purpose handyman.

SELECTION AND THE CAMPAIGN OF 2008

In January 2007, Delaware Senator Biden announced his intention to seek the Democratic nomination for president in 2008.[1] Biden had previously aspired to win his party's nomination in 1988, but his campaign became derailed amid accusations that he plagiarized sections of a speech by a British politician and exaggerated his academic record.[2] In 2008 he was one of several aspirants, including heavy favorite Hillary Clinton, 2004 vice presidential nominee John Edwards, and the Democratic Party's rising star, Barack Obama. Biden seemed to sabotage any chance for success almost immediately by saying that Obama was "the first mainstream African-American who is articulate and bright and clean and a nice-looking guy." Long known for making verbal gaffes, he spent most of the first official day of his campaign apologizing.[3] He never quite vaulted into the top tier of candidates and withdrew from the race after finishing fifth in the nation's first nominating event, the Iowa caucuses.[4]

He had, however, emerged from the process with his reputation and stature somewhat enhanced. There was discussion among his inner circle about endorsing Clinton or Obama. He was close to Clinton, and although originally skeptical of Obama, he had come to respect the first-term senator during the campaign. In the end it was decided to endorse neither so as not to alienate the eventual winner. The hope was that he might secure a position in the administration of the winner, perhaps even a spot on the presidential ticket. Throughout the spring he talked frequently with each, eventually being seen as an honest broker of sorts between the two. In fact at one point he told Obama—to the horror of his aides—that Clinton would be his best choice for vice presidential nominee.[5]

Biden's original skepticism of Obama was reciprocated. The nominee felt that Biden was often condescending and patronizing toward him and his staff. But Obama's appreciation for Biden grew throughout the spring of 2008 and by the time he had secured the nomination he was leaning toward tapping him for the ticket. Even though aides went through the process of vetting several names, notably Virginia Governor Tim Kaine and Indiana Senator Evan Bayh, the process was largely a formality.[6] In an interview with two key Obama campaign strategists, Biden claimed he did not want to be vice president, concerned that he would find himself in the vice presidential void into which so many of his predecessors had fallen. At the same time he explained why he would be a good selection.[7]

The two met in Minneapolis in early August to discuss Biden's interest in and expectations of the job. Team Obama's main concern was whether Biden could show the necessary restraint of tongue on the campaign trail. Biden was equally reluctant. He had "been his own boss" for better than three decades and did not necessarily want to work for someone else. Moreover, he did not want to be forgotten like previous vice presidents. In the end, his wife Jill helped persuade him to accept the offer.[8] Still, he wanted to be assured that he would play a significant role in the administration, be part of every major policy discussion[9]—that he would be "part of the deal."[10] He was looking, in short, to be Obama's "advisor in chief."[11]

Making full use of new technologies Obama first announced the selection in an e-mail to campaign Web site subscribers.[12] Biden brought several things to the ticket. First, he had thirty-five years of experience in Washington as opposed to Obama's four. Second, Obama had virtually no foreign policy experience, whereas Biden had (alternately) been the ranking minority member and Chair of the Foreign Relations Committee in the Senate. Finally, Biden's ability to appeal to middle class and Catholic voters, traditional Democratic constituencies, balanced Obama's appeal to the more intellectual progressive-liberal base of the Democratic Party.[13]

On the Republican side, John McCain won the Republican Party's nomination without too much difficulty, despite suspicions by the far right concerning his conservative credentials. There was much speculation in the media that McCain might select his friend, Democratic senator and Al Gore's vice presidential candidate Joe Lieberman as his running mate. Lieberman had endorsed McCain for president based on compatible views on the war on terror. Although McCain was strongly leaning toward selecting Lieberman, aides were fearful that selecting a candidate from the opposing party would alienate the conservative base even further. The last time a presidential ticket included a vice presidential candidate from the opposing party was during the Civil War, when former Democrat Andrew Johnson ran with Republican Abraham Lincoln. In the end McCain's aides prevailed.

Also considered for the nomination were former Pennsylvania Governor Tom Ridge, Minnesota Governor Tim Pawlenty, former Massachusetts governor Mitt Romney, and Alaska Governor Sarah Palin.[14] The latter was a late addition to McCain's list and—fatefully—not fully vetted. She met briefly with McCain three days before the selection was to be announced, and knowing there was some risk involved he offered her the spot.[15] The announcement was made the day before the start of the Democratic national convention at the end of August. Reaction from the right was enthusiastic; others were surprised and somewhat wary. By early September doubts were already being raised regarding her suitability for the nation's highest office. A *Newsweek* poll indicated that only 45 percent of respondents believed she was qualified to assume the presidency—as opposed to 71 percent for Biden (exit polls of voters after the election painted a similar story).[16]

Both Palin and Biden proved to be energetic campaigners, but each violated the Richard Nixon doctrine of "do no harm." In Palin's case this was because she was insufficiently vetted and not well prepared by the McCain team for what to expect during a presidential campaign. Moreover, she appeared to lack the focus needed to master the issues. This became apparent in two nationally televised interviews early in the campaign. She subsequently became the butt of the joke in six classic *Saturday Night Live* skits in which she was masterfully portrayed by Tina Fey.[17]

In Biden's case the problem centered on his lack of discipline speaking on the campaign trail. Simply put, the vice presidential nominee almost immediately began making a number of gaffes. In mid-September he told reporters that he thought he was more qualified than Obama to be president. When Obama and his aides heard this remark an immediate frost set in between the Obama camp and Biden. But Biden wasn't finished.

More Biden gaffes (which the Obama campaign team came to refer to as "Joe Bombs"[18]) from the campaign included the following:

- "Hillary Clinton is as qualified or more qualified than I am to be vice president of the United States of America. Quite frankly, it might have been a better pick than me" (Nashua, New Hampshire, in early September).
- "Stand up, Chuck, let 'em see ya" (speaking to wheelchair-bound Missouri state Senator Chuck Graham, at a rally in Columbia, Missouri, in early September).
- "Look, [McCain's] last-minute economic plan does nothing to tackle the number-one job facing the middle class, and it happens to be, as Barack says, a three-letter word: jobs. J-O-B-S, jobs" (Athens, Ohio, in October).
- "When the stock market crashed, Franklin D. Roosevelt got on the television and didn't just talk about the, you know, the princes of greed. He said, 'Look, here's what happened" (interview with Katie Couric, September 22).[19]
- "Mark my words, it will not be six months before the world tests Barack Obama like they did John Kennedy. . . . Watch, we're gonna have an international crisis, a generated crisis, to test the mettle of this guy" (Seattle, Washington, October 20).[20]

At one point Obama became so angry he asked aides (perhaps rhetorically), "How many times is Biden gonna say something stupid?"[21] It was not until two weeks before the election, when Biden called Obama to apologize and promised to be more disciplined that the relationship between the two was put back on track.[22]

The debate between Biden and Palin took place on October 2. Reports suggest the governor had some trouble staying focused during preparation. Biden, who practiced with Michigan Governor Jennifer Granholm, had two interrelated tasks. Because he was so much more experienced than Palin the fear was that if he steamrolled her he would be perceived as a bully. In addition, he needed to be concise so as to avoid any further gaffes. Therefore, he concentrated on being concise and restrained, even in the face of provocation.[23] The debate was watched by 66 million people, the only time in history that the vice presidential debate had a larger viewing audience than the presidential debates.[24] Throughout the debate Palin was evasive, in many cases avoiding the questions posed by moderator Gwen Ifill. She painted McCain and herself as mavericks and attempted to appeal to the middle class by speaking to "Joe six-pack" and "hockey moms." Biden tried to link the Republican ticket to Bush. Although some observers believed the outcome to be fairly even, a few instant polls suggested otherwise.[25] CBS reported that 46 percent of viewers thought Biden won, compared with 21 percent for Palin; CNN had Biden on top by a margin of 51 to 36.[26]

As a final note on the campaign, Biden was up for reelection for his seat in the Senate in 2008. Delaware law allowed him to run for both the Senate and the vice presidency. In the end he won both races and resigned from the Senate before assuming the vice presidency.[27]

IN OFFICE: THE FORMAL VICE PRESIDENCY

As of 2015 there were no presidential succession concerns facing the Obama administration. A minor stir was caused in early 2013 when both Obama and Biden were briefly out of the country at the same time (in different places). This however was not an actual succession issue as much as it was a historical first.[28] Biden has cast no tie votes in the Senate during his tenure either.

He has, however, presided over the Senate on several occasions. For example, like all vice presidents, Biden presides when newly elected senators are sworn into office.[29] And perhaps because he is a veteran of the Senate he has presided over several important votes during his tenure, including the vote for the Affordable Care Act (December 2009), ratification of the New START Treaty (December 2010), the Democratic tax plan of 2012, an "amendment to gun control legislation [which] would have expanded background checks to include sales at gun shows and over the Internet and . . . authorized a $400-million upgrade to the national background check database,"[30] and immigration reform (in June 2013).[31] All of these votes were considered important by the White House.

One development worth noting with regard to Biden's role in the Senate is that before being sworn in, the Democratic Senate Majority Leader Harry Reid made it clear that the new vice president would not be welcome in internal party meetings in the body. This tradition of excluding the vice president dates back to Lyndon Johnson, who as Majority Leader had assumed he might be able to take part in party deliberations in the Senate while in office as vice president. He was quickly disabused of this notion by party leaders. Reid's comments were significant because Dick Cheney had regularly attended convocations of Republican legislators in the Senate, a practice that some viewed as a violation of the principle of separation of powers and congressional independence.[32]

Although advised by Walter Mondale to avoid taking any line assignments, Biden was tasked with tracking and reporting progress on Obama's 2009 economic stimulus bill. For several months he traveled the country speaking with governors, mayors, and local officials about their projects.[33] In May of that year he gave his first report, claiming that 150,000 jobs had been generated or saved, only seventy-seven days after the measure was implemented. In addition the report claimed that 95 percent of working families had seen tax credits, unemployment compensation had increased by $25 per week, and $88 billion was available to local governments across the country for various (mainly transportation) projects. The report went on to claim that a half a million more jobs would be generated or saved in the subsequent one hundred days.[34]

Biden was also asked by Obama to chair a White House Task Force on Working Families comprised of administration policy makers. The objective was to seek a way to create new initiatives and identify reforms that would help middle-class families, particularly with child and elderly care, college costs, and retirement savings. The panel used input and ideas solicited from various business and government sectors.[35] Biden also headed a Gun Violence Task Force that was created by the president within days of the December 2012 shootings at Sandy Hook Elementary School in Newtown, Connecticut. Finally, in his 2014 State of the Union address Obama charged Biden with heading an "across-the-board" review focused on reforming "federal training programs to help make them more job-driven."[36] Six months later the review led to the signing of the "Workforce Innovation and Opportunity Act."[37]

IN OFFICE: THE INFORMAL VICE PRESIDENCY

Biden has been extremely active during his tenure as vice president. Like other vice presidents he has gone to his share of funerals. Some of these funerals have been for notable political figures in the United States. In fall 2012 he attended services for long-term South Carolina Senator Fritz Hollings.[38] In July 2014 he was present at the service for Howard Baker Jr., who served in the Senate (from Tennessee) and was, for a time, Senate Majority Leader, White House Chief of Staff, and Ambassador to Japan.[39] In February 2014, with former President Jimmy Carter, he paid his respects at the funeral of Former Second Lady Joan Mondale.[40] Like Cheney, funerals seemed to hold the potential to generate controversy for Biden. For example, the Vice President attended the funeral of former Israeli Prime Minister Ariel Sharon in 2014, but many wondered why Obama himself did not attend. Similarly, neither Obama nor Biden were present at the funeral for former British Prime Minister Margaret Thatcher, claiming that domestic politics precluded their leaving the country.[41] Some of the funerals Biden attended were more personal in nature, like that of his ninety-two-year-old mother in 2010[42] or the services of a friend and Syracuse University law school classmate in early 2012[43]

Despite the increased responsibilities of the vice president as assistant to the president there is still a strong ceremonial component to the job. Biden, for example, conducted a ceremonial swearing in of Central Intelligence Agency (CIA) Director David Petraeus at CIA Headquarters in Langley, Virginia, in 2011.[44] In 2013 he attended the groundbreaking ceremony of a shelter for battered women in Chicago[45] and joined in a "Celebration of Freedom" naturalization ceremony in Atlanta, Georgia in 2013.[46] In 2014 he marched in the Independence Day parade in Philadelphia,[47] honored victims of the 2013 Boston Marathon bombings,[48] and spoke "at the opening ceremony for the 2014 Asian American and Pacific Islander Heritage Month"[49] and of the National Governors Association meeting in Nashville, Tennessee.[50] He delivered the keynote address at the progressive activist Netroots Nation conference.[51] In 2014 alone Biden delivered commencement addresses at Miami Dade College, the University of South Carolina, the University of Delaware (his alma mater), and spoke at commencement ceremonies for the graduating classes of the Coast Guard and Air Force Academies.[52] Biden also represented the United States at the opening of the 2010 World Cup.[53]

Finally, and perhaps uniquely among recent vice presidents, Biden does not ignore his roots in the fulfilling of his ceremonial duties. For example "on St. Patrick's Day [in 2014 he] spoke at the Greater Pittston Friendly Sons of St. Patrick dinner at the Woodlands Inn and Resort in Plains Township but first swung by Scanlan's Restaurant on Linden Street in his home town of Scranton Pennsylvania and Terry's Diner in Moosic."[54]

Like most previous vice presidents Biden has also been a presence in the aftermath of natural disasters. In fall 2009 he "toured the metro Atlanta area by helicopter"[55] and the Grand Ole Opry House in Nashville, Tennessee, in 2010[56] after flooding in those areas. In spring 2011 he toured north St. Louis County with Missouri Governor Jay Nixon after a tornado hit the area.[57] In fall 2012 he surveyed the damage wrought by hurricane Sandy in New Jersey.[58]

Biden has been particularly active in his diplomatic role. His foreign policy experience was part of the reason he was selected by Obama. While in the Senate Biden had traveled abroad extensively, particularly in his capacity as ranking minority leader (2004–2006) and chair of the Senate Committee on Foreign Relations (2001–2003, 2007–2009). In fact his first trip after the election came before his inauguration, when as chair of the Senate Foreign Relations Committee he went on a "fact-finding" mission to Iraq, Afghanistan, and Pakistan.[59] On his return he recommended that the new administration establish clear objectives for U.S. involvement in each theater in addition to renewing a focus on stopping Al-Qaeda in Afghanistan.[60] In the spring he traveled to "Bosnia, Kosovo, and Serbia, where peacekeeping efforts had been one of his major interests as Chairman of the Senate Foreign Relations Committee."[61] There he encouraged the Bosnian parliament to resolve ethnic differences peacefully. In July the vice president was off to Georgia and Ukraine. His visit was an attempt to allay fears that the United States was reducing its support of the two countries in favor of bettering relations with Russia.[62]

In spring 2010 Biden traveled to Israel hoping to improve the somewhat strained relations that had developed between the Obama administration and the Jewish state. He was only partially successful. He started off pledging complete support for Israel, proclaiming there is "no space between the US and Israel when it comes to Israel's security."[63] However he also suggested that Israel stop building "more settlements, dismantle existing outposts, and allow the Palestinians freedom of movement based on their first actions."[64] Unfortunately, while the vice president was there the Israeli government announced plans to build new homes for citizens residing in Arab East Jerusalem. Biden publicly condemned the plan, suggesting it ran counter to his hope to reinvigorate peace talks. While Israel's Interior Minister claimed that the announcement of the project could have waited until after Biden's visit and Biden himself suggested there would be time in the future to discuss this and other subjects,[65] the trip ended on a somewhat sour note. In July of that same year Biden traveled to Iraq to hold talks with Iraqi Prime Minister al-Maliki. Although by this point most U.S. troops had been withdrawn, the vice president reinforced American commitment to the country and pressed the prime minister to accelerate progress on new election laws, cooperation with differing political interests, revenue sharing, and more.[66]

In spring 2011 the vice president met with the Russian president to further efforts at restoring U.S.–Russian relations (in his words, to "push the reset button") and strengthening economic ties.[67] That summer saw Biden in Asia, meeting with representatives of the Japanese and Chinese governments. While in Tokyo the vice president assured Prime Minister Naoto Kan that the United States was resolving its ongoing budget challenges. During his visit to Beijing Biden met with Chinese Premier Wen Jiabao. Again he attempted calm fears and provide reassurance about American fiscal matters, assuring the Chinese that they had "'nothing to worry about'" when it came to the U.S. economy.[68] In summer 2013 Biden was in India for four days trying to strengthen U.S. "economic and defense ties" with the Asian giant.[69] In December he visited Japan, China, and South Korea as a way of reaffirming "America's commitment to the region."[70] In spring 2014 he met with the leaders of Poland, Estonia, Latvia, and Lithuania to ease their concerns "about Russia's takeover of Crimea."[71] He also visited Ukraine to offer a small aid package and reassure the government (and show Russia) that the United States was supporting them; he later made a return trip for the inauguration of newly elected Ukranian president Poroshenko.[72]

In all Biden has "traveled to more than two dozen countries . . . in every region of the world" during his vice presidency.[73] He visited several of these countries more than once. For example he has been to Iraq eight times during his tenure, serving as the point man in keeping Iraqi leadership apprised of how the administration viewed their progress.[74] Unlike his predecessors in the transitional era, on most of these trips he is charged with a substantive policy mission. Obama, in Biden's words, "sends me to places that he doesn't want to go."[75] In this respect he has been, for the most part, a true asset to the Obama administration. The partial exception to this rule may be, perhaps predictably, those occasions when he has made controversial remarks (as in his trip to Israel in 2010).

Biden has also been, by all accounts, virtually indispensible to the Obama administration on the legislative front. Over the past several decades he has developed numerous relationships with legislators from both houses and on both sides of the aisle. In this regard his ties are wide and deep. He was, for example, the only person who was asked to eulogize both Strom Thurmond and Jesse Helms at their respective funeral services.[76] And although he has been excluded from Democratic caucus meetings in the Senate, he often interacts with Democratic lawmakers and makes the effort to maintain good relations with members of both parties. He regularly exercises in the Senate gymnasium (where he maintains his old locker) and when Congress is in session he frequently works in the ceremonial office of the vice president in the Capitol Building. Biden's relationships with key players on Capitol Hill have been vital to securing support for much of Obama's legislative agenda. He has helped establish and fortify Obama's status within Congress and has been responsible for helping the administration navigate through the congressional and political minefields endemic to Washington politics.[77]

For example, in early 2009 he vigorously lobbied Republican Senators Susan Collins and Arlen Specter for their votes to help pass Obama's $787 billion American Recovery and Reinvestment Act stimulus package.[78] In fact his influence was critical in convincing Specter to abandon the Republican Party and run for reelection in 2010 as a Democrat. Specter's reelection helped the Democrats secure another seat in the Senate, boosting the president's partisan advantage in that body.[79] As noted previously, Biden's efforts were critical in persuading two-thirds of the members of the Senate to ratify the new START Treaty in 2010. He was also involved in the negotiations that led to the passage of the repeal of the military's policy on gays, "Don't Ask, Don't Tell."[80] The fall of 2010 saw Biden working closely with Republican Senate Minority Leader Mitch McConnell to craft a bipartisan tax bill that temporarily extended tax cuts enacted under the George W. Bush administration, then led efforts to sell the agreement to congressional Democrats (in addition to helping first sell the president on the plan).[81]

In 2011 an informal "Biden panel" made up of the vice president and six members of Congress worked to negotiate a deal to raise the federal debt ceiling and set spending limits in the face of a looming government shutdown and a default on federal loans. The vice president's relationship with McConnell—and his own reputation within Congress as a man of his word—was central in the passage of the Budget Control Act of 2011.[82] He again worked closely with McConnell in fall 2012 to negotiate a deal that led to the passage of the American Taxpayer Relief Act of 2012 in early 2013.[83]

One indication of how invaluable Biden has been to Obama in working with members of Congress is that Biden was shut out of direct talks with Congress during the government shutdown and debt ceiling crisis in fall 2013. Although continuing appropriations were eventually passed, Biden played little part in the compromise deal because Senate Majority Leader Reid and other Democrats believed Biden had given away too much in previous deals.[84] Biden, in other words, works for Obama.

In his political role Biden has been quite active as well. In the face of polling and predictions that suggested major losses for the Democrats in the 2010 midterm elections (including loss of majority status in the House) he remained publicly confident throughout the summer and fall, at one point claiming that "the day after the election, there will be a Democratic majority in the House and a Democratic majority in the Senate. If it weren't illegal, I'd make book on it."[85] The fact that his party suffered huge losses in the House, losing their majority, and six seats in the Senate, does not detract from the fact that he was a workhorse throughout the campaign, traveling all over the country stumping for Democratic candidates.

Of course Biden made a few gaffes while on the campaign trail. For example he twice referenced the $200 "billion" dollars being spent by conservative groups in political ads throughout the campaign, clearly meaning "million."[86] One interesting side story in the 2010 campaign was the candidate who did *not* run. Amid a good deal of speculation, and some encouragement, Biden's son Beau, serving as Attorney General of Delaware, opted not to run for the seat previously occupied by his father. It was widely believed that he would have been a competitive candidate. His decision to stay out of the race was based on a stated desire to finish what he started as Attorney General.[87]

Biden was also active in the Obama–Biden reelection effort in 2012. Perhaps naturally there were rumors that Obama was considering replacing him on the ticket (with, for example, Hillary Clinton) to improve his chances for reelection, but nothing came of this.[88] To reiterate a point made previously, vice presidents are not dropped during reelection efforts in the modern era, primarily because doing so would be a public relations disaster. The negative effects would almost certainly outweigh any possible positive effects from having a new, presumably more electorally attractive running mate.

Obama's opponent was Mitt Romney, the former Republican Governor of Massachusetts. Romney had made a credible run for the Republican nomination for president in 2008 but fell short. This was in part because conservatives distrusted him. As governor he had advocated policies more in line with liberal or moderate Republicans—or even Democrats. Nonetheless he had an enormous advantage in funding in 2012, the experience and organization from his 2008 effort, and a relatively weak field of competitors. Even this was not enough to guarantee him victory, but in the end he prevailed.[89]

Romney formally began his search for a running mate in early April. Long-time aide Beth Myers compiled and presented the presumptive candidate with a list of twenty names. After winnowing several of these out,

> calls were made to each of the [remaining] individuals . . . asking if they would like to be considered. By July Romney was presented with the results of the vetting process, and by the end of the month only three candidates were still under consideration, namely, former Minnesota Governor Tm Pawlenty, Ohio Representative Rob Portman, and Wisconsin Representative Paul Ryan. In meeting with Myers and his top advisers on August 1 he let it be known that of the three, he was leaning toward Ryan. He then called Ryan, setting up a secret meeting between the two for August 5. The selection was officially announced at 8:00 a.m. on August 11.[90]

The selection illustrated, again, that the historical model of vice presidential selection does not serve well to understand the process in the modern era. Although all three individuals on the short list balanced the ticket regionally, Portman's Ohio brought more Electoral College votes to the ticket and was far more competitive than Wisconsin. The selection process was also somewhat unusual in that in the previous fifty years only two other members of the House of Representatives have been selected as vice presidential candidates (William Miller in 1964 and Geraldine Ferraro in 1984); in 2012 two of the three finalists were from the House. It was also the first major party ticket in American history in which neither the presidential nor vice presidential candidate was a Protestant: Romney is a Mormon, Ryan a Catholic. What Ryan did bring to the ticket was a reputation as a fiscal conservative. In this sense his selection was similar to the selection of Palin in 2008, made to bring conservative credibility to a presidential candidate who was perceived as being more moderate than the Republican base might otherwise prefer.

Biden was vigorous on the campaign trail. The challenge for the ticket in 2012 was to present the previous four years as having been a success. This was not necessarily an easy task, primarily because while the economy had improved, it had yet to fully recover from the crash of 2008. Perhaps the pithiest summary of the administration's message could be found in Biden's frequent refrain throughout the campaign: "Bin Laden is dead and GM is still alive."[91] The former was a reference to the raid that killed U.S. nemesis Osama Bin Laden in 2011, and the latter, to the successful federal government bailout of distressed car making giant General Motors. Perhaps remarkably, Biden remained—for the most part—gaffe-free throughout the campaign. Ryan focused primarily on the issue of the flagging economy throughout the campaign. Given his role as Chair of the House Budget Committee this was understandable.

The debate between Biden and Ryan took place on October 11, 2012, at Centre College in Danville, Kentucky (the same location as the Cheney–Lieberman debate in 2000). Although viewership was below that for the three presidential debates, it was the third-highest watched in the history of vice presidential debates (behind the 2008 Biden–Palin and the 1984 Bush–Ferraro debates). Given Obama's lackluster performance in the first presidential debate, Biden's mandate was to act more aggressive to halt perceptions that the campaign was flagging. This he did—perhaps, overdid. He portrayed an air of superiority, frequently smiling and laughing while Ryan made his points. Ryan, on the other hand, had only to demonstrate that he was worthy of being elected to the second-highest office in the land and assuming the presidency if need be. He succeeded. The debate may have been a draw, although some snap polls conducted immediately afterward gave Ryan a slight edge.[92]

Unlike his predecessor Biden does not shy away from the press or the public, carrying the administration's banner on the tough issues of the day. The vice president has been Obama's leading advocate on foreign policy, military efforts, and the domestic agenda, including gun control, fiscal policies, and more.[93] For example after being named to head the Gun Violence Task Force in the aftermath of the Sandy Hook shootings, Biden took to the road again publicly promoting stricter gun control measures.[94]

He has granted interviews to and made appearances in a wide variety of media outlets. Major magazines such as *The New Yorker*, *Rolling Stone*, *GQ*, and *Time* have all published interviews with Biden, as have *Field & Stream* (regarding gun rights)[95] and *Car and Driver*.[96] Digital outlets that have featured Biden interviews include Parents.Com,[97] BloombergTV, Radio Free Europe/Radio Liberty, and a fledgling Cuban dissident online newspaper named *14ymedio*.[98] He has also appeared on a number of television news outlets, including CNN, CBS, and PBS, as well as all of the Sunday morning talk shows and radio networks like NPR. Biden has even found time to make appearances on entertainment (or "infotainment") programs like *The Daily Show, The View, Late Night with Seth Meyers,* and *Rachael Ray.* At the 2014 White House Press Correspondent's Dinner he demonstrated what a good sport he is by appearing in a pretaped skit (as the actual VP) with Julia Louise Dreyfus, the star of HBO's *Veep.*

Of course there is some risk involved for the administration when Biden grants interviews and makes these appearances. This was perhaps nowhere more evident than in the spring of 2012 when during an appearance on *Meet the Press* Biden stated, "I am absolutely comfortable with" gay marriage.[99] This public proclamation was not well received by the administration because the president had yet to make his own support of gay marriage public, which put Obama on the hot seat. The statement all but forced him to publicly express his own support or risk being perceived as out of step with his vice president.[100]

It is in the final informal role of modern vice presidents, the advisory role, that Biden has perhaps distinguished himself the most. The partnership between he and Obama took some time to develop, in part because by nature Biden is typically blunt and straightforward and the president is more cautious.[101] But it has, over time, developed into a true partnership, quite different than the relationship between Bush and Cheney or Clinton and Gore.[102] Biden himself suggests that the two are "co-captains."[103] Although this may overstate his own influence somewhat, the fact remains that the two are quite in step with each other.

Why does the relationship between the two work so well? Because at the most fundamental level Biden fully understands the nature of the modern vice presidency. As he correctly noted, "There is no inherent power in the office of the vice presidency. Zero. None. It's all a reflection of your relationship with the president."[104] Biden's condition for taking the job was that he could play a part in the administration, and he clearly understands that this depends on his relationship with Obama. And by all accounts Biden's first interest was to help Obama succeed.[105] Moreover, Biden and Obama are, in the vice president's words, "ideologically simpatico."[106] Biden and "the president see eye to eye on [most all] policy issues."[107] This obviously makes it easier for the two to agree. He is also fiercely loyal to the president in his interactions with others. For example he has been known to shut down conversation when others begin to be too critical of Obama.[108] This is a quality that the president cannot help but appreciate. Finally, it helps that the two have become friends.[109]

The relationship is further enhanced as the result of the fact that their staff and aides are so closely integrated with each other. "Theirs is by all accounts a conjoined administration."[110] At minimum this prevents infighting within the administration and allows for both men and their assistants to work more closely together. The top advisers of each man gather together almost every day to discuss and set the agenda for the day.[111] For example, "Obama's press secretary used to be Biden's communications director. Biden's strategist is the brother of Obama's former national-security adviser; Biden's chief of staff co-authored a book with Obama's former chief of staff."[112] There is little room for dissension to grow between the two men with regard to strategy and messaging.

The partnership is even strong enough to withstand the seemingly inevitable Biden gaffes. In spring 2009 Biden responded to a question about the outbreak of swine flu by saying he would advise against his own family members traveling on airplanes or subways. This led to a swift and public retraction on the part of the White House.[113] Later that summer Biden publicly confessed that the administration may have "misread how bad the economy was" and downplayed Russia's status as a world power.[114] Senior Obama aide Valerie Jarrett has suggested that Biden's gaffes, which come when he speaks frankly and off-script, are "part of what makes the vice president so endearing," going on to add that Obama "wouldn't change him one bit."[115] Obama seems, in other words, to have accepted the gaffes as part of the Biden package.

Like Gore and Cheney, Biden interacts frequently with his president. Every morning Obama and Biden (and both men's senior staff) are briefed on intelligence matters and the economy and they set the day's agenda. Biden also has an open invitation to attend regular sessions with the president and Secretaries of State and Defense.[116] Whereas Cheney always attended meetings of the National Security Council Principals Committee, Biden attends approximately one-third of the time.[117] And as noted, Biden is frequently the "last person in the room" before a major decision is made. This gives him enormous potential for influence.

> When I first got asked to do this job, I said, "No, thank you. I'll do anything I can to help you, but I'm not interested. . . . I wanted a commitment that I get to be the last guy in the room on every major decision—not generally, but specifically. . . . [so,] literally, every meeting he has, I'm in. . . . I spend an average of four to five hours a day with him, every single day. . . . [and] once a week, no matter what, we sit down for between 35 minutes and as long as an hour and a half, depending on what we have to say.[118]

Biden has had his hand in any number of the Obama administration's decisions. This began before they were inaugurated. He was, for example, a pivotal member of the incoming administration's transition team. He aided the incoming president by providing input and feedback on filling cabinet positions. This included supporting the nomination of former foe Hillary Clinton as Secretary of State.[119] Early in the administration he led meetings focused on developing an economic recovery plan. This comprehensive plan evolved into a stimulus package that Biden helped sell to the country and to Congress.[120] When Obama was presented the opportunity to nominate his first appointment to the U.S. Supreme Court it was Biden who coached the nominee, Sonia Sotomayor, a Federal Appellate Court Judge from New York, and helped secure approval from the Senate.[121]

Biden's biggest influence on foreign policy was on the Afghanistan debate, where in 2009 he influenced the president in developing a compromise plan for managing the remaining troops in Afghanistan.[122] For him the focus in Afghanistan was always Al-Qaeda. The strategy that evolved was a hybrid: a small surge of ground forces and drones. President Obama said that his vice president "was enormously helpful in guiding those discussions."[123] He also became the key player in refining and reshaping the Obama administration's evolving strategy in Iraq. Biden vigorously challenged the status quo, seeking to ensure that whatever course of action was chosen, it wasn't selected because it was what had always been done.[124] He was given the task of managing the withdrawal of American forces from Iraq and substituting them with economic and diplomatic measures.

EVALUATING THE BIDEN VICE PRESIDENCY

So what to make of the tenure of the nation's forty-seventh vice president? On the one hand one could note that Biden has his share of critics. For example Former Secretary of Defense Robert Gates was harshly critical of Biden's foreign policy judgment in a recent book (Biden has been equally critical of Gates's judgment).[125] Documents seized in the raid that killed bin Laden show that the terrorist advised assassins to spare the vice president and target Obama, stating that "Biden is totally unprepared for that post [the presidency], which will lead the U.S. into crisis."[126] A poll from 2012 revealed that when respondents were asked for a single word that describes Biden, the two most frequent—and nearly equal—responses were "good" and "idiot."[127]

On the other hand Obama has openly praised Biden on any number of occasions. For example after Biden convinced Senator Specter to switch party affiliation from Republican to Democrat, giving the Democrats sixty votes in the Senate, Obama labeled Biden "employee of the month."[128] The title of one recent article claimed that "Biden May Be the Most Influential Vice President Ever,"[129] which would be consistent with Biden's stated wish "to be the best vice president ever." Unlike the majority of his predecessors he clearly revels in the job.[130] Although it may be the case that like Cheney, Biden has become less central to Obama's decision making in terms of foreign policy in his second term, he is a major player in the Obama administration.[131]

An open question as of the writing of this book is whether Biden will run for president in 2016. When he joined the ticket in 2008 he told Obama, "I'm sixty-five and you're not going to have to worry about my positioning myself to be president." However by 2011 he was meeting with his family and closest advisers about a possible run in 2016.[132] If he does, there are several obstacles in his way. First, Hillary Clinton remains the odds-on favorite to capture the Democratic nomination should she decide to run. Second, he would have to overcome the perception that he is too old: If elected he would be seventy-four at the time of inauguration, or one year older than Ronald Reagan was at the start of his second term.[133] Finally, there does not seem to be much support for a Biden run among sitting senators. This is perhaps surprising, inasmuch as many were his colleagues for a long time.[134] Whether he runs, and the result if he does, does little to detract from the fact that his has been a successful vice president.

NOTES

1. Dan Balz, "Biden Stumbles at the Starting Gate," *Washington Post*, January 31, 2007, www.washingtonpost.com/wp-dyn/content/article/2007/01/31/AR2007013100404.html.

2. James W. Caesar, Andrew E. Busch, and John J. Pitney, Jr., *Epic Journey: The 2008 Elections and American Politics* (Lanham, MD: Rowman & Littlefield, 2009), 102.

3. John Heilemann and Mark Halperin, *Game Change: Obama and the Clintons, McCain and Palin, and the Race of a Lifetime* (New York: Harper, 2010).

4. Stephen J. Wayne, *The Road to the White House, 2012*, 9th ed. (Boston: Wadsworth).

5. Heilemann and Halperin, *Game Change*, 336–37.

6. Ibid., 338, 340.

7. Jules Witcover, *Joe Biden: A Life of Trial and Redemption* (New York: Morrow, 2010), 410.

8. Evan Osnos, "The Biden Agenda: Reckoning with Ukraine and Iraq, and Keeping an Eye on 2016," *The New Yorker*, July 28, 2014, 41.

9. Ibid., 340–41.

10. Witcover, *Joe Biden*, 410

11. Witcover, *Joe Biden*, 432; Richard Yon, "Vice President Joe Biden," in *The Obama Presidency*, Robert P. Watson, Douglas M. Brattebo, and Jack Covarrubias, eds. (Albany: SUNY Press, 2012), 363–377, 368.

12. Wayne, *The Road to the White House, 2012*, 145.

13. Caesar, Busch, and Pitney, Jr., *Epic Journey*, 140–41; Paul R. Abramson, John H. Aldrich, and David W. Rohde, *Change and Continuity in the 2008 and 2010 Elections* (Washington D.C.: CQ Press, 2012), 33.

14. Jody C Baumgartner, "The Veepstakes: Forecasting Vice Presidential Selection in 2008," *PS: Politics and Political Science*, 41 (2008): 765–72.

15. Heilemann and Halperin, *Game Change*, 358–64.

16. Abramson, Aldrich, and Rohde, *Change and Continuity in the 2008 and 2010 Elections*, 44–45, 52.

17. Jody C Baumgartner, Jonathan S. Morris and Natasha L. Walth, "The Fey Effect: Young Adults, Political Humor, and Perceptions of Sarah Palin in the 2008 Presidential Election Campaign," *Public Opinion Quarterly* 76 (2012): 95–104.

18. Osnos, "The Biden Agenda."

19. Daniel Kurtzman, "Bidenisms—Joe Biden Gaffes and Biden Quotes," Politicalhumor.About.com, http://politicalhumor.about.com/od/joebiden/a/bidenisms.htm.

20. Heilemann and Halperin, *Game Change*, 413.

21. Ibid., 413.

22. Ibid., 411–13.

23. Wayne, *The Road to the White House, 2012*, 265.

24. Ibid., 263.

25. Abramson, Aldrich, and Rohde, *Change and Continuity in the 2008 and 2010 Elections*, 47.

26. William J. Crotty, "Electing Obama: The 2008 Presidential Campaign," in *Winning the Presidency 2008*, William J. Crotty, ed. (Boulder: Paradigm, 2009), 20–47, 40.

27. Abramson, Aldrich, and Rohde, *Change and Continuity in the 2008 and 2010 Elections*, 17.

28. Juliet Eilperin, "With Obama and Biden Both Overseas, Who's in Charge?" *Washington Post*, March 19, 2013, www.washingtonpost.com/blogs/post-politics/wp/2013/03/19/with-obama-and-biden-both-overseas-whos-in-charge/.

29. Kristen A. Lee, "Vice President Biden Presides over Senate Swearing-in Ceremony with Sometimes Awkward Jokes and Hugs," *New York Daily News*, January 4, 2013, www.nydailynews.com/news/politics/biden-swears-new-senators-awkwardness-ensues-article-1.1233004.

30. Nicole Gaudiano, "Biden Presides as Senate Votes Down Gun-Control Provision," *Delawareonline.com*, April 17, 2013, www.delawareonline.com/article/A7/20130417/NEWS/304170108/Biden-presides-as-Senate-votes-down-gun-control-provision.

31. Matt Vasilogambros, "With Joe Biden at the Senate, Immigration Reform Is Passed," National Journal, www.nationaljournal.com/congress/with-joe-biden-at-the-senate-immigration-reform-is-passed-20130627.

32. Lisa Mascaro, "Biden Unwelcome in Senate Huddles, Where Cheney Wielded Power," *Las Vegas Sun*, December 7, 2008, www.lasvegassun.com/news/2008/dec/07/biden-unwelcome-senate-huddles-where-cheney-wielde/.

33. Michael Scherer, "Mo Joe," *Time*, June 11, 2012, 26–30.

34. Witcover, *Joe Biden*, 452.

35. Yon, "Vice President Joe Biden," 372.

36. Nicole Gaudiano, "Biden to Lead Job-Training Effort," *USA Today*, January 31, 2014. www.usatoday.com/story/news/nation/2014/01/31/biden-to-lead-job-training-effort/5078423/.

37. Jeff Mason, "Obama, Biden Highlight Job-TRAINING in Middle-class Push," *Reuters*, July 22, 2014, www.reuters.com/article/2014/07/22/us-usa-obama-training-idUSKBN0FR0XF20140722.

38. "Vice President Biden Stops in Charleston for Funeral," *WLOX*, October 16, 2012, www.wlox.com/story/19833483/police-source-vice-president-joe-biden -flying-into-n-charleston.

39. *News Sentinel* staff, "Honoring a Statesman: Howard Baker Recalled as Warm, Uniting Leader," *Knoxville News Sentinel*, July 1, 2014, www.knoxnews .com/news/biden-mcconnell-reid-among-dignitaries-coming.

40. Emily Shapiro, "Biden, Carter Attend Funeral for Former Second Lady Joan Mondale," *ABC News Radio*, February 8, 2014, http://abcnewsradioonline.com/ politics-news/biden-carter-attend-funeral-for-former-second-lady-joan-mond .html#ixzz398cJxjEj.

41. David Jackson, "Obama Sends Former Officials to Thatcher Funeral," *USA Today*, April 16, 2013, www.usatoday.com/story/theoval/2013/04/16/obama -margaret-thatcher-james-baker-george-schultz/2087011/.

42. Randall Chase, "Jean Biden's Funeral: Joe Biden Eulogizes Mother, Calls Her Courageous," *Huffington Post*, January 12, 2010, www.huffingtonpost .com/2010/01/12/jean-bidens-funeral-joe-b_n_420553.html.

43. Terri Weaver, "Vice President Joe Biden Attends Funeral in Syracuse for Law School Classmate," *Syracuse.Com*, March 13, 2012, www.syracuse.com/ news/index.ssf/2012/03/vice_president_joe_biden_atten.html.

44. "Vice President Biden Visits CIA Headquarters for Ceremony with Director Petraeus," Central Intelligence Agency, October 12, 2011, www.cia.gov/news -information/press-releases-statements/press-release-2011/vice-president- biden-visits-cia-headquarters-for-ceremony-with-director-petraeus.html.

45. John Byrne, "Biden Visits Chicago for Women's Shelter Ceremony, Fundraisers," *Chicago Tribune*, November 26, 2013. http://articles.chicagotribune .com/2013-11-26/news/ct-biden-womens-shelter-met-1126-20131126_1_chicago -lawn-vice-president-joe-biden-fundraisers.

46. Felicia Escobar, "Vice President Biden Celebrates Citizenship at King Center Naturalization Ceremony," WhiteHouse.Gov, November 15, 2013. www .whitehouse.gov/blog/2013/11/15/vice-president-biden-celebrates-citizenship -king-center-naturalization-ceremony.

47. Natalie Pompilio, "Vice President Joe Biden Celebrates Independence Day in Philly," *The Delaware County Daily Times*, July 4, 2014, www.delcotimes.com/ general-news/20140704/vice-president-joe-biden-celebrates-independence-day -in-philly.

48. Lloyd Young, "Boston Marathon bombings: One Year Later," *Boston.Com*, April 15, 2014, www.boston.com/bigpicture/2014/04/boston_marathon_bomb ings_one_year_later.html.

49. "Vice President Joe Biden Honors Asian Americans and Pacific Islander Heritage Month at Opening Ceremony," *VoiceOfAsiaOnline.com*, May 8, 2014, http://voiceofasiaonline.com/blog/vice-president-joe-biden-honors-asian-amer icans-and-pacific-islander-heritage-month-at-opening-ceremony/.

50. Emily Ledbetter, "VP Biden to speak at NGA meeting in Nashville," *GCANews.Com*, July 9, 2014, www.gcanews.com/vp-biden-to-speak-at-nga-meet ing-in-nashville/.

51. Sabrina Siddiqui, "Joe Biden: Malaysia Plane 'Apparently Shot Down' Over Ukraine, 'Not an Accident'," *Huffington Post*, July 17, 2014, www.huffingtonpost .com/2014/07/17/joe-biden-malaysian-airliner_n_5596775.html.

52. Michael Vasquez, "Biden to Speak at Miami Dade College Commencement," *Miami Herald*, April 23, 2014, www.miamiherald.com/2014/04/23/4076223/biden-to-speak-at-miami-dade-college.html; Megan Sexton, "Vice President Joe Biden to Deliver UofSC Commencement Address," University of South Carolina, April 9, 2014. www.sc.edu/uofsc/announcements/2014/04_biden_to_speak_at_uofsc_commencement.php#.U9vtYeNdW30; "Commencement Speaker," *UDaily*, University of Delaware, April 7, 2014. www.udel.edu/udaily/2014/apr/commencement-040714.html; Daniela Altimari, "Vice President Addresses Coast Guard Graduates," *The Courant*, May 22, 2013, http://articles.courant.com/2013-05-22/news/hc-biden-coast-guard-graduation-20130522_1_vice-president-joe-biden-graduates-u-s-coast-guard-academy; Don Branum, "Biden to Class of 2014: 'You Carry America on Your Back'," Af.Mil, May 28, 2014, www.af.mil/News/ArticleDisplay/tabid/223/Article/485107/biden-to-class-of-2014-you-carry-america-on-your-back.aspx.

53. Scott Baldauf, "Joe Biden at World Cup: 'We're Going to Beat England,'" *CSMonitor.Com*, June 11, 2010, www.csmonitor.com/World/Africa/Africa-Monitor/2010/0611/Joe-Biden-at-World-Cup-We-re-going-to-beat-England.

54. Borys Krawczeniuk, "Biden Visit to NEPA Cancelled," *CitizensVoice.Com*, June 13, 2014, http://citizensvoice.com/news/biden-visit-to-nepa-cancelled-1.1702415.

55. "Catoosa, Walker and Chattooga Added to Flooding Disaster Declaration," *Associated Press*, September 25, 2009, www.northwestgeorgianews.com/rome/news/catoosa-walker-and-chattooga-added-to-flooding-disaster-declaration-biden/article_7df62296-a459-591c-be30-e87c369b0388.html.

56. "Vice President Joe Biden Tours Flood-Damaged Opry," *WATE.Com*, July 16, 2010, www.wate.com/story/12822041/vice-president-joe-biden-tours-flood-damaged-opry.

57. Jo Mannies, "Biden, Nixon Tour Tornado-damaged Berkeley," *St. Louis Beacon*, May 11, 2011, www.stlbeacon.org/#!/content/16213/biden_nixon_touring_tornado_damaged_berkeley_.

58. Patty Hill, "Vice President Joe Biden Tours Hurricane Sandy Damage in New Jersey," *WhiteHouse.Gov*, November 20, 2012, www.whitehouse.gov/blog/2012/11/20/photo-gallery-vice-president-joe-biden-tours-hurricane-sandy-damage-new-jersey.

59. Carol E. Lee, "'Senator' Biden's Trip Raises Concerns," *Politico,* January 6, 2009, www.politico.com/news/stories/0109/17136.html.

60. Witcover, *Joe Biden*, 440–41

61. Ibid., 453.

62. Ibid., 455.

63. Herb Keinon, "Veep Shows Israel Some Love," *The Jerusalem Post*, March 10, 2010, 1.

64. Reihan Salam, "Biden's Disastrous Israel Trip," *The Daily Beast*, March 10, 2010. Available at www.thedailybeast.com/articles/2010/03/10/bidens-disastrous-israel-trip.html#sthash.JP2PIfAK.dpuf.

65. Donald Macintyre, "Palestinians Threaten to Quit Talks over Settlements; US Vice-President Joe Biden Battles to Keep Both Sides at the Negotiating Table," *The Independent (London)*, March 12, 2010, 28.

66. Witcover, *Joe Biden*, 454

67. Will Englund, "In Moscow, Biden Gets Specific on Corruption," *Washington Post,* March 10, 2011, www.washingtonpost.com/wp-dyn/content/article/2011/03/10/AR2011031003861.html.

68. MJ Lee, "Biden's Asia Message: Don't Worry," *Politico,* August 26, 2011.

69. Aru Pande, "Biden's India Visit Is Key in Asia 'Rebalance' Strategy," *Voice of America,* July 23, 2013, www.voanews.com/content/biden-meets-indian-counterpart-in-new-delhi/1707286.html.

70. Patrick Goodenough, "Biden Heads to Asia to 'Reaffirm' U.S. Presence as a 'Pacific Power,'" *CNS News,* December 2, 2013, http://cnsnews.com/news/article/patrick-goodenough/biden-heads-asia-reaffirm-us-presence-pacific-power.

71. Scott Wilson, "Biden in Europe to 'Reassure Our Allies' Over Russia's Moves in Ukraine," *Washington Post,* March 18, 2014, www.washingtonpost.com/politics/biden-in-europe-to-reassure-our-allies-over-russias-moves-in-ukraine/2014/03/18/ff05b5be-ae84-11e3-9627-c65021d6d572_story.html.

72. Osnos, "The Biden Agenda."

73. "Vice President Joe Biden," *WhiteHouse.Gov,* www.whitehouse.gov/administration/vice-president-biden.

74. Jeanne Cummings, "Joe Biden, 'the Skunk at the Family Picnic,'" *Politico,* September 16, 2009, www.politico.com/news/stories/0909/27211.html.

75. Osnos, "The Biden Agenda."

76. Ibid.

77. Michael A. Mimoli, "Biden Forged Bond with Obama through His Loyalty," *Los Angeles Times,* September 6, 2012, http://articles.latimes.com/print/2012/sep/06/nation/la-na-biden-20120906.

78. Witcover, *Joe Biden,* 441.

79. Ibid., 451–52.

80. Yon, "Vice President Joe Biden," 375–76.

81. Helene Cooper, "As the Ground Shifts, Biden Plays a Bigger Role," *New York Times,* December 11, 2010, www.nytimes.com/2010/12/12/us/politics/12biden.html?pagewanted=all; Carl Hulse and Jackie Calmes, "Biden and G.O.P. Leader Helped Hammer Out Bipartisan Tax Accord," *New York Times,* December 7, 2010, www.nytimes.com/2010/12/08/us/politics/08deal.html?pagewanted=all.

82. Glenn Thrush, Carrie Budoff Brown, Manu Raju, and John Bresnahan, "Joe Biden, Mitch McConnell and the Making of a Debt Deal," *Politico,* August 2, 2011, www.politico.com/news/stories/0811/60463.html; Tim Reid, "Q+A: Debt and Deficit Talks in Early Stages," *Reuters,* May 16, 2011, www.reuters.com/article/2011/05/16/us-usa-debt-talks-idUSTRE74F26V20110516.

83. Karoun Demirjian, "It's Over: House Passes 'Fiscal Cliff' Deal," *Las Vegas Sun,* January 1, 2013, www.lasvegassun.com/news/2013/jan/01/its-over-house-passes-fiscal-cliff-deal/.

84. Nicole Gaudiano, "Biden Mostly Out of Sight as Shutdown Drags On," *USA Today,* October 13, 2013, www.usatoday.com/story/news/politics/2013/10/13/biden-mostly-out-of-sight-during-shutdown-showdown/2968373/.

85. Jeff Zeleny, "Biden Urges D.N.C. to Reject Grim Election Forecast," *The New York Times,* August 20, 2010, www.nytimes.com/2010/08/21/us/politics/21dems.html?ref=joseph_r_jr_biden.

86. Michael D. Shear, "$200 Billion in Ads, Mr. Biden? That's Real Money," *New York Times*' "The Caucus," October 22, 2010. Available at http://the caucus.blogs.nytimes.com/2010/10/22/200-billion-in-ads-mr-biden-thats-real -money/?_php=true&_type=blogs&ref=politics&_r=0.

87. Carl Hulse, "Biden's Son Will Not Run for Delaware's Open Senate Seat," *New York Times*' "The Caucus," January 25, 2010. Available at http://thecaucus .blogs.nytimes.com/2010/01/25/bidens-son-will-not-run-for-delaware-senate -seat/.

88. Edward Klein, *Blood Feud: The Clintons vs. the Obamas* (Washington D.C.: Regnery, 2014).

89. James W. Ceaser, Andrew W. Busch, and John J. Pitney, Jr., *After Hope and Change: The 2012 Elections and American Politics* (Lanham, MD: Rowman & Littlefield, 2013).

90. Baumgartner, "The Post-Palin Calculus: The 2012 Republican Veepstakes," 608.

91. Ceaser, Busch, and Pitney, *After Hope and Change*, 107.

92. Jody Baumgartner, "Column: Biden, Ryan Both Accomplish Goals," *USA Today*, October 12, 2012, www.usatoday.com/story/opinion/2012/10/12/vice -president-debate-romney-biden-baumgartner/1626609/; Ceaser, Busch, and Pitney, *After Hope and Change*, 114.

93. David Rothkopf, "The Bidenization of America," *foreignpolicy.com*, January 14, 2013, www.foreignpolicy.com/articles/2013/01/14/the_bidenization_of_ america.

94. Leigh Ann Caldwell, "Obama Sets Up Gun Violence Task Force," *CBS News*, December 19, 2012, www.cbsnews.com/news/obama-sets-up-gun-vio lence-task-force/.

95. Anthony Licata, "The *F&S* Gun Rights Interviews: Joe Biden, Vice President of the United States," *Field & Stream*, www.fieldandstream.com/articles/ guns/2013/02/gun-control-joe-biden-interview.

96. John Phillips, "What I'd Do Differently: Vice President Joe Biden," *Car and Driver*, October, 2011, www.caranddriver.com/features/what-id-do-differently -vice-president-joe-biden-interview.

97. Michael Kress, "Joe Biden on Shotguns, Safeguards, and Smart Parenting," www.parents.com/kids/safety/joe-biden-shotgun-gun-safety/.

98. Kyle Munzenrieder, "Joe Biden Gives Interview to Cuba's First Independent Digital News Site," *Miami New Times*, May 27 2014. http://blogs.miaminew times.com/riptide/2014/05/joe_biden_gives_interview_to_cubas_first_indepen dent_digital_news_site.php.

99. Glenn Thrush and Carrie Budoff Brown, "Biden Blamed; Politics Drove Timing," *Politico*, May 9, 2012.

100. "Joe Biden," *The New York Times*, January 2, 2013, http://topics.nytimes .com/top/reference/timestopics/people/b/joseph_r_jr_biden/index.html; Glenn Thrush and Carrie Budoff Brown, "Biden Blamed; Politics Drove Timing," *Politico*, May 9, 2012; Michael A. Mimoli, "Biden Forged Bond with Obama through His Loyalty," *Los Angeles Times*, September 6, 2012, http://articles.lat-imes.com/print/2012/sep/06/nation/la-na-biden-20120906.

101. Mark Leibovich, "For a Blunt Biden, an Uneasy Supporting Role," *New York Times*, May 7, 2012, www.nytimes.com/2012/05/08/us/politics/for-a-blunt-biden-an-uneasy-supporting-role.html?_r=2&pagewanted=all&.

102. Edward-Isaac Dovere and Darren Samuelsohn, "The Joe Biden Factor," *Politico*, September 5, 2012, www.politico.com/news/stories/0912/80621.html.

103. Jeanne Marie Laskas, "Have You heard the One About President Joe Biden?" *GC*, July, 2013, www.gq.com/news-politics/newsmakers/201308/joe-biden-presidential-campaign-2016-2013.

104. Zeke J Miller, "Interview: Vice President Joe Biden On Amtrak, Obama and Pot," *Time*, February 10, 2014, http://time.com/5647/joe-biden-interview-2016-presidential-campaign/.

105. Laskas, "Have You heard the One About President Joe Biden?"

106. Ibid.

107. Douglas Brinkley, "Joe Biden: The Rolling Stone Interview," *Rolling Stone*, May 23, 2013, www.rollingstone.com/politics/news/joe-biden-the-rolling-stone-interview-20130509.

108. Osnos, "The Biden Agenda."

109. Leibovich, "For a Blunt Biden, an Uneasy Supporting Role."

110. Laskas, "Have You Heard the One about President Joe Biden?"

111. Ibid.

112. Ibid.

113. Mark Silva and Christi Parsons, "White House Adjusts Biden's Swine Flu Advice," *Los Angeles Times*, May 01, 2009, http://articles.latimes.com/2009/may/01/nation/na-biden1.

114. Peter Nicholas and Paul Richter, "Despite Fumbles, Biden's a Player," *Los Angeles Times*, August 18, 2009, http://articles.latimes.com/2009/aug/18/nation/na-biden18.

115. Nicholas and Richter, "Despite Fumbles, Biden's a Player."

116. Laskas, "Have You Heard the One about President Joe Biden?"; Osnos, "The Biden Agenda."

117. Osnos, "The Biden Agenda."

118. Brinkley, "Joe Biden: The Rolling Stone Interview."

119. Witcover, *Joe Biden*, 432.

120. Yon, "Vice President Joe Biden," 372.

121. Witcover, *Joe Biden*, 454; Osnos, "The Biden Agenda."

122. Witcover, *Joe Biden*, 449; Osnos, "The Biden Agenda"; "Joe Biden," *The New York Times*, January 2, 2013, topics.nytimes.com/top/reference/timestopics/people/b/joseph_r_jr_biden/index.html.

123. Witcover, *Joe Biden*, 468

124. Ibid., 459

125. Osnos, "The Biden Agenda."

126. Ibid.

127. Ibid.

128. Dovere and Samuelsohn, "The Joe Biden Factor."

129. Michael Hirsch, "Biden May Be the Most Influential Vice President Ever," *National Journal*, December 31, 2012, www.nationaljournal.com/whitehouse/biden-may-be-the-most-influential-vice-president-ever-20121231.

130. Jeanne Marie Laskas, "Have You Heard the One about President Joe Biden?" *GC*, July, 2013. Available at www.gq.com/news-politics/newsmakers/201308/joe-biden-presidential-campaign-2016-2013.

131. Osnos, "The Biden Agenda."

132. Ibid.

133. Ibid.

134. Manu Raju and Maggie Haberman, "Senate to Joe Biden: We Want Hillary Clinton," *Politico*, June 19, 2014. Available at www.politico.com/story/2014/06/joe-biden-senate-want-hillary-clinton-108040.html.

10

+

Making Sense of It All: The Future of the Vice Presidency

In the previous three chapters we looked in some detail at the vice presidencies of Al Gore, Dick Cheney, and Joe Biden. Together, these three men have occupied the office for more than two decades, closing out one millennium and moving into the next. How do they compare in terms of their tenures in office? We begin this chapter by examining this question. We then summarize what we know about the modern vice presidency. After identifying trends in the institution in the modern era and commonalities in how recent vice presidents have approached their job we look to the future. What will the vice presidency look like in the future? What types of men or women will occupy the office? How will future presidents and vice presidents see the job of vice president?

Finally, we look at some of the normative questions that emerge in light of the development of an active, executive vice presidency. What should we expect from a vice president? Are the increased duties for the vice president, however informal, in keeping with the spirit of the Constitution? To whom are they accountable, the president or the people? In fact, can the vice president be held accountable?

COMPARING VICE PRESIDENCIES: GORE, CHENEY, AND BIDEN

The modern era is generally characterized by an active vice presidency, and Gore, Cheney, and Biden all approached the job with a high degree of energy and vigor. Beyond the symbolic activities associated with the office (or, for that matter, with virtually any political office) all three men took the job seriously. This alone sets the modern era apart from previous times, when the vice presidency was seen as little more than a joke.

All three were active on the diplomatic front. Gore (presumably with Bill Clinton's blessing) was actually responsible for a good deal of the administration's foreign policy. Cheney took fewer trips abroad than did either Gore or Biden, but foreign and security policy was his focus. And one of the reasons Barack Obama selected Biden was for his foreign policy expertise and his relationships with various foreign leaders. All three also did tireless work on the legislative front for their president and political party.

Importantly, all three men enjoyed the trust of their respective presidents, at least implicitly, to a relatively high degree. The relationship between Clinton and Gore seemed to suffer as the Monica Lewinsky scandal dragged on; George W. Bush and Cheney still enjoy a good professional relationship, although they have never mixed socially; and it appeared to take a while before Obama was fully comfortable with Biden. This said, the relationship between each vice president and his president was, for the most part, good. Building on precedent set by previous administrations in the modern era, this allowed for a great deal of meaningful interaction between president and vice president. This in turn led to Clinton, Bush, and Obama relying, to some extent, on the insight and advice of their respective vice presidents. This was particularly true during their first terms, when each president was leaning on his vice president to help understand the nuances of Washington politics. To some degree, reliance on all three vice presidents in their advisory role waned during their second terms.

Several differences are evident among the three as well. For example, Gore seemed to treat much of his time in office as preparation for a presidential run in 2000. For the most part this is consistent with the vice presidency in the modern era through the end of the century. The office has come to be seen as a "stepping stone" to the presidency. To be fair, Gore's focus on 2000 affected his vice presidency only marginally (the fund-raising scandals), but it seemed clear that later in his second term he was promoting himself—rather than Clinton or his policies—a great deal. Cheney, on the other hand, made it clear from the start of his vice presidency that he had no interest in running for president. And although he has remained in the public light, frequently criticizing the Obama administration's foreign policy, he seems to have no interest in returning to elective office. Theoretically Cheney's disinterest in running for president left him freer to focus on the president's goals and objectives without concern for his political future. It remains to be seen (as of this writing) whether Joe Biden will run for president in 2016, but there is every indication that he has not ruled out the possibility.

Cheney was also more secretive in his approach to the job, not only with respect to dealing with the press and the public, but with other members of the administration and Congress as well.[1] The lengths he went to in this regard are the stuff of (mostly negative) legend. For example he had his own safe in his office and was often known to withhold important information from his own staff. This penchant for secrecy also manifested itself in his public persona. Cheney was clearly one to avoid the public spotlight, as a rule avoiding the press and public appearances, preferring to work "in the shadows." As just one example, if either Gore or Biden had been involved in a hunting accident like Cheney's, it is virtually impossible to imagine them not speaking to the national press in fairly short order.

Another difference between the three was their relative popularity. An impressionistic survey of media accounts (with the exception of Fox News and other more conservative outlets) of the Cheney vice presidency would reveal an overwhelmingly negative view. Accounts of Gore and Biden seem to be generally positive. This is not to say that Gore and Biden were universally liked or approved of, nor is it to suggest that there were no low points during their tenures. But taken on the whole, the consensus view seems to be that Gore and Biden did a better job than Cheney. Is this the case? The answer may depend on how one sees the job of the vice president.

THE JOB OF THE VICE PRESIDENT

In 2007 Cheney and his chief legal counsel David Addington seemed to suggest that the vice presidency was not part of the executive, but rather the legislative branch. The claim was made in response to requests from the National Archives and Records Administration for information that Cheney was not willing to provide. Although technically the claim may have had some merit, this was clearly a legal hair-splitting exercise.[2] During the 2008 presidential campaign, Sarah Palin claimed that the vice president "is not a member, or a part of the legislative branch," then seemed to contradict herself by continuing, "except to oversee the Senate." Palin claimed that in that role a vice president "can really get in there with the senators and make a lot of good policy changes."[3] Although technically she was not completely incorrect, her response ignored the realities of more than two hundred years of Senate practice.

But what *is* the job of the vice president? One of the main objectives of this book is to illustrate that the minimal constitutional description of the functions of the vice president are not consistent with the current reality. "Even casual observers of the presidency understand that these two functions no longer define the job of modern vice presidents."[4] So how do we—how should we—evaluate a vice president? Several possibilities suggest themselves. The first is how the vice president is viewed by the public. The rationale for this approach is fairly simple. Vice presidents are elected by the people, and therefore we can look to public opinion data to see how well they are perceived. By this measure, both Gore and Biden were better vice presidents than Cheney.

Historically, vice presidential job approval and favorability were only sporadically tracked by opinion pollsters (if at all), and then mainly during election years. Since 1997 various polling organizations have fairly consistently been tracking each. Although each of these concepts seems fairly clear, various organizations use different questions to measure them. For example, ABC News asked respondents the following question to gauge favorability toward Biden: "Overall, do you have a favorable or unfavorable impression of Joe Biden?" Respondents could select either "favorable," "unfavorable," or state that they were unsure. CBS News asked a slightly different question: "Is your opinion of Joe Biden favorable, not favorable, undecided, or haven't you heard enough about Joe Biden yet to have an opinion?" Here, respondents were given choices of "favorable," "not favorable," "undecided," or "I haven't heard enough." Questions about job approval (CBS News: "Do you approve or disapprove of the job Joe Biden is doing as vice president?") have similarly minor variations.

Despite the fact that these slightly different questions are attempts to get at the same concept, strictly speaking, they cannot be collapsed together and compared. To resolve this problem public opinion researchers rely on an algorithm developed by James Stimson. Using input from various question sources measuring a similar idea (in this case, favorability or job approval) the algorithm constructs a single, generalized measure of opinion over time.[5] Figures 10.1 to 10.3 show both favorability and job approval for Gore, Cheney, and Biden. Each relies on public opinion data from several respected polling organizations.[6]

Data for Gore only cover the period from early 1997 through the end of his term. Figure 10.1 shows that Gore's favorability rating averaged about 46 percent, from a low of 39 percent in the late summer of 1999 to a high of 56 percent in September of 2000, the start of the fall presidential campaign. One thing that becomes apparent is that Gore's favorability was relatively immune to news about the Lewinsky scandal and the impeachment of the president. The former broke in January 1998 and the latter occurred in December of that same year. Gore's average favorability rating for the twelve-months of 1998 was 48.4 percent, slightly higher than his forty-month total average. His job approval rating averaged 51 percent from January 1997 through November 2000, slightly higher than his favorability rating. The low job approval rating of 44 percent came

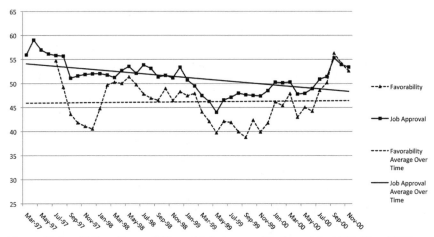

Figure 10.1. Al Gore Favorability and Job Approval Ratings, July 1997–Nov. 2000

in May 1999, while the high of 59 came in February 1997, the start of his second term. Examining trend lines for each set of data suggests that both were relatively stable over time. Although his favorability ratings trended marginally (approximately 1 percent) higher over this time period his job approval ratings trended slightly downward (approximately 5 percent).

Included in Figure 10.2, favorability and job approval ratings for Cheney, are data for his entire term. In both cases he averaged approximately 35 percent, much lower than Gore, but this only tells a small part of the story. In both cases there is a precipitous decline of more than 20 percentage points over the course of his tenure. His favorability rating peaked at 50.8 percent in April 2002, while his job approval rating hit its high mark of 59.8 percent in November 2001, shortly after the attacks of 9/11. By the end of his time in office he had bottomed out at 29.4 percent favorability and 30.3 job approval. Although these figures are comparable to those of George W. Bush, one wonders what effect Cheney's aversion to public appearances and the media may have had on the public's perception of him.

Biden's numbers, seen in Figure 10.3, are similar to Gore's. His favorability ratings, which cover the period from his inauguration through February 2014, average approximately 47 percent. His low point was in December 2010, when his favorability was at 36.6 percent, whereas the high point of 59 percent was during the month after he took office. Overall his numbers are fairly constant throughout his time in office. Like Gore (and Cheney), Biden's job approval is slightly higher than his favorability, averaging 50 percent and trending slightly upward as his second term

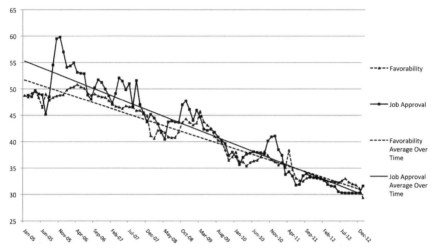

Figure 10.2. Dick Cheney Favorability and Job Approval Ratings, Jan. 2001–Jan. 2009

progresses. His low point came in December 2009, when his job approval rating was at 45.8 percent. The Biden data is somewhat surprising considering that his tendency to put his foot in his mouth is the only thing many people know about him. He seems to enjoy a respectable degree of public approval despite this.

A second approach to evaluating vice presidents can be thought of as policy-oriented. In this view a vice president can and should be measured by the policies he or she advocated, helped implement, and so on. There are two problems with this approach. The first is that it likely gives too

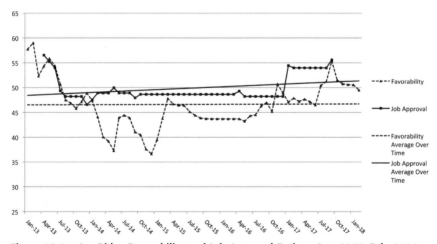

Figure 10.3. Joe Biden Favorability and Job Approval Ratings, Jan. 2009–Feb. 2014

much credit to vice presidents for policies adopted during their tenures. Regardless of how visible, active, and influential a vice president may be, in the end the president is the president, and therefore responsible for failures and deserving of credit for successes. Vice presidents may share in this accountability, but to assign it solely to them would be to give them too much credit. Secondly, any approach to evaluating a vice presidency that focused too much on policy would flounder, based on the partisan leanings of the individual doing the evaluation. What one observer sees as a policy success, or good policy, another might view as a policy failure, or bad policy.

Another way to assess a vice president might be thought of as a legal-constitutional approach. In this view the vice president is evaluated according to whether the vice president behaved in a legal or constitutional manner. For example a strict reading of the Constitution might lead one to conclude that the vice president is a legislative officer. If this is the case then all active modern vice presidents "might be considered unconstitutional"[7] inasmuch as they actively take part in executive branch affairs. From a legal standpoint a vice president will fall short to the extent that he or she has circumvented (or appeared to circumvent) the law. Many consider Cheney to have been a poor vice president because of his alleged "war crimes" (e.g., defending the use of waterboarding during the interrogation of terrorism suspects), advocating wiretaps of questionable legality, his role in the Valerie Plame affair, and more. One problem with this standard is that there is often enough disagreement over the interpretation of an action's legality (e.g., was waterboarding of terror suspects illegal?) to leave us asking more questions. Moreover, some of our greatest presidents themselves have circumvented the law (e.g., Abraham Lincoln's suspension of *habeas corpus* during the Civil War, Franklin Roosevelt's internment of U.S. citizens of Japanese descent during World War II).

A final approach can be thought of as the practitioner's approach. There is by now a fairly well-developed set of norms that guide both presidents and vice presidents with regard to the job of the vice president. According to this view a vice president "serves a constituency of one: the president."[8] This view conforms precisely to our description of the modern vice presidency.[9] A vice president is expected to serve and assist the president. A concise version of how the job is and should be approached can be found in George H. W. Bush's memoirs and is expanded on here.

1. *The President is in charge.* This is probably the most important rule, especially when considering the issue of vice presidential influence. Vice presidents will only have as much influence as their president

will allow. "Vice presidential power still is largely a function of the president's willingness to confer it."[10]

2. *Loyalty to the president is assumed.* Advice given to the president should be given confidentially, and a vice president's public statements should mirror those of the president's. The vice president is expected to toe the presidential line, so to speak, in public. Relatedly, the vice president should never upstage the president. The American people should never be confused about who the president is. Finally, if the president does happen to take the advice of the vice president, the vice president should never take credit for it.[11]

3. *The vice president's role should be well-defined.* At some point prior to taking office, the president and vice president should have worked out an understanding of what will be expected of the vice president, and conversely, what the vice president can expect from the president in terms of access and opportunity for input. This has been standard practice for most modern vice presidents. The corollary to this is that the president must clearly convey to his staff what the role of the vice president is, since presidential staff tend to be protective of their president.

4. *Vice presidents must "share the dirty work."* Whether campaigning for members of Congress, working with Congress, or publicly speaking out to promote the president's policies, vice presidents must be willing to promote the president's agenda. All other things being equal, the more he or she does so, the greater the chance the president will come to value their input.[12]

5. *Vice presidents should avoid special appointments.* This was Walter Mondale's maxim. A vice president's political capital is better spent trying to personally assist the president.[13] Being in charge of special commissions, task forces, etc., will likely embroil the vice president in bureaucratic struggles, waste time and resources, and if it is a trivial assignment, undermine his or her reputation.

6. *The president and vice president should complement each other.* If the president has little or no experience in Washington politics (e.g., Jimmy Carter, Ronald Reagan, Clinton, and George W. Bush), a vice president who does has a greater opportunity to affect policy.[14] In addition, if the two are personally compatible, it is more likely that the working relationship will flourish and the vice president will have even more opportunity to affect decision making.

There are several benefits that result from thinking about the vice presidency in this way. First, a great deal is expected from modern presidents. Vice presidents can share the workload. This is hardly a new concept. In 1937, Roosevelt's Committee on Administrative Management (the Brownlow Committee), tasked with making recommendations to reorganize the executive branch, famously declared in its report that "the President needs help."[15] Vice presidents provide that help. And, unlike Cabinet secretaries, top aides, advisers, and others who help modern presidents in their day-to-day management of the executive branch, they are elected by the people and thus (technically) accountable to the people.

Secondly, giving vice presidents meaningful tasks and exposure to the full range of presidential information and duties allows them to become familiar with the job and the issues facing the country. This is important in the event that a vice president is forced to fill a presidential vacancy. The example typically used to justify this view is the fact that Harry Truman knew nothing about the Manhattan Project on succeeding to the presidency. It is unreasonable to expect that a vice president who assumes the presidency should do so with less than complete exposure to the intricacies of the office. Moreover, it is quite arguably simply a bad idea for the country.

Third, making the vice presidency a substantive and meaningful job quite likely attracts better qualified, higher-caliber individuals. Hard evidence of this assertion would be difficult to find, but there is plenty of anecdotal evidence to support it. One need only look through history to find examples that may support this claim. Before the premodern era there were any number of well-known politicians who refused a place on the ballot as vice presidential candidate, at least partly on the grounds that it was an empty office. This is no longer the case. Examples of good people who decline invitations to run for the office are now few and far between, and many lobby for the chance. Of course this might be the result of the fact that the office is now perceived to be a stepping stone to the presidency. In other words the office may be attractive despite the job itself. Individuals run for the vice presidency with the idea that if they serve their time they can move on to the presidency. If this is the case then it is not simply higher-caliber individuals but those with political ambition that are attracted to the job. However ambition and quality are not mutually exclusive characteristics in politicians.

A final justification for the adoption of this view of the vice presidency is somewhat more abstract. As one of the nation's only two elected officials, why *not* expect the vice president to have a meaningful role in governance? This argument is more persuasive if combined with the idea that a vice president is a presidential successor-in-waiting.

Of course there are arguments against this perspective as well. The primary objection is constitutional in nature. Although the Constitution does not proscribe against an active, executive vice president, it does not provide for one either. In fact, some might argue that because the vice president has actual legislative tasks assigned to the office there is no place for an executive role. Moreover, beyond impeachment and removal, vice presidents are not, strictly speaking, subject to the same checks and balances as is the president. This is particularly important when we remember that modern vice presidents operate in a para-constitutional netherworld. They are at once part of the legislative and executive branches but can call neither home. Cheney was partly correct when he claimed he was "not part of the executive branch," except for the fact that he was so patently wrong. How are actors in such an institutional arrangement held accountable? This argument effectively counters and negates all of the supposed benefits the activist vice presidency model brings to the system.

CONCLUSION: THE FUTURE OF THE VICE PRESIDENCY

Despite any constitutional or other arguments against an active vice presidency it is highly unlikely that future vice presidents will revert to their premodern passive roles. Although Biden, for example, claimed he would not be another Cheney, he has been (if anything) more active than Cheney was during his tenure in office. The reality is that the vice president is now one of the president's most valued assistants, and this reality is unlikely to change.

Regardless of how we look at it, the American vice presidency is a fundamentally changed institution. To begin with, the method of selecting vice presidential candidates has changed in the modern era. This has had a profound effect on the types of individuals selected for the vice presidential nomination, why they are selected, and thus on the institution of the vice presidency itself. In the modern era, presidential candidates, not the party, choose their running mates. With a frontloaded primary season they have ample time to research, interview, and consider their choice. This helps ensure that competent candidates will be selected. This is important because of increased concerns in the modern era over the issue of presidential succession. In addition, it all but guarantees that vice presidents will be loyal to and compatible with their presidents. The former has virtually become part of the vice presidential job description, while the latter is important if a vice presidents hopes to have a meaningful role or any influence in the administration.

Vice presidential selection has also changed with respect to the role of the media. Rather than just reporting, the press now aids in the vetting of potential candidates. This not only increases the chance that a competent running mate will be selected, but also that the eventual nominee will have a scandal-free past. In fact, having had previous exposure to the national media has almost become a minimum requirement for the vice presidential nomination. This means that presidential candidates and their campaign organizations need to take the demands of the national media (access, information) seriously. The controversial candidacies of Spiro Agnew, Thomas Eagleton, Geraldine Ferraro, Dan Quayle, and Sarah Palin nominations are good examples of what happens when this is ignored. The media also serves to generate publicity for the vice presidential choice, and thus the campaign, by way of covering the veepstakes.

In the modern era the vice presidency has become attractive enough that few refuse the nomination, and many individuals now campaign for it, albeit quietly. The attractiveness of the office is enhanced by the fact that it has become politically unfeasible to dump sitting vice presidents from the ticket in the president's reelection effort.

Individuals who now aspire to and are considered for the vice presidency differ in many significant ways from their premodern counterparts. They are more diverse, especially with respect to religion, ethnic, and socioeconomic backgrounds. This trend will continue. Vice presidential candidates are also somewhat more qualified than those in the premodern era in terms of their political experience. They are better educated and have on average of almost twenty years in public service, relatively little of which is at the subnational level. Most have, in other words, a good working knowledge of how national politics works. Modern-era vice presidential candidates are also typically politically ambitious. Many have previously run for the presidency or were doing so the year they were nominated for the vice presidency.

Changes in the selection process have altered the way in which presidential tickets have traditionally been balanced. Although regional and ideological balance remain important, it seems to have become less so in the past few election cycles. The candidate-centered nature of modern presidential campaigns also means that vice presidential candidates must, and do, actively take a central role in the presidential campaign. The primary role of vice presidential candidates is that of aggressor, attacking the opposing presidential (and vice presidential) candidates in a way that presidential candidates cannot. Finally, with respect to the campaign, the now-standard vice presidential debate is a visible event for the vice presidential candidate, and, if not prepared for properly, can result in negative publicity for the campaign. The Nixon doctrine, that vice presidential candidates can hurt but not help the campaign, still prevails in the modern era.

Finally, the institution of the vice presidency itself has been transformed. The office has expanded to the point where it would now be all but unrecognizable to the framers of the Constitution. This has been in part the result of the aforementioned changes. The institutional resources (staff, budget, access to the president, salary, and more) available to modern vice presidents have increased gradually to the point where vice presidents now have, in effect, an independent power base. As important in the growth of the office has been the role of precedent and institutional memory. New vice presidents take office knowing what their predecessors had and did and expect the same. In fact, the public has come to expect this as well (as much as any of us think about the vice president).

Modern vice presidents spend little time discharging their formal duties in the Senate. As the modern era progressed, we saw an increase in their statutory and appointive duties, but starting with Mondale, vice presidents have generally avoided these as well. The job of vice president now amounts to that of presidential alter-ego, and in the best of scenarios, right-hand man, or assistant-in-chief. Vice presidents now actively work to promote the president's policies at home and abroad, as well as doing service for the party in the form of campaigning for congressional candidates. Perhaps most importantly, presidents now turn to their vice presidents for advice. This advisory vice presidency is significant inasmuch as it better prepares vice presidents to assume the presidency in the event of presidential vacancy, as well as giving presidents a valued and trusted source of policy input.

In the 1970s, Arthur Schlesinger predicted that the vice presidency would remain "a resting place for mediocrities."[16] Nothing, it appears, could be further from the truth. In the past several decades we have seen a wholesale change in the institution and the individuals who aspire to and occupy it. Although vice presidents remain *vice* presidents, it is no longer possible to see them as political hacks, occupying an irrelevant office, and performing meaningless tasks. Hopefully this book has made it clear that this view can and should be relegated to the history books.

NOTES

1. Baumgartner, "Scoundrel or Über-Lieutenant?"

2. Scott Shane, "Cheney in Dispute on Oversight of His Office," *New York Times*, June 22, 2007. Available at www.nytimes.com/2007/06/22/washington/22cnd -cheney.html?pagewanted=all&_r=0.

3. Nitya, "Palin Says Vice President 'In Charge of' Senate," ABC News, October 22, 2008. Available at http://abcnews.go.com/blogs/politics/2008/10/palin-says -vice/.

4. Baumgartner, "Scoundrel or Über-Lieutenant?" 236.

5. James A. Stimson, *Public Opinion in America: Moods, Cycles, and Swings* (Boulder: Westview Press, 1991).

6. These data are available publicly at PollingReport.Com. For Al Gore, www .pollingreport.com/g.htm; for Dick Cheney, www.pollingreport.com/A-B.htm; and for Joe Biden, www.pollingreport.com/C.htm.

7. Glenn Harlan Reynolds, "Is Dick Cheney Unconstitutional?" *Northwestern University Law Review Colloquy*, 102 (2007): 110–16, 110.

8. Baumgartner, "Scoundrel or Über-Lieutenant?" 236.

9. Jody Baumgartner, *The American Vice Presidency Reconsidered*; Joel Goldstein, *The Modern American Vice Presidency*; Paul Light, *Vice Presidential Power*.

10. Nelson, *A Heartbeat Away*, 23; Light, *Vice-Presidential Power*, 131.

11. Cronin, "Rethinking the Vice-Presidency," 339–40; Light, *Vice-Presidential Power*, 233–34.

12. Light, *Vice-Presidential Power*, 234.

13. Cronin, "Rethinking the Vice-Presidency," 339–40.

14. Light, *Vice-Presidential Power*, 138–39.

15. U.S. President's Committee on Administrative Management. *Report of the President's Committee.* Washington, DC: Government Printing Office, 1937, p. 5.

16. Pika, "The Vice Presidency," 497.

Index

About the Authors

Jody C Baumgartner is associate professor of political science at Eastern Carolina University and the author of *Politics is a Joke!* (2015); *Conventional Wisdom and American Elections: Exploding Myths, Exploring Misconceptions,* second edition (2010); and *Laughing Matters: Humor and American Politics in the Media Age* (2007, coedited with Jonathan Morris). He has also written or collaborated on over two dozen articles and book chapters on political humor, the vice presidency, and other subjects.

Thomas F. Crumblin is an independent researcher and author who received a Bachelor's Degree in Political Science from Syracuse University. His interests include American and British politics along with Media and politics. A native of Staten Island, New York, he is married and lives in Tarpon Springs, Florida.